Elmdon

Continuity and change in a
north-west Essex village
1861-1964

Elmdon

*Continuity and change in a
north-west Essex village
1861-1964*

JEAN ROBIN

WITH A FOREWORD BY
AUDREY RICHARDS

CAMBRIDGE UNIVERSITY PRESS

CAMBRIDGE
LONDON   NEW YORK   NEW ROCHELLE
MELBOURNE   SYDNEY

Published by the Press Syndicate of the University of Cambridge
The Pitt Building, Trumpington Street, Cambridge CB2 1RP
32 East 57th Street, New York, NY 10022, USA
296 Beaconsfield Parade, Middle Park, Melbourne 3206, Australia

First published 1980

Printed in Great Britain at the University Press, Cambridge

Library of Congress cataloguing in publication data
Robin, Jean.
Elmdon: continuity and change in a north-west
Essex village, 1861-1964
Bibliography: p.
1.   Elmdon, Eng. — History. I. Title
DA690.E319R6   942.6'712   79-12964
ISBN 0 521 22820 4

Contents

Illustrations

Maps

Figures

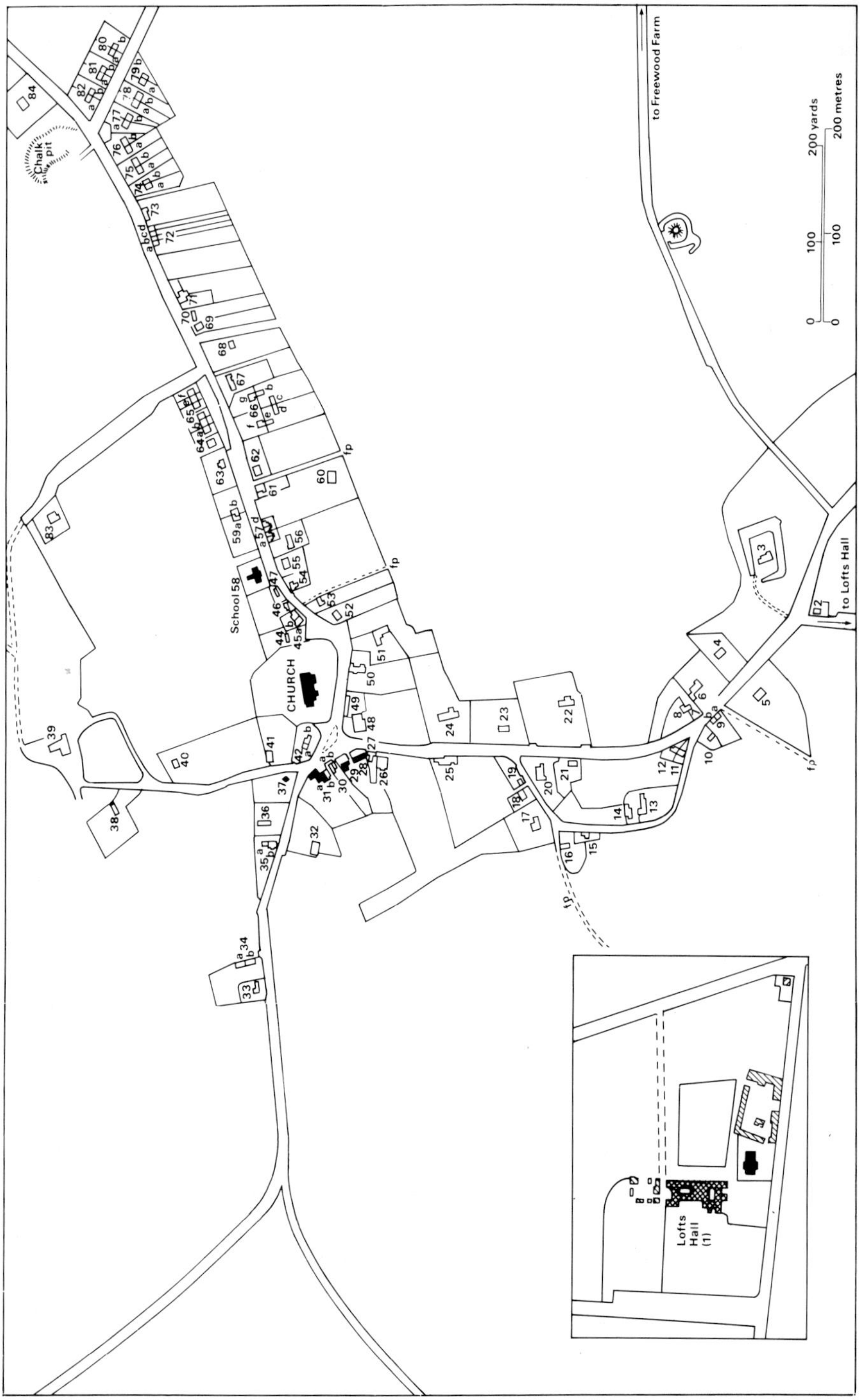

Map 1 Elmdon village in the 1960s

Elmdon Village in the 1960s

Key

1 Lofts Hall
2 Lofts Hall Lodge
3 Pigots
4 Pigots Lodge
5 Serenity
6 Wilkes Barn (formerly the Wilkes Arms)
7 and 8 Rose Cottage (two dwellings)
9 (a) and (b) Unnamed cottages
10 Elm Cottage
11 Vine Cottage
12 Pilgrim's Cottage
13, 14, 15, 17, 18 Cottages in King's Lane
16 Shepherd's Hay
19 Humphrey's Green
20 Hillside
21 The Forge (formerly belonging to the Brands)
22 Hill Farm
23 Laburnum View
24 The Bangles (four dwellings)
25 The Old Stores (formerly the Crisps' shop)
26 T-Meadow (formerly the Brands' shop)
27 Dormer Thatch (formerly the Gamgee/Greenhill bakery)
28 The Carrier
29 Village Hall (formerly the Reading Room)
30 (a) and (b) Cross Hill cottages (formerly butcher's shop)

31 (a) The King's Head
   (b) King's Head Cottage
32 Elmdon Lodge Farm (formerly Baker's Farm)
33 Frondirion
34 (b) Whitehall
34 (a), 35 (a) and (b), 36 Cottages in Heydon Road
37 Caravan
38 Bury Lane Cottage
39 Elmdon Bury
40 Bury Lodge
41 The New Vicarage
42 (a) Crawley House } (formerly the
   (b) Crawley Cottage } grammar school)
43 Church of St. Nicholas
44 Church Cottage
45 (a) Rose Cottage
   (b) School House Cottage
46 South View
47 Unnamed cottage
48 The Old Vicarage
49 Old Vicarage Cottage
50 Farthing Green (formerly The Colony)
51 Church Farm
52 Ilgars
53 Violet Cottage
54 Pump Cottage
55 Gayfield
56 Post Office Cottage

57 (a) to (d) School Row
58 School
59 (a) Mount View
   (b) Dalorin
60 Bridleway
61 Baker's Stores (formerly George Hopwood's pork butcher's shop)
62 Wheelwrights (formerly Isaac Rollings' premises)
63 Bury Garden Cottage
64 Police House
65 (a) - (f) Bury Cottages (council bungalows)
66 (a) - (f) The Glebe (council houses)
67 Mulberry Cottage
68 Unnamed cottage
69 The Firs
70 Unnamed cottage
71 The Limes (butcher's shop)
72 (a) - (d) Manor Row
73 The Hoops
74 (a) - 76 (b) Ickleton Road Council Houses
77 (a) - 79 (b) Hollow Road Council Houses
80 (a) and (b) and 82 (a) and (b) Unnamed houses
81 (a) Glenroy
   (b) Trevose
83 Little Elmdon Bury
84 Alfredshot

Note: Poplars Farm and Elmdon Lee farm both lie some two-and-a-half miles from the centre of Elmdon village, to the north-east and south-east respectively.

Foreword

The character of Elmdon village

Elmdon is one of a small group of villages set on the chalky uplands of north Essex. These rolling hill-tops are mostly covered with boulder clay which becomes thicker on the lower slopes, a soil suited to the arable farming typical of East Anglia. Road works or cuttings in the area reveal the thick layer of chalk beneath the clay and show how near to the surface it is.

This chain of villages, Strethall, Elmdon, Chrishall, Heydon and the two Chishills, stands on top of a ridge which is about 400 feet above sea level, with another line of villages, Melbourn, Fowlmere, Thriplow and Whittlesford, below. The ridge villages have remained curiously isolated, though this part of Essex is quite densely settled and there are, for instance, twenty-four villages within a five-mile radius of Elmdon itself. Even during the Roman occupation of Essex the main thoroughfares passed elsewhere. The Icknield Way, for instance, ran through Strethall and Littlebury Green to the south and east of Elmdon but not through the village itself. Map 3 (p.31) shows that somewhat the same kind of semi-isolation was found in nineteenth-century Elmdon (see chapter 2) and still exists. Elmdon lies in the middle of a cluster of villages linked by second-class roads and lanes, but the main motor-roads from Royston, Bishop's Stortford and Saffron Walden miss it. The village is not on the direct route to anywhere.

Elmdon is very much a border village. Some of the inhabitants will tell you that the boundaries of Essex, Hertfordshire and Cambridgeshire intersect at its highest point, the hill-top on which the old manor-house of Elmdon Bury stood and where the farm-house which replaced it stands today. The map does not quite confirm this view, although the point of intersection of the boundaries is very near. Nevertheless, the inhabitants of Elmdon definitely consider themselves to be 'Essex people'. Their links are with Saffron Walden, some six-and-a-half miles to the east, which is their market town and administrative centre, and not with Cambridge, their largest nearby city, which lies fourteen miles to the north. It is difficult to know what makes for a feeling of county loyalty among people who are largely uninterested in local administration and who do not differ markedly in dialect or ways of living from the people of neighbouring counties, but the feeling is certainly there. I have heard an Elmdon mother, distressed at the thought of her daughter marrying a man living as far away as Chelmsford, console herself with the thought that 'anyhow he is an Essex man'. County loyalties are certainly intermittent. They flare up and die down in situations of competition, such as sport, or of cooperation, such as the need to remove snow from a road running over the border between Essex and Cambridge, but on such occasions Elmdon stands firmly, and even aggressively, on the Essex side.

Elmdon has always been an agricultural community, though in the seventeenth and eighteenth centuries its inhabitants were evidently deeply involved in the textile industry centred in Saffron Walden, which specialised in the production of fustian cloth and of fine yarn for the Norfolk worsteds.[1] Spinning was widespread in the villages near Saffron Walden and the inhabitants of Elmdon were described in 1770 as being 'supported by husbandry and spinning'.[2] The village is also listed among twelve villages including Littlebury, Clavering and Newport, which were engaged in wool-combing and in weaving worsteds and fustians.[3] There are one or two seventeenth or eighteenth-century houses in the village which do not seem to be farms and which might well be textile merchants' houses. But the industry had collapsed by the beginning of the nineteenth century, owing to a mechanisation of the textile processes in the north. Jean Robin's account of village life in the middle and end of the nineteenth century shows how few openings outside agriculture there were for the inhabitants at that time (chapter 6).

Arable farming seems always to have predominated; the crops were mainly wheat and barley with some oats, peas and beans, whilst a family of twentieth-century farmers introduced beet. But here as elsewhere in East Anglia the economy has been mixed. The Domesday register listed 26 swine and 288 sheep on the lord's demesne and 250 swine in the valley forest land to which all had access. Sheep have been kept from time to time. Seven shepherds were listed in Elmdon in the 1861 census (see p.6) though only one farmer was keeping sheep in 1964 when work on this book was begun. Beef cattle, pigs and poultry appear in the records and are still kept. A few dairy cattle have supplied the village, especially during the two world wars, but in the main East Anglian conditions do not suit dairy farming. The largest farmer in Elmdon has, however, built up a pedigree herd of Jerseys since the late forties and has become the Secretary of the Quality Milk Production Society. The establishment of this herd has been a notable development in Elmdon of recent years.

It is difficult to estimate the population of Elmdon from the census since the figures for Elmdon and Duddenhoe End, which are both in the same parish, are given jointly. However, our survey made in 1964 showed that the population was 321 persons all told. Elmdon therefore falls into the bottom end of the medium-sized parishes in this part of Essex, with nearby Littlebury and Barley numbering 511 and 515 respectively in 1961; Ickleton, Fowlmere and Great Chesterford reaching the 600s, and Thriplow 836. Villages with some industrial development, such as Whittlesford, Duxford, Newport and Melbourn had populations between one and two thousand. Elmdon must be reckoned a small to medium-sized village for this part of the country and it is likely to remain so since it is not in the town-planners' phraseology, a 'development area'. For those interested in comparing its size with other recently-studied East Anglian villages, the population of 'Akenfield' was a little smaller, 298 in 1961; Blaxhall was larger in 1966 'about 400'; and Foxton a good deal larger, 680 in 1961.[4]

This has been an area of large landowners since the sixteenth century, when successive Tudor magnates united some rather numerous local manors by purchase. Elmdon village lies between two hills, each of which formerly had its own manor-house, home-farm, church and a pond which provided the water supply. On the southern hill was the manor-house of Wenden Lofts bought by Sir Thomas Meade in 1567. He built, or rebuilt, the house, which was subsequently called Lofts Hall, finishing it in 1579. He also bought Pigots manor, lying a quarter of a mile away, which soon ceased to exist as a separate manor. The Meade family also purchased the second important manor, Elmdon Bury, lying three-quarters of a mile away on the northernmost hill, and from then on both these two manors, Wenden Lofts and Elmdon Bury had one owner, with Wenden Lofts generally acting as the owner's 'seat'. The property remained in the Meade family from 1554 to 1717 when it was sold to a merchant to George I, Robert Chamberlain, who in turn sold it to another London business man, Nathaniel Wilkes. This transaction included part of Elmdon village as we now know it, and much of Duddenhoe End. The growth of the Wilkes estate from 1739 to 1927 by purchase and additions after the Enclosure Act of 1824 is the main theme of this book. By 1927 when the Lofts Hall estate was finally sold, there were practically no small-holders left, as Jean Robin explains. Thirty-five years later when our study began, the land in and around Elmdon village was held by five farmers owning 705, 300, 300, 200, and 70 acres respectively. Elmdon can therefore be classified as a district of capitalist farming. There are no small-scale farms, allotment schemes or farmers' cooperatives.

Industrial development in the surrounding district has been rapid of recent years. In 1905 the Ciba-Geigy company set up works at Duxford, five miles away from Elmdon, and Spicers paper factory was started at Sawston in 1914. Both firms were actively recruiting labour in the late fifties and Spicers provided a bus service to bring in workers from the village. But Elmdon seems to have turned more slowly to industrial work than some neighbouring villages, though here we have to rely on impressions only. School-leavers were attracted by the high wages and easier work at Duxford and Sawston, but some of the older men had almost a sense of guilt or disloyalty at leaving the land and there were still as many as 40 per cent Elmdon men engaged in agriculture or related employment in 1964. Elmdon seemed to me still to have the air of an agricultural community when I first went there in 1957, and indeed this continued for many years afterwards. Tractors rattled through the village and lined up outside the council houses for the lunch break. Village events such as fêtes were arranged to fit in with the different harvests — wheat, beans or beet — and children worked on the farms in the school holidays. Industrial work is now the norm rather than the exception for Elmdon villagers, yet in the early sixties the change of an older man from farm to factory was still the subject of comment and criticism. As late as 1966, a farm worker spoke with concern of his mate who had gone to work at Spicers a week previously, saying 'I daresay he is all right so far but he is bound to suffer, cooped up inside all day'.

It is difficult to classify the composition of the population of

Elmdon, or of any other English village for that matter. Our present typologies are still very rough and ready. There is a general and increasing interest in the study of rural communities as soaring house prices in urban areas drive so many families from town to country. Popular papers and magazines publish articles on 'commuter villages', 'squire's villages' or 'traditional communities'. With so little comparative knowledge available it is difficult to put Elmdon into one of these loosely-defined categories, and such rapid changes were taking place in the village during our study that what seemed an accurate description at one time appeared quite misleading two or three years later.

In 1964 Elmdon could certainly not have been called a commuter village — 41 per cent of the inhabitants had been born in the village (44 per cent males and 37.5 per cent females). There were of course a few outsiders who had bought holiday cottages in the years between the wars and there may have been more immigrants who came and went and are not all remembered. In the late fifties a small group of outsiders settled permanently in the village because they had local jobs. This group included the director of a local industry, a land agent, two Cambridge University lecturers, and a Christian Science practitioner and writer. There was also another small group of people who had retired to Elmdon in order to enjoy a peaceful life. It included a sculptor, two bank employees, two teachers, two nurses and three people with private means. In 1964 there were four retired couples and nine women, single or widowed, living alone. But the commuting group proper had only reached 11 per cent of the working population in 1964. It included stockbrokers, insurance agents, journalists, art designers, secretaries and teachers. Nine years later the figure had risen to 25 per cent. The period before 1964 is sometimes described as the time 'before the commuters came'.

The social organisation of the village changed in 1957, the year I arrived in Elmdon as a week-end and vacation resident. This turned out to be the last year of a squire-type organisation, even though the attitudes appropriate to this kind of situation lingered on for a number of years. The late Mr Jack Wilkes, the seventh Wilkes to succeed to the ownership of the Lofts Hall estate, was still alive. Admittedly, he had sold the estate in 1927 and had left Elmdon temporarily, but he had returned to the village in 1932, bought back Elmdon Bury, one of the two old manor-houses and lived there for a further twenty-six years, though no longer farming.

After acting as a squire for the years from 1887 to 1927 and working the Elmdon Bury and Freewood farms, it is not surprising that he continued to act as Elmdon's squire and that this situation was accepted by most of the villagers. He died in September 1958 but in that time I was able to see how closely his behaviour followed the pattern of his predecessor but one, the Reverend Robert Fiske Wilkes (1818–1879), as described in such interesting detail in this book.

Elmdon is a Church village, without a non-conformist chapel, and Jack Wilkes was a great supporter of the Church, playing an active part on the parochial council. The village also had a Church school, which he regularly visited, taking an interest in the children's progress. He furthered the village sports clubs by financial contributions and advice. He lent his garden for Conservative party rallies and presided over fêtes. During the war he had helped in the organisation of the Home Guard. Like his predecessor he headed the list of subscriptions to village activities (see chapter 8) and urged others to subscribe. He entertained newcomers to the village if he thought them worthy of inclusion in the upper ranks of the small Elmdon society. Agricultural labourers still touched their caps to him and repeated his comments and views. Those who had voted for the Labour Party in elections were anxious that Jack Wilkes should not be told for fear he might disapprove. After his death in 1958 the paternalistic organisation of village activities continued for some years. His widow lived until 1976 and continued to exercise the duties of a squire's wife. She entertained and took part in fêtes and bazaars, distributed 'meals-on-wheels' and washed up for school dinners right into her old age. She joined the Evergreen Society outings open to all over 60 years, not because she enjoyed them but because she thought it was her duty.

The vicar, farmers and others who had also taken part in this paternal organisation of activities continued their roles for many years after the death of the Squire and were certainly functioning in much the same way in 1964 and after. Of the seven farmers listed, two were on the parochial council and three on the parish council in 1964. One ran a boy-scout troop prior to 1957. Farmers' wives were also active, particularly, it seems, during the war, when the making of jam and preserving of fruit was organised. They were joined by some of the women who had retired to Elmdon and bought small cottages there and also by some of the newer house-owners who had arrived in Elmdon in the late fifties, one of whom started the Evergreen Society.

All these facts justify us, I think, in classifying Elmdon as a traditionally-organised village when we started our work in 1964, even though it was to change so rapidly in the next ten to fifteen years.

Elmdon in 1964

Elmdon is generally described as a pretty village. Indeed I do not remember ever hearing a visitor using another adjective for it. This is perhaps because it has a number of beautiful and interesting old buildings such as the guildhall (42a and b on map 1, p.viii) which was bought and given to the village as a grammar school in 1559, but must have been built considerably earlier. It has also three farmhouses of age and distinction, 'Pigots' (3), a seventeenth-century building erected on the site of an old manor-house which is finely timbered and moated all round; Hill Farm (22), reckoned as the oldest building in Elmdon with a fifteenth-century wing and two ancient barns on the slope of the hill below; and Church Farm (51), another building of interest, dated 1626. These three houses are still used as farms. Elmdon Bury, the old manor of Elmdon, is also used as a farm but its house has been greatly restored. Another large and beautiful Tudor house is 'Bangles' (24), which was possibly the home of a wealthy merchant. It was divided into four tenements in 1964, all fast falling into decay. Above it is an imposing vicarage (48), early Victorian, and probably one of the first Elmdon houses to be built in brick.

This is not an unusual number of ancient buildings to survive in an Essex village. In fact, according to the report of a Royal Commission on Historical Monuments published in 1908,[5] Elmdon, with twenty-four recorded 'monuments', reached about the average figure for the area. The number is now probably less, since the attempt to list and preserve old buildings of merit dates only from the passing of the Town and Country Planning Act of 1947.

But, of course, a reputation as a 'pretty' village depends greatly on the siting of the 'monuments'. Elmdon is a linear village with its buildings along its three main roads. Even the farms, usually built outside the village in England, and approached by small access roads, are here almost all standing just a few hundred yards back from the street, so that the old Tudor buildings can thus be clearly seen.

But a 'pretty' village may merely mean one with many old cottages, since the white and pink colour washes common in East Anglian villages, together with the greys and browns of thatch and old slate roofs, make an artist's scene. A sales catalogue of 1927 states that Elmdon was 'well-known for the number of its Tudor cottages' and this was in the days before British architects had begun to specialise in the 'conversion' of old cottages, and, later, barns, to modern standards of comfort. The survival of seventeenth- and eighteenth-century cottages to the twentieth century is a matter of the care taken to preserve them. This is particularly the case in Essex where there is little or no building-stone, and brick does not seem to have been used till the nineteenth century. There is nothing so derelict-looking as a Tudor cottage built of timber, lathe and plaster, which has fallen into disrepair. Cottages are said to have been better looked-after when the landlord was resident, and Elmdon was fortunate in this respect since the Wilkes family was resident in the village from 1739 onwards and did a good deal of building of houses as well as repairing. There were in Elmdon in 1964: 14 per cent seventeenth-century and earlier houses; 23 per cent of eighteenth century; 14 per cent of nineteenth century; and 49 per cent of twentieth-century dwellings, but the count was difficult to make as many houses contain additions from two or even three centuries.

Again, it is the placing of the old houses which is the important thing from the aesthetic point of view. Is a picturesque old cottage standing next to a particularly ugly garage or a derelict house? Do the cottages which have such charm for the commuter stand side by side or scattered between modern bungalows? This is a matter of sociological as well as aesthetic importance. Even in a village as small as Elmdon, neighbourhood groups develop quickly and people are referred to, whether in anecdotes of the past or in present-day gossip, as, for instance, the 'Kings Lane lot', 'the Pilgrim hill people', or 'the council houses people'. In 1964 house-purchasers' money was chasing after old houses rather than new, and therefore a group of sixteenth- and seventeenth-century cottages tended to give rise to a commuter's neighbourhood, very much recognised by the village as such.

The central point of Elmdon is Cross Hill with its small triangular

Cross Hill, 1979

green, just large enough to hold the inevitable brick and wood bus shelter, the war memorial cross and a signpost. Small as the green is, it is the stopping place for buses; the shelter is the courting place for the young; and boys whirl around it in motor-cycle displays on Sundays. Here the British Legion, in ever decreasing numbers, meet on Armistice Day and blow their Last Post; the Thaxted Morris dancers assemble from time to time; and the revellers on New Year's eve used to stream out of the two pubs and sing 'Auld Lang Syne' round the cross, while one of the oldest inhabitants used to imitate a cock's crow and try to wake the village cocks, as I once heard him do.

The little green is on a sharp slope. North of it is the guildhall and the church, while to the south is the old vicarage, the Carrier (28), the village hall (29) presented to the community in 1905, two Victorian brick cottages (30a and b), and the King's Head (31).

Three roads meet at the Cross Hill signpost. The road to the west is labelled Chrishall and Heydon; the High Street, running south, goes to Wenden Lofts, Audley End and Saffron Walden; and the road to the east is the Ickleton Road. Each had its own distinctive character in 1964.

The road to Heydon was dominated by a late Victorian, red-brick farmhouse, Elmdon Lodge (32). Opposite stood a cluster of cottages, some of which were tied and housed the Elmdon Lodge labour force. In 1964, this was in no sense a commuter centre.

The central road leading south from Cross Hill, the High Street, is lined with old houses and cottages. In 1957 seven of these cottages were occupied by Elmdon people, forming a neighbourhood group of eleven local families with the addition of the four tenants of 'the Bangles', but by 1977 the number of indigenous inhabitants had dropped to two. The other dwellings had been bought by outsiders and by 1970 they had been 'converted' with loving care by their mainly commuter owners, and had acquired new bow windows, additional rooms, garages, car ports, cedar doors and outside hanging lamps. Tied cottages which might well have been condemned as unfit for habitation had blossomed forth into an elegance which would have surprised their Tudor builders. No wonder this part of Elmdon is known as the 'posh' or 'toffs'' end of the village.

A turning off the High Street leads into Kings Lane, perhaps one of the most romantic sites in Elmdon, and one over which bitter controversy raged when speculative builders twice attempted to 'spoil Kings Lane' by putting up bungalows there. The lane runs steeply uphill, its surface scored by rain gutters, with cottages on either side, both white and pink. Two of these must be the smallest dwellings in Elmdon of the 'two up and two down' type, in one of which a labourer is said to have brought up a family of ten. Kings Lane must have been a busy place in earlier days. There was a forge and a beer-shop at its junction with High Street. The forge was dismantled in 1944 when the attached house became a private dwelling. Opposite was a cottage said to have been the village bakehouse, while Sarah Freeman, formerly a children's nurse in high society, inherited a laundry at the top of the lane from her aunt, and ran it for many years with village labour. But Kings Lane today is a quiet place. In the silence that falls on the village at mid-day it has an almost dreamlike quality. Only two Elmdon families lived in it in 1964, an old couple who rented a cottage set back from the road from an owner who lived in America, and a mother and unmarried son who were tenants of an immigrant couple who owned another cottage in the village as a holiday home. The other cottages were inhabited by three single women and two couples, all retired from occupations pursued elsewhere.

The Ickleton Road, the third road to leave the Cross Hill junction, runs east. On this route out of Elmdon there is a lively

King's Lane, 1979

mixture of house-styles and all the social services — the police
station, the post office, the school and the shop. Eleven of the
Ickleton Road houses would be called 'old', that is to say built
before the nineteenth century, and some of the larger of these
houses were in the past occupied by craftsmen, such as the wheelwright, or beer-sellers. There were also some Victorian buildings,
mostly made of brick, and two small blocks of terraced houses,
Manor Row (72 a-d) and School Row (57a-d), which are of interest
as they were never tied cottages but rentable accommodation. In
the early twentieth century the Squire built no fewer than seven
houses for his senior employees and one for a relative. They were
apparently constructed of a mixture of chalk and cement by
Wilkes' own workmen in 1904. They were much derided at the
time, and were called the houses 'that Jack built'. But they have
acquired a certain dignity with age and now seem to 'fit' in the
street. Houses were also put up by individual purchasers in the
earlier twenties, some on the sites of decrepit cottages. There
was a bungalow built by a farmer in the late fifties, on the site of
some tied cottages of great age, which were dark and damp, sunk

below the level of the street, and known as the Wurzel Clamp because of their shape. There were also a few newer houses put up by individual purchasers in the sixties. The days of the speculative builder did not come till much later when Elmdon was attached to the main-drainage system in 1975.

The council houses, built in blocks at intervals of some years and in a great variety of styles, are also situated on the Ickleton Road. The Glebe (66a-f) was the first to be built (1922). It is constructed round three sides of a square which is open to the road and filled with tenants' vegetable patches. The Glebe has now a comfortable, lived-in appearance and an air of quite venerable age. It also has a central position near the shop. Further down Ickleton Road are the main council blocks (74a-79b) which are built in the grimmer style of council architecture of 1948, together with six houses similar in style, which either belong to a farmer or are individually-owned. In this group of twenty new houses, mostly council built, Elmdon people who left tied cottages were housed. As in other English villages, these two housing blocks are on the edge of Elmdon as there was nowhere else to build. This geographical isolation, slight as it is, accounts for the use of the term 'the council people' to describe the inhabitants, and perhaps explains the resentment some of them feel at being, as they say, 'cooped up in the council houses' without the means to buy themselves a house at the present exorbitant rates elsewhere in the village.[6]

The more recent council housing does not have this defect. The six Bury cottages (65a-f), known originally as the 'old people's bungalows' are built on a ridge on the north side of the road next to what was then the school. These bungalows fulfilled such an obvious need that two more were built in 1967. The bungalows have a fine view, not only over the hillside opposite, but over the shop (61) which was certainly the centre of village life in 1964 and is even more so of recent years since the store has taken over the post-office. The shop is the place for gossip and information and is the most useful meeting place in the village. The school, next door to the old people's housing, was also a centre of social life in 1964 before it was closed and the school transferred to Chrishall. It was the place where meetings, wedding receptions, whist drives and jumble sales were held, as the present village hall had not been enlarged sufficiently to fulfil these functions by 1964.

This then is the Ickleton Road, a mixture of Tudor, Victorian, and twentieth-century buildings, early and late; a set of houses built by landowners, private individuals, council authorities and, recently, speculative builders that is probably typical of Essex villages and perhaps of those of other counties as well. It has certainly not got the beauty of harmony but it is a street full of activity where all the inhabitants of Elmdon go to and fro.

As to its amenities Elmdon probably reaches the level of other small villages in this part of the world. It has no street-lighting and this is felt to be a grievance because old people still remember the time when the streets were lit with gas lamps, one on Cross Hill, one at the church corner, one at the entrance to Kings Lane and one opposite the Old Forge which was once the post office. Some inhabitants were still drawing water in buckets from the pump in the High Street in 1966 and these were carried on a wooden yoke as Swiss milkmaids used to carry buckets of milk. There was another pump in the Ickleton Road near the house now called 'Pump Cottage'. Elmdon was not attached to the main-drainage system till 1975 — households used Elsan sanitation or had septic tanks. Seventeen households had no interior sanitation in 1970.

Elmdon may build and rebuild its houses, add a bit here and take away a bit there, 'spoil' its ancient appearance or 'improve' it, but its site will remain. Medieval English villages tend to have been built on the slopes of fortified hills where these existed and this gives them their variety and charm. Elmdon between two such hills is a fine example. Its most beautiful view is seen from the site of a medieval castle on top of Elmdon Bury hill — 'Castle hill' on the Ordnance map. Here a rectangular moat survives intact and there is a sweeping view over rolling fields as far as Ely in one direction and over the hills behind Ickleton and Gt Chesterford in the other. Below Castle hill the land falls abruptly to Elmdon Bury Farm and then to the road junction, Cross Hill. The Saffron Walden road then plunges down-hill into the valley of the High Street, before rising steeply up the opposite hill, Wenden Lofts. It is surely the switch-back roads of many English hill villages which gives them their distinctive beauty, and Elmdon on top of its chalk ridge is typical in this respect.

Origins of this book

This book was never planned as a conventional social survey. It grew out of a teaching experiment. In 1962 Edmund Leach and I, both then members of the Department of Social Anthropology of Cambridge University, decided to provide some practical fieldwork training for some of our students. Many of them were going to work in what would be to them very unfamiliar environments, in, for instance, Africa, Asia, South America or Oceania, and they would have to face difficult and exacting tasks in their fieldwork. We felt they should have some first-hand experience of a few of the basic techniques of anthropological research, such as interviewing and the taking and keeping of notes. We decided that the collection of genealogies and family histories, usually considered an essential part of anthropological fieldwork could well be undertaken in an English village within the short span available in student vacations. We chose Elmdon for this experiment because I had acquired a house there some two years earlier, and because we were impressed by the number of householders with the same surname who appeared in the current electoral rolls. Some of these names were also to be seen on tombstones in the churchyard, dating in some cases to the eighteenth century.[7] This seemed to indicate a continuity in at least part of the village population and these were the families which we thought it would be profitable to study. I had one neighbour who belonged to one of these old Elmdon families and another who had been a teacher in the village school for forty-four years. Both were interested in the project and willing to help us.

The students were asked to collect the genealogies of some families which were chosen because of their long association with Elmdon, namely the Clarks, Gamgees, Greenhills, Hammonds, Hayes, Hoys, Laws and Reeves -- all names which appear in the present book. We also asked the students to get as much information as possible about the life-histories of living members of the selected families. We hoped they would get data on three generations of a family by interview and would be able to trace lines back as far as the fourth and fifth or even the sixth generation with the help of the parish registers and other documents.

It soon became clear that we were handling a very large group of people. This was specially the case when an ancestor had had a number of children who had all survived the hard conditions of the nineteenth century and had remained resident in Elmdon. Robert Hammond, for instance, who had a child baptised in Elmdon in 1816 according to the register, had a son, a second

Robert (1824–72) who had six sons and three daughters who all remained in Elmdon, married there and produced children. Therefore the descendants of the first Robert Hammond form a large group in Elmdon today. A student calculated there were as many as fifty living adults, out of a population of 321, who had relationships by blood or marriage to the Hammonds. We were dealing, in fact, with six or seven large groups, much intermarried as it turned out, and this is one of the reasons why our family case-history method proved so useful, not only in providing experience for students, but as a means of reconstructing the history of an English village, its changes in occupation, emigration and immigration patterns and lifestyle.

Four student parties worked in the village during the next few years. Four second-year students of anthropology were in Elmdon for a week to ten days in August 1962,[8] five for a period of two weeks in December 1963,[9] two for a fortnight in July 1965,[10] and another two for a fortnight in August 1967.[11] I was able to provide some continuity by making week-end and vacation visits to Elmdon until I became a permanent resident in 1964. I made notes, for instance, on village events such as weddings, funerals, Christmas celebrations, and meetings, whether of the parish council or the village hall committee. Edmund Leach was obliged to leave the work in 1967 when he became Provost of King's College, Cambridge, but he left us valuable notes on the history of Elmdon and many ideas.

The student visits were of course extremely short but a surprising amount of fascinating material was collected, owing both to the enthusiasm of the students and also to the fact that our informants seemed to enjoy the informal and quite unstructured interviews, and particularly liked to describe their childhood and youth in the Elmdon of 'old days', actually the early twenties.

The teaching experiment was, I think, successful but it certainly took a long time, as the dates of the students' visits show. This is not the place to discuss the history of the project with its achievements and failures, though our experience will certainly be of interest to the numerous students of anthropology and sociology now embarking on village surveys. More material will be given in the more directly anthropological volume on Elmdon, *Kinship at the core* by Marilyn Strathern. Suffice it to say here that we soon found it necessary to extend our study of the old Elmdon families and to take a census of the village as a whole. This was completed in 1964, mainly by Ann Whitehead. We thus had the genealogies and histories ·of six selected families, and data on the birth, the residential and occupational history, marriage and offspring of all the adult inhabitants of the village. It is for this reason that 1964 was selected as the terminal date of the present study. But the changes in the composition of the population were rapid after 1964 and we made further checks in 1971, 1974 and 1977. This material appears in a chapter on recent changes in Elmdon society contributed by Frances Oxford to Marilyn Strathern's book.

As the years went on, it became clear that in spite of our original modest intentions we had enough material to produce a book. We therefore had to systematise the work. In 1969 Julian Laite and Paul Atkinson did a preliminary housing survey and completed the village map and in 1971, Hilda Kabushenga, a student from Uganda, checked our figures for a month. In 1972 we were able to appoint our first whole-time investigators, D. Woodhill, a sociologist, and R. Taylor, a historian, who both worked almost entirely on documentary material and produced preliminary studies of the Lofts Hall estate and of the farming families of Elmdon, together with histories of some of the other families no longer represented in Elmdon, and a history of the school.

At the same time Jean Robin, a geographer, agreed to put order into our genealogical material and to make sense of the scattered bits of information contained in field-notes, the preliminary analyses of parish registers, and the other documents. She and I decided as an interim measure to prepare a small book for the people of Elmdon containing the history of six of our selected families — the Gamgees, Greenhills, Hayes, Hammonds, Hoys and Reeves — all still represented in the village. This little book under both our names was published privately in 1975 with the title of *Some Elmdon Families.*

By then Jean Robin had become an expert in the nineteenth-century history of Elmdon and had worked and re-worked the census material to produce an unexpected amount of information on the social and economic history of Elmdon as a whole, its population changes, its emigration and immigration rates, the transformation of Elmdon occupations during the past hundred years, and the education and employment of women in the late nineteenth century, together with detailed material on the history of the Lofts Hall estate and of the changes in farming ownership and farming organisation. It went far beyond the scope of *Some*

Elmdon Families. After a short period of work with the Cambridge Group for the History of Population and Social Structure, she started to write a history of a hundred years of change in the economic and social life of Elmdon as a whole. The study has been based on two sets of data. Firstly the documentary material, mainly the official records and the surveys of the Lofts Hall estate, 1927 and 1860. Secondly, the verbal information provided by the inhabitants of the village, together with their views and comments. This combination of written and oral information may well be the first experiment of its kind yet made. One of its advantages became obvious once the work for the book about the six families had begun. It was clear that the oral information enlarged the historical span of the selected kinship groups both in time-depth and geographical distribution.

The national census provided a wealth of information on family size, household composition, occupation and, by deduction, on population changes, emigration and immigration, as Jean Robin's statistics show so clearly, but the last census available to scholars is that taken in 1871. Parish registers, of course, continued to be kept after that date and give us details on the birth, marriage and death of all Elmdon inhabitants who were baptised, married or buried in the village. But the genealogies produced by interview were completed in most cases up to 1972 because our informants insisted that we put in the names of children recently born, as the family trees in *Some Elmdon Families* show. This gives a very long time-depth in the history of village kinship groups. The documentary plus the verbal information gives a longer historical span than most anthropologists have been able to use. It also enabled Jean Robin to provide information on the whereabouts of family members who had left Elmdon and had therefore ceased to appear in the census, together with their occupations, marriages and children. Had the emigrants raised their economic position and social status or lowered it as judged by their occupations, most of them in urban areas? Had the girls who went into domestic service in London, married policemen or milkmen on the round, or returned home to marry childhood sweethearts? Both occurred, as the interviews showed.

The field notes also enabled us to study the persistence of the sense of kinship identity under modern village conditions. How far are those who left Elmdon remembered and for how long? *Kinship at the core* gives interesting data from the parish registers on the return of Elmdon men and women to have their children baptised in St Nicholas Church, or to bury their relatives there. I was able to note the number of absentee relatives who came back to Elmdon for holiday visits, weddings and funerals. Students of migratory labour in South Africa and Zambia have often wanted such information but the official records are not adequate for the purpose. In an English village, by contrast, it would be possible to make some estimation of the persistence of kinship links over one or two, or even three generations both in the case of absentees in nearby villages as well as those who have gone further afield.

This whole question of the persistence of the sense of kinship identity of course depends on people's memories and the means they take to preserve them. The accuracy of the Elmdon people's power of recall of genealogical facts as compared to the records in the parish register is a fundamental piece of knowledge for anthropologists, and one still to be worked out.

Another interesting result of our work was a continual and useful kind of cross-fertilisation between the records and the material obtained by interview. This was stimulating. Take, for instance, the question of marriage. Living people told us that they remembered inter-village fights, one resulting in a death, and that these were mainly 'about women'. Some also gave an impression that wives were difficult to get and that it was a friendly act to produce a bride for a mate. Brother and sister exchange marriage went on in Elmdon over several generations and such marriages often indicate a shortage of either men or women in other societies, a shortage which leads families to claim rights over suitable spouses for their sons or daughters. Did something of the kind exist in Elmdon or did the isolation of the community lead to large numbers of intra-village unions, of which brother and sister marriages were one form? What was the sex ratio in Elmdon at different periods of its history? Was there a shortage of marriageable girls in fact as well as imagination, and if so was it due to the emigration of girls to London and elsewhere to take posts in domestic service? How many girls from London found husbands in Elmdon? Anecdotes sometimes pose questions to the records and the records sometimes send the fieldworker back to ask questions of the living.

It is because Jean Robin has been able to use these different sources of information so fruitfully that I believe this book will

make a valuable contribution to the increasing number of studies
of English village life.

Audrey Richards

Preface

A newcomer to Elmdon would quickly find his way round the village, for it is not a large community. In 1964, the year in which this study ends, it contained 114 households, one less than it had done just over a hundred years earlier at the beginning of the period under consideration. In 1861, as now, agriculture was the only industry of any importance not only in the village itself but in the parish in which it lay. Even the rate of population turnover was almost unchanged, being marginally greater in the mid-nineteenth century than it was in the 1950s. The question must be asked whether a study of continuity and change in such a small and apparently stable community can have any relevance outside the confines of the immediate area.

This book does not set out to assess how typical an English village Elmdon may be. Yet its recent history does throw light on matters of interest to rural societies in general. For all its dependence on agriculture and its lack of physical growth since 1861, Elmdon lies not in some remote border area but within fifty miles of London, with a mainline station less than five miles away which was already in operation in 1861 and which provided then, as now, a service to the heart of the City. While it made little personal difference to the men working on the land in Elmdon in the nineteenth and early twentieth centuries whether the capital was fifty or five hundred miles off, London and its environs offered opportunities to those who had to seek employment elsewhere; and soon after the First World War the village began to be drawn into the commuter belt. The maintenance of Elmdon's stability as late as 1964, while it was so open to influence by the largest conurbation in the country, is a matter for remark.

Because Elmdon's population has been a comparatively small one throughout the period of this study, it has been possible to follow the lives of individuals and families in a degree of detail which can illuminate many areas not always thoroughly explored. For example, the annual registers of electors available from the end of the nineteenth century onwards provide a tool by which overall population turnover can be assessed; but because the numbers of individuals concerned are few, it has also been possible to discover what kind of people entered the village, how long they stayed, and what influence events such as the two World Wars had on the old-established Elmdon families. Again, analysis of marriage data can reveal not only the proportion of intra-village marriages, but also the degree to which the different occupational groups 'kept themselves to themselves', and kinship links can be traced and their influence assessed in a way that would be inhibited by a considerably larger sample.

Finally, for the first sixty-six years of the period covered, Elmdon's history provides an opportunity to consider the effect on a village of a squire who owned only half its farms and cottages. In Elmdon, the other half of the land and houses belonged to a number of different owners, many of whom let their properties, so that whatever the social influence of the Squire throughout Elmdon, in economic terms the villagers had an alternative to employment and housing on his estate. Some of the advantages and disadvantages of being inside or outside the squirearchical system can therefore be seen by comparing the fortunes of the Squire's tenants on the one hand, and those living outside the estate on the other. The sale of the Squire's property to a number of new owners between 1927 and 1930 provides an opportunity to observe how far changes in land and property ownership affected Elmdon's agricultural population, and to what extent the Squire's paternalism towards his farm-labouring tenants, most of whom he had known all his life, was replaced by paternalism of a rather different kind exercised at one remove by the local authority through their housing programme, and from even further away by the national government through its rent acts.

This book attempts to look at all sections of Elmdon's population, and to assess the effect on their daily lives of external events, whether personal, local or national. In so doing, it provides a framework of basic information for use by Marilyn Strathern in her companion volume *Kinship at the core,* which considers the nature of community in Elmdon from an anthropologist's viewpoint. The two approaches are necessarily different, and in some cases result in different interpretations of terminology. For example, to say in this book that an incomer marrying an Elmdoner, and taking up permanent residence in the village as a result, has become 'established' in Elmdon implies no more than the inescapable fact that he or she is physically present there. The question as to whether, or to what extent, such an incomer is accepted as part of the community is one of the matters explored by Marilyn Strathern.

In writing this book I have been greatly indebted to Audrey Richards who not only supervised the study of Elmdon village, undertaken by students of the University of Cambridge Department of Social Anthropology, from its inception in 1962, but also gave ungrudgingly of her time and knowledge while the book was in preparation. I am also grateful to Edmund Leach who, with Audrey Richards, directed the survey in its early years and whose notebooks, like hers, have proved so valuable, and to the students themselves. Without their interviews with long-established Elmdon residents, it would have been impossible to piece together in any detail the history of Elmdon from the sale of the Squire's property in 1927 onwards, and these same interviews gave many leads back into the more distant past. My thanks go to David Woodhill for his very useful work on the history of the Lofts Hall estate, and to Rosaleen Taylor for her study of the Wilkes family. Marilyn Strathern has been unfailingly helpful in her comments on the manuscript.

I would also like to thank the late Mrs Wilkes, and her nephew Major Rippingall, for access to family papers; the Rev. Francis Dufton, who bore so patiently with repeated requests for inspection of the parish registers and who provided much information on local affairs; Mr and Mrs Walter Brand of Chrishall for showing me their collection of family documents and allowing the reproduction of a page from Robert Brand's arithmetic book on page 175; Mr Jack Cross for his help on the agricultural history of Elmdon; Mr Weeden for his recollections of the early days of the bus services; and all those who so kindly made available the title-deeds of their properties and provided photographs. I am particularly grateful to the people of Elmdon, too numerous to mention individually, who have given so much of their time to helping the project through their knowledge of the past.

My thanks go to Mr Peter Laslett, Miss Elaine Lingham, Dr Alan Macfarlane, Dr Mary Prior and Dr Edith Whetham for their helpful suggestions and comments on the manuscript; to Mr Michael

Young who designed the. housing map on p. viii; and Dr Lucy Adrian who not only organised this map, but who also gave continual help and advice to the survey throughout the period.

Finally, financial help in the earlier stages of the Elmdon survey from 1962 onwards is gratefully acknowledged from the Esperenza Trust, the Wenner-Gren Foundation and the Nuffield Foundation. This assistance led to the private publication in 1975 of *Some Elmdon Families* by Audrey Richards and Jean Robin, which has been used as a major source. Publication of the present volume has been made possible through the generosity of the Wenner-Gren Foundation and the British Academy, to both of which I am most grateful. My thanks also go the the Department of Social Anthropology, University of Cambridge, for the purchase of essential documentary material, and for allowing me the use of a microfilm reader throughout the preparation of the book.

Cambridge, November 1978   Jean Robin

I

Elmdon in 1861

If an observer in 1964 standing on the sloping green at Cross Hill in the centre of Elmdon, had had the power to take himself back a hundred years or so to 1861, he would have noticed remarkably little change in his immediate surroundings. The roads of course would look different, for they would be unmetalled. The High Street running down the hill towards Wenden Lofts, and the roads eastward to Ickleton and westward to Chrishall would be dry and dusty if it were summer, rutted and muddy in winter. But the church would look much the same, its square tower standing out against a background of trees; the King's Head and the Carrier, rival public houses in 1964, were both selling beer in 1861; the Old Vicarage would be instantly recognisable on the corner of Ickleton Road; and down the curve of the High Street the outside of the houses would look relatively unchanged. If the outward appearance of much of Elmdon seemed little different, however, the same cannot be said of the society it contained. What kind of a place was it to live in, in 1861, and who were the people who made their homes there?

The Squire

There were 520 people living in Elmdon in 1861,[1] but it must be said straightaway that the man with the most power and influence over the village was not among them. He was the Reverend Robert Fiske Wilkes, and as owner of the Lofts Hall estate, he lived in the neighbouring parish of Wenden Lofts, though the Hall itself lay only half a mile from Cross Hill.

Robert Wilkes had not always expected to come into the owner-ship of the estate. He was born Robert Fiske, son of a clergyman who was both Rector of Wenden Lofts and Vicar of Elmdon. His relationship to the previous Squire, John Wilkes, was somewhat

1

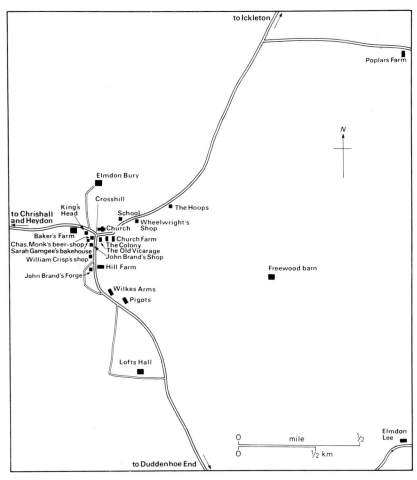

to Ickleton

Poplars Farm

N

Elmdon Bury

Crosshill

King's
Head

to Chrishall
and Heydon

Baker's Farm
Chas. Monk's beer-shop
Sarah Gamgee's bakehouse
William Crisp's shop
John Brand's Forge

School

The Hoops

Wheelwright's
Shop

Church

Church Farm
The Colony
The Old Vicarage
John Brand's Shop

Hill Farm

Freewood barn

Wilkes Arms

Pigots

Lofts Hall

Elmdon
Lee

0   mile   ½
0   ½ km

to Duddenhoe End

Map 2   Elmdon village in 1861

2

remote, since he was the latter's mother's great nephew. But John Wilkes died, childless, in 1848, and when his widow also died ten years later, Robert Fiske succeeded to the property, changed his name to Wilkes, left the vicarage in Elmdon village, where, like his father before him, he had been carrying out his parish duties, and moved into Lofts Hall. On the day the 1861 census was taken, he was living there with his wife, one son and five daughters. His elder son was away from home, probably at school. The family was supported by a butler, a cook-housekeeper, a trio of carefully graded housemaids — upper, ordinary and lower — a kitchenmaid, a nursemaid, and a governess, all living in. His coachman occupied one of the lodges, and his head gardener had rentfree quarters in Pigots homestead near the lodge gates.

There was no problem in finding room in the Hall for this large group of people. Built on the site of an older house by Sir Thomas Meade in 1579, Lofts Hall had been through the usual series of alterations and improvements common to large country houses of any antiquity. It was to undergo further changes after 1861 before it was finally burned down in 1934[2] (some say as a result of a fire lighted to destroy jackdaws' nests in the billiard room chimney, others less romantically blaming a faulty electric light switch). For example, Sir James Bailey, who leased the Hall during the early part of the twentieth century, built on an extra wing. The exact size of the Hall in 1861 is therefore not known, but when it was put up for auction in 1927, it was described as containing twenty principal and secondary bed and dressing rooms, as well as five servants' bedrooms; a drawing-room, 30 feet by 19 feet panelled in old oak with a gilded frieze; a dining-room of similar size with windows running the length of the apartment; a library, a morning-room, a smoke room, an outer hall measuring 45 feet by 17 feet, and a billiard room some 36 feet by 26 feet.[3] This last room was probably the 'ballroom' described in 1964 by an elderly lady in Elmdon who occasionally worked at the Hall in her youth. She recalled 'a lovely room — huge — with a glass roof and white walls with pheasants all over them'. Even without Sir James Bailey's new wing, it is clear that in 1861 the Rev. Robert Wilkes was living in some style. The panelling indeed was so fine that after the 1927 sale it was stripped from the walls and sold in London, ending up in the Hearst collection in the United States.

It was not simply his ownership of Lofts Hall that made Robert Wilkes such an important figure in Elmdon. With the Hall went

3

Rev. Robert Fiske Wilkes

the estate, which at that time consisted of 3,782 acres of land in
the parishes of Wenden Lofts, Elmdon and Chrishall, along with a
smaller estate of 851 acres at Chishill, a mile or two west of
Chrishall.[4] However, while he owned most of the property in the
southern half of Elmdon parish, centred on Duddenhoe End,
Robert Wilkes had acquired only half the farm land and cottages
in and around Elmdon village itself. The history of the estate up

4

to its dispersal in the late 1920s will be outlined in chapter 3, but in 1861, its future seemed secure.

As landowner, Robert Wilkes had considerable power over his tenant farmers, for he could terminate or renew their leases when these fell in after their seven-year term. He also had direct influence on the lives of the 240 inhabitants of Elmdon, nearly half the population, who in 1861 were living in houses or cottages owned by him. All Elmdoners were his parishioners, for in 1861 he remained Vicar of Elmdon, as well as Rector of Wenden Lofts, though he had a curate living in Elmdon to help him. Even the children came into contact with him, since he had a close association with the village school which had been rebuilt on land presented by his predecessor at Lofts Hall, John Wilkes, in 1843.[5] And finally he held the sonorous titles of Lord of the Manor of Mountneys and Dagsworth, otherwise Elmdon Bury, Lord of the Manor, or reputed Manor, of Duddenhoe, Lord of the Manor of Rockells, Wiggpitts and Coggleshalls, and Lord of the Manor of Flanders with Chiswick, although to the villagers he was simply 'the Squire'. Even in 1861, incidentally, his titles were not entirely empty, since the Manor Courts were still sitting, largely over land transactions and inheritance matters, and indeed the Elmdon Bury Court continued until 1899.[6]

Other property owners

Although Robert Wilkes owned nearly half the land and houses in Elmdon in 1861, the rest of the property in and around the village was distributed among a miscellany of owners.

The three farms not included in the Lofts Hall estate covered some 1,140 acres. Two of them, Poplars Farm and The Lee, both on the eastern borders of the parish, were the property of absentee landlords who seem to have played no part in village affairs. The third, Baker's Farm, was bought in 1858 by James Hayden.[7] He and his father before him had been tenants at the homestead, and with its purchase he became the first recorded owner-occupier of a farm in Elmdon.

We do not know the ownership of each of the remaining houses and cottages but some were owner-occupied by craftsmen or tradesmen, like the blacksmith John Brand and the tailor James Walters; some were owned by the tenant farmers, like Miss Perry at Poplars, who held a life interest in one of the houses in the High

Table 1
Elmdon village occupations, 1861

	male	female
Clergymen	2	—
Farmers, and	5	1
working sons	3	—
Blacksmiths/wheelwrights	8	—
Thatchers	3	—
Builders/bricklayers	9	1
Bricklayers' apprentices	2	—
Bricklayers' labourers	3	—
Painters	—	1
Carpenters	5	—
Tailors	3	—
Shoemakers	2	—
Dressmakers	—	4
Straw-bonnet makers	—	2
Victuallers, beer-sellers	2	2
Bakers	1	1
Bakers' working sons	2	—
Butchers	1	—
Butchers' boys	1	—
General shopkeepers	1	—
Drapers, upholsterers	1	—
Shop assistants	—	2
Postmaster	1	—
Carriers	2	—
Schoolmistress	—	1
Farm bailiffs	2	—
Farm labourers - 15 years and over	80	—
14 years and under	24	—
Shepherds - 15 years and over	5	—
14 years and under	2	—
Cowmen	1	—
Female field workers	—	12
Gentlemen's servants	1	—
Gardeners	1	—
Gardeners' labourers	2	—
Grooms	2	—
Companions	—	1
Domestic servants, living-in	—	10
Domestic servants, living-out	—	5
Domestic servants home on holiday	—	2
Nurses/nursemaids	—	2
Laundresses	—	1
Totals	177[i]	48

(i) This figure includes 3 cases of dual occupation, i.e. baker and beer-seller, farmer and shopkeeper, shopkeeper and postmaster. The total number of individual men is therefore 174.

Source: 1861 census

6

Street, which she let to a village shopkeeper;[8] and some belonged to small-scale property investors such as James Ward who was listed as owning six cottages in Elmdon at the time of the Enclosure Award in 1829.[9] Very few cottages were owned by farm labourers, who made up a large part of the population, and no individual property-holder stood out as a rival to the Squire in power and influence.

The clergy

The work of the community, however, had to go on whether or not an individual owned his house, rented it or occupied a tied cottage. Surprisingly enough, there were no well-do-do upper- or middle-class families in Elmdon itself living entirely from investments without any kind of paid employment, and only two household heads could be described as professional people, as table 1 shows. Both these men were clerics. The curate of Elmdon lived in what is now the Old Vicarage at Cross Hill. Today it is in private hands, having been replaced by a smaller and more convenient vicarage behind the church, but then it housed the curate, his 11-year old nephew who had been born in India, and a solitary living-in servant. Next door lived the Rector of Strethall, a small parish two miles away. The rector's stipend was only £155 per annum,[10] but his family had private means, for his widowed mother and two sisters, who were living with him, were all described in the census as holding investments in government funds, and the household ran to two living-in domestic servants. Strethall had its own perfectly adequate rectory, and its incumbent probably came to live in Elmdon through friendship with the Squire, who charged him no rent for his house. When this house, now called 'Farthing Green', was put up for sale in 1927 with the rest of the Lofts Hall estate, it was described as 'The Colony', a name which was the result of a particularly atrocious Victorian pun. The rector in question was the Rev. Joseph Collin, and it was from his name that 'The Colony' was derived. The little boy from India may well have had a rather depressing time while he was with his uncle, for, apart from the domestic servants, no one else in the two neighbouring clerical households was under 41 years of age and, apart from Mr Collin's widowed mother of 72, all were unmarried.

7

Croquet at The Colony, *c.* 1870

The farmers

Next to the rector and curate in the village hierarchy came the farmers. They may have been below the clergy in the social scale, but they had considerably more economic power, since in 1861 they directly employed six out of every ten men working in the village. Their holdings were big, four out of the six being of 300 acres or more. Then as now, the farms were largely arable, and therefore labour intensive in the days before the widespread use of machinery.[11] The size of each farm and the number of men and boys employed are shown in table 2.

Farmers such as John Rolfe, with his 705 acres, were clearly comparatively wealthy men. Rolfe was paying an annual rent of £1,040 for the use of Elmdon Bury in 1860, as well as his share of £130 for shooting rights over 1,160 acres, which he held jointly with his cousin, James Rolfe, an estate tenant in Wenden Lofts.[12] Elmdon Bury farmhouse was a fine building, containing a parlour, hall, keeping room, dairy, kitchen, scullery, pantry, cellar, laundry and six bedrooms, and there were two living-in house servants to help Mrs Rolfe with her domestic duties.

8

Table 2
Elmdon village farms, 1861

farmer	farm	acres	no. of employees men	no. of employees boys
John Rolfe (LHE tenant)	Elmdon Bury (including Freewood)	705	28	12
Charles Mickley (non-LHE tenant)	The Lee	480	21	8
James Hayden (owner)	Baker's	360	11	5
Rebecca Perry (non-LHE tenant)	Poplars	300	10	3
Edward Hayden (LHE tenant)	Church	209	8[i]	-
John Brand (LHE tenant)	Hill	116	3	5
Totals		2,170	81	33

(i) This figure has been taken from the 1851 census for Church Farm, since no return of employees was made in 1861.

LHE = Lofts Hall estate

Source: 1861 census

The homesteads of Church Farm and Hill Farm, both belonging to the Lofts Hall estate, lay right in the heart of the village, only 250 yards apart across the fields which separated them. Church Farm was just over 200 acres, but the farmhouse, next to The Colony, was similar in size to that of Elmdon Bury. The tenant, Edward Hayden, must have had no difficulty in filling the six bedrooms, since he had the largest household in Elmdon, consisting of twelve people in all - himself, his wife, his son and six daughters, his widower-father, a young nephew, Robert Pigg, who was working as a labourer on the farm, and a 16-year-old domestic servant. Hill Farm was occupied by another of Edward Hayden's nephews, John Brand, a young man whose great-great-great-grandfather had been the common ancestor of himself and of the other Elmdon John Brand, the blacksmith living in the High Street to whom reference has already been made. The farm only covered just over 100 acres, and John, with his sister Caroline, also kept a grocer's shop as a supplement to his income.

Baker's Farm, too, was close to the village, lying just to the west of Cross Hill. Its owner, James Hayden, was a bachelor, whose unmarried sister lived with him as his housekeeper. Both were born in Henham, Essex, and no connection has been traced between them and the other Haydens in the village.

The two remaining farms, Poplars and The Lee, lay well outside Elmdon. Poplars indeed was comparatively isolated, being nearly threequarters of a mile from another house. The farm was created after the Enclosure Award of 1829, and a farmhouse was built alongside the barns and sheds which were already on the site. The house is still there, smaller than the other Elmdon homesteads and seeming rather dark, being shadowed by the belt of trees around it. Miss Rebecca Perry, an elderly spinster, was the tenant of this 300-acre farm in 1861. She was helped by an equally elderly general servant, and supported by a companion. A farm worker and a groom also lived on the premises. The Lee farm, covering 480 acres and tenanted by Charles Mickley, was larger than Poplars, and it stood considerably closer to the hamlet of Littlebury Green than it did to Elmdon itself.

As well as being major employers, the farmers filled most of the positions on the vestry, a village organisation which preceded the parish council and which was responsible for the allocation of parish relief, as well as for the supervision of the highways and other parish matters. Minutes of vestry meetings held under the chairmanship of John Rolfe of Elmdon Bury in March 1861, listed those eligible for election to the offices of constable, overseer, surveyor, assessor and churchwarden. All but one of those named were farmers, the exception being a shopkeeper.[13] All in all, the farmers made their presence felt.

Those employed in private households

The group of people employed in private households varied from the London-born governess at Lofts Hall, who may well have found that she was short of companionship in her off-duty hours, feeling herself above the house servants in social status, to 13-year old Eliza Challis, daughter of an Elmdon roadman, who lived with her widowed mother and worked by day as a nursemaid.

The Squire's ménage at Lofts Hall was the grandest in the immediate vicinity. Although the Hall was in Wenden Lofts, and therefore the living-in servants do not figure in table 3, they cannot be left out of any account of domestic service in Elmdon in 1861, for Wenden Lofts scarcely existed as a village, containing as it did

Table 3
Proportion of working population in different occupational groups, Elmdon village 1861

	male		female		total	
	no.	% (i)	no.	%	no.	%
Professional	2	1	–	–	2	1
Farmers	8	5	1	2	9	4
Employees in private households	6	3	21	44	27	12
Craftsmen, tradesmen and their workers (ii)	44	25	14	29	58	26
Farm employees	114	66	12	25	126	57
Totals	174	100	48	100	222	100

(i) Because of the small numbers involved, percentages in this and some other tables have been expressed to the nearest whole number. For this reason, percentages do not always total 100.

(ii) includes apprentices, 3 bricklayers' labourers, and the village schoolmistress.

Source: 1861 census

only a dozen scattered households. As a result, the Hall servants were very much part of the Elmdon community, and several of the young women working there over the years married Elmdon men and settled down for good in the village. The very fact that they were employed at the Hall must have given the staff there a certain cachet, and to this was added the distinction that all male head servants, the cook-housekeeper, and the five living-in maids came from outside Elmdon or Wenden Lofts. Only the lesser jobs went to Elmdoners. Thus Richard Peck from Norfolk was the gardener, but his two labourers, a father and son team, were from Elmdon. James Huvet, the coachman, came from Stansfield, but his groom was an Elmdon boy. The butler, who was the husband of the cook-housekeeper, was born in Bishop's Stortford. Robert Pilgrim, who had been employed by one or other member of the Wilkes family for at least twenty years, and who lived in an estate house at the top of King's Lane which to this day is known as Pilgrim's Cottage, came from Great Chesterford. This pattern was repeated in the only two households of the gentry in Elmdon, those of the clergy families. Neither could rise to the employment of men-servants, but their maids came from outside the village. It seems very likely that the Squire's chief male employees were regarded as at least the equals of the craftsmen and tradesmen, and there is

11

some evidence of intermarriage between their families, as we shall see in chapter 7.

The next group of servants to be considered are those working on the farms. Miss Perry at Poplars was exceptional for two reasons; firstly, because she employed a groom — possibly because as a 68-year-old she could not attend to her pony and trap herself — and secondly, because her general servant was elderly. The other six female servants living-in at the farms were all young, ranging from 15 to 23 years of age, and all single. At The Lee and Baker's Farm the girls were specifically described as house servants, but at Elmdon Bury and Church Farm they were classified only as 'servants', so they may well have had to undertake certain duties in the dairy or with the poultry, as well as their indoor work. Only one of these six girls was Elmdon-born, though the other five all came from within a five-mile radius and show a common pattern of employment for girls in the mid-nineteenth century. They left home, before marriage, for a spell of domestic service within walking distance of their own village; and on the rare occasions when a holiday occurred they were able to visit their families and friends. As a result, they often ended by marrying a boy from their home area.

This pattern was repeated by Elmdon girls. Indeed, two girls in their 20s who were employed elsewhere as house servants, were visiting their homes on the day the census was taken. As a further illustration, the 1851 census for Elmdon recorded five 4-year-old girls, but by 1861 only one was still in the village. As the families of the other four were still living there, these four girls can reasonably be supposed to have emigrated to work. On the other hand, eleven of the twelve 3-year-olds in 1851, whose families remained, were still in Elmdon ten years later, which suggests that while 14 was a suitable age for leaving home, 13 was considered too young. This is borne out by the fact that no living-in domestic servant in Elmdon in 1861 was under 15 years of age.

A third group of five servants were sleeping at home, but working by day. This group included three girls of 13, 14 and 15, who might well have gone on to living-in posts later. Finally, three widows, all over 50, kept their houses going by working as a charwoman, a nurse and a laundress respectively. It is not known where these day-workers were employed, but we can safely say that only the Squire, the clergy and the farmers employed living-in domestic help in 1861.

12

Craftsmen and tradesmen

In common with many other country villages, Elmdon in the nineteenth century was more self-sufficient than it is today. Visits to the market town of Saffron Walden, six miles away by road, were necessarily time-consuming, and not to be undertaken lightly.

Elmdon's two former shops in the High Street

T-Meadow - formerly the Brands' shop in the High Street

13

As a result, in 1861 the village enjoyed considerably more services than it did in 1964. There were two shops next door to each other in the High Street. One, which has already been mentioned, was a grocery store run by John Brand of Hill Farm and his sister Caroline. The proprietor of the second was William Crisp, who was also the postmaster. Mr Crisp was the enumerator for the national censuses which were held at ten-year intervals, and he took particular care in describing his own work. In 1851 he entered 'Cabinet Maker and Shopkeeper' against his name, but by 1861 this has been amended to 'Draper, Upholsterer and Post Master'. There were five carpenters in Elmdon, who with the nine brick-layers, the three thatchers and the painter, formed a work force which could take care of most of the building and repair work needed in the village and on the Lofts Hall estate in general. Eight blacksmiths and wheelwrights dealt with the shoeing of horses for private use as well as for farm work, or undertook the repair of machinery, carts and wagons. There were three tailors, two of them being the Walters brothers, John and Jimmy, who lived with their widowed mother at the Hoops beerhouse, which they ran as a side-line. Both of them were musical, John playing the organ and Jimmy the violin. Jimmy lived on into the twentieth century and is remembered as being a fine-looking old man 'with fingers as white as a lady's', who entertained the village with trios played by himself as first violin and his two sons as second fiddle and double bass. The third tailor, Gabriel Rollings, was husband of one of the four dressmakers, and brother of two others. There were two shoe-makers, and two girls made straw bonnets, an occupation which was a throw-back to the time, a few years before, when there had been a straw-bonnet manufactory in Elmdon employing eight young women.[14]

Apart from the grocery store, Elmdon in 1861 had a butcher's shop and two bakeries. There was no mill to provide flour, but grain could be taken either to the Wenden Lofts mill, or down to Duddenhoe End. There were four establishments selling beer. One of these, later to become the Carrier, was also a bakery; another was at the Hoops. The other two were public houses. The King's Head was practically next door to the beer-selling bakery, while the Wilkes Arms, serving the other end of the village, was placed almost at the gates of Lofts Hall. Because it was so close to the Hall, the Wilkes Arms was let on a yearly tenancy, as an incentive to the landlady, Sarah Smoothy, to keep her customers

14

in order, so that the Squire should not be disturbed by roistering and rowdy villagers pouring out at closing time.[15]

Nor was Elmdon deprived of what would nowadays be called public services. Transport was in the hands of two carriers, Joseph Gamgee and Thomas Miller, who were in partnership. Between them, they ran a weekly service to Royston, and sent two carts to Cambridge on Saturdays and one on Wednesdays.[16] A roadman, who lived in Duddenhoe End, looked after the highways and Elmdon shared a policeman with Wenden Lofts. The post office was located in Mr Crisp's shop in the High Street. Finally, a young woman from Islington was in charge of the sixty or so children in the village school, who came from Duddenhoe End and Wenden Lofts as well as Elmdon. She was helped by a nineteen-year old assistant who lodged in the next parish.

Financially, most of this group of craftsmen and tradesmen were better off than the majority of Elmdoners, who worked on the land as labourers. William Crisp and John Brand, the blacksmith, in particular stood out above the others, for John Brand owned his own house and forge, while the Crisps saved enough capital for Mrs Crisp to buy the shop and house, which they had rented for so long, when the opportunity came up in 1877.[17] In addition, both men were the only non-farmers to be included in 1852 in the list of those qualified and liable to serve as constables of the parish, and a year later, William Crisp was serving the vestry as an assessor.[18] Again, the better cottages in the village tended to be rented by this group. But even so, none of the craftsmen or tradesmen in 1861 employed living-in domestic servants, and it is doubtful if the standard of living of the thatchers or carriers, for example, was markedly higher than for the agricultural labourers. The question of how far these craftsmen and tradesmen formed a social as well as an economic group will be seen in chapter 8.

The farm workers

As table 3 shows, the solid base of Elmdon's labour force in 1861 was made up of the 114 male and 12 female farm workers, representing 57 per cent of those gainfully employed in the village. This group was headed by two bailiffs, one almost certainly working for Miss Perry at Poplars Farm, and the other for John Rolfe at Elmdon Bury, and included seven shepherds and one cowman. But the rest were largely concerned with the routine of ploughing,

15

sowing, harvesting and threshing imposed by the pattern of arable farming carried on in the district.

Although the term 'agricultural labourer' may bring to mind a vision of a stalwart man in the prime of life walking behind a plough this is a very one-sided picture. In Elmdon the ages of the farm workers ranged from 7 to 75 years - and the 7-year-old was a girl, who accompanied her widowed mother to the fields. Although it was exceptional for a girl to be employed so young, it was less unusual for a boy. Two 8-year-old boys, out of the seven of that age - in Elmdon, were described as 'agricultural labourers' and neither was marked out, as the 7-year-old girl was, by obvious adversity at home. Indeed, all the boys of 10 years of age and over were at work except for three, of whom two, the cousin of the village schoolmistress and the curate's nephew, were not really Elmdoners. In Elmdon, boys' work was synonomous with work on the land, and all the working boys aged 10 to 14 were employed by the farmers except for one, who was an apprentice bricklayer with the family firm.

At the other end of the scale came the very old farm workers. Their jobs were not sinecures. One Elmdon resident in 1964 could remember watching his 79-year-old grandfather threshing corn with a flail in Freewood barn, a task which he kept up for hours at a time - 'and he did it all on dry bread and water, except that sometimes the water would have a spoonful of milk in it'. Clearly the elderly continued to work as long as they could. Indeed, in 1861 only two agricultural labourers had retired on parish relief, one being over 70 and the other in his 80s. The term 'agricultural labourer', then, covered a very wide age range and only just over half those so described in Elmdon in 1861 were between 20 and 59 years old.

As the age of the 'agricultural labourers' varied, so did the work they were employed on. The children were used on a variety of odd jobs, such as bird-scaring, taking stones off the plough land, leading the horses, and generally fetching and carrying for their elders. Some of the men themselves did specialised work. The shepherds and cowmen have already been mentioned, but the horsemen must not be overlooked. They played an important role in the days before farms were mechanised. An early intimation of their ultimate fate, however, may be found in the survey of the Lofts Hall estate carried out in 1860 by the firm of Carter Jonas, which recorded that John Rolfe had improved Elmdon Bury farm

16

by putting up a 'machinery and engine house'.

Another example of at least temporary specialisation lies in the teams, up to 21-men-strong, who spent four or five weeks each summer bringing in the harvest. More is said about them in chapter 4.

The farm workers were not highly paid for their labours. The average earnings for the midsummer quarter, 1861, in the Dunmow division of Essex were recorded as 10-11 shillings a week for men, 4 shillings a week for women and 3 shillings a week for children under 16, with a shilling's worth of beer also provided.[19] Evidence from a local farm at a rather later period shows that beer was not handed out on an equal basis to all workers, but that different workers received different rations. A horsekeeper, for example, was given beer only on Sundays, while a stockman got it every day, and thatchers and threshers had extra beer for special work. Beer distribution, therefore, was really used as a means of introducing occupational differentials among the work force, and no doubt questions of prestige came into it as well as the pleasure of drinking the beer itself.

Although most agricultural labourers were paid the same weekly wage, and differentials for skill and responsibility were very small in terms of money payments, yet the total income of a household could vary considerably between one family and another. The reason for this lay mainly in the early age at which boys started work. One often hears praise of the parents who brought up a family of ten on 11 or 12 shillings a week, and no one would deny that to do so was a triumphant achievement. But in fact a large family would often have a higher income per head than did the members of a much smaller unit. For example, in 1861 Henry Jeffery, his wife and seven children were living in a tied cottage belonging to Elmdon Bury Farm. If we assume that Elmdon's agricultural workers were receiving the average wages for Essex which have already been quoted, then Henry would have brought home 11 shillings a week, and so would his son Benjamin who was 16, and thus over the age at which he would have been paid as a child. Henry's 15-year-old daughter Henrietta was employed as a field worker, and two more sons aged 11 and 8 were also on the land. If these three were paid the normal wage of 3 shillings a week each for children, the cash going into the household each pay-day would have totalled 31 shillings or 3s 5¼d for each of the nine family members. If, on the other hand, we look at Joseph

King's family, we see that although he and his wife only had two daughters, the four of them had to subsist on a single wage of 11 shillings a week earned by the head of the household, giving them a weekly cash income per head of only 2s 9d.

These were regular wages, but extra money was earned at harvest time. In 1860, Essex men were averaging 21 shillings a week for five weeks over the harvest period, or 9-10 shillings a week more than usual, and in addition they received 5 shillings worth of beer a week, or the money in lieu.[20] These harvest payments helped the labourers to pay their cottage rents, of around £3 0s 0d per annum in Elmdon, which fell due each Michaelmas.

The contribution of the twelve female field workers in 1861 can have had little significance compared with the work done by the men. Outdoor work on the land for women was becoming unfashionable, for it was believed that it encouraged a general coarseness, and would unfit any girl who undertook it for domestic service later in life.[21] The girls and women working on the farms in Elmdon in 1861 fell into two classes; those who were handicapped in some way, and those who were simply carrying on an old tradition. The first group comprised two widows and two fatherless children; a deaf girl of 25 who might well have found both marriage and domestic service closed to her because of her disability; and a single woman in her 20s who was helping to support her elderly pauper grandfather. In the second group came the daughter of an Elmdon Bury farm worker, and five girls, all with the same surname, who lived almost next door to each other and ranged in age from 8 to 25 years. In view of the fears expressed that field work would damage a girl's prospects in domestic service, it is interesting to see that two of the three younger girls among the fieldworkers remaining in Elmdon in 1871 had managed to acquire jobs as living-in servants.

Up to this point, Elmdon society in 1861 has been represented as a pyramid, the apex being formed by the gentry and the base by the farm workers. The people at work, however, comprised less than half the total population of the village. The remaining 57 per cent cannot be ignored. Except for five men on parish relief and an elderly retired farmer, all of them were women and children.

18

Children

The numerical importance of children in bringing Elmdon's population up to its total of 520 individuals in 1861 can be seen from table 4, which shows that two out of every five people in the village were less than 15 years old. The national average for this age range in the same year was rather lower, being 35.6 per cent[22] against 41 per cent in Elmdon, although as chapter 9 shows, this was not because Elmdoners had more children than people in other parts of the country, but rather because emigration of girls in their late teens and young men in their 20s meant the 15-44 age group was under-represented in Elmdon in comparison with the country as a whole.

Like present-day children who do not live near a nursery school or play group, all the under-5s were at home, except for one 4-year-old who was staying temporarily with a farm bailiff's family and attending school. The rest of the children, from 5 to 14, fell into three main groups — those who were being educated, those at work, and those who simply lived at home waiting until they were old enough to do a paid job.

In 1861, compulsory education still lay fifteen years in the future,[23] but schooling was no novelty in Elmdon. Over 300 years earlier, in 1559, a local landowner called Thomas Crawley had founded a grammar school in the former guildhall, still standing, next to the church at Cross Hill. In his will he left £14 0s 0d a year to pay 'one honest, convenient, meet and able schoolmaster, being a priest, to be chosen by the patron of the vicarage of Elmdon, the vicar of Elmdon, the parson of Heydon, vicar of Chrishall and parson of Wenden Lofts . . . to keep and teach a grammar school within the town of Elmdon, within which school I will there shall

Table 4
Age structure, Elmdon village 1861

Years	0—14		15—29		30—44		45—59		60+		total	
	no.	%	no.	%	no.	%	no.	%	no.	%	no.	%
Males	97	39	63	25	35	14	34	14	21	8	250	48
Females	117	43	60	22	33	12	31	11	29	11	270	52
Totals	214	41	123	24	68	13	65	12	50	10	520	100

Sex ratio: 92.59

Source: 1861 census

19

be taught freely, in grammar and in good and virtuous manners, all children and scholars as shall repayre or be sent thither, born of parents living in Elmdon, Chishill, Strethall, Nether Chrishall, Arkesden, Barling, Barkway, Manuden, Langley and Clavering'.[24] As a result of Thomas Crawley's generosity, free education had been available in Elmdon for many generations.

By 1843, it was felt that a new school-building was needed, and the Squire, John Wilkes, gave some land to the east of the church, along the Ickleton Road, as a site. Plans were drawn up for a building containing two rooms, measuring 25 feet by 18 feet, to accommodate both boys and girls, at an estimated cost of £620. John Wilkes donated £100, and a further £230 was promised from local sources. The sum of £290 was still needed, and an approach for a grant was made to the National Society for Promoting the Education of the Poor in the Principles of the Established Church. The Society agreed to give £75, the Education Department matched this donation with a similar sum, the rest of the money was found somehow, and work started on the new building in the spring of 1844. Six months later the school opened, being maintained at an annual cost of about £80 0s 0d per annum by subscriptions, the income from the old grammar-school fund, and a weekly contribution of a penny from each child.[25] The poorer people certainly had to pay for progress, and the abolition of the free school must have had its effect on attendance. It was not until 1891 that schooling in Elmdon was again provided without charge.

The initial investment of £620 proved a very sound one. Solidly built, the building remained in use as a school for 129 years, up to its closure in 1973, and it has since been sold for conversion to a private house. After 414 years of having their own school close to their own homes, Elmdon children now have to leave the village each day in order to be educated.

Table 5 shows that forty-nine Elmdon children between the ages of 5 and 14 were receiving schooling in 1861, or 38 per cent of all the children in that age group, which is a figure around the national average for rural areas at the time. They were not the only pupils at the school, since children from Duddenhoe End and Wenden Lofts also came there. Unfortunately the attendance registers for this period have not survived, but it looks as if the pupils, entered in the census as 'scholars', came from all classes of Elmdon society, including two children of John Rolfe from the large Elmdon Bury Farm. From later records,[26] it would seem that

Table 5
Occupations of children aged 5–14 years, [i] *Elmdon village 1861*

	Boys		Girls		All	
	no.	%	no.	%	no.	%
Receiving education	18	33	31	42	49	38
At work	27	50	7	9	34	27
At home	9	17	36	49	45	35
Totals	54	100	74	100	128	100

(i) The total number of children aged 0–4 was 86 (43 boys, 43 girls) making a total of 214 children aged 0–14.

Source: 1861 census

attendance may not always have been regular, for in the 1880s children were absent on such varied grounds as 'picking acorns, gleaning peas, picking up wood, picking stones from the fields, attending Chrishall fete, potato picking, potato planting, gleaning wheat fields, going to a house sale, watching soldiers marching through the village, and haymaking'.

To return to the children of 1861, it can be seen from table 5 that girls stood a better chance of being educated than boys, since roughly two out of every five girls were at school, as compared to one in three of the boys. Further analysis of the figures reveals that girls got their education later than the boys, for only one Elmdon-born boy over the age of 9 was at school, as against eighteen girls, four of whom were 13 years old; and also that daughters of agricultural labourers had twice as good a chance of schooling as their brothers, since 14 per cent of the Elmdon agricultural labourers' sons were at school, as against 28 per cent of their daughters. So the girls had a better chance of education than the boys, and were likely to take it at a later age, probably because the boys were able to get work when they were considerably younger than their sisters.

The difference between what was expected of the girls and boys comes out even more clearly in the percentages of each sex at work in 1861. Exactly half the boys were earning their livings, and as we have already seen, all boys born in Elmdon who were over 9 years old were at work on the farms, except for one who was an apprentice bricklayer, and another, 10 years old, who was still at school. But less than one in ten of the girls aged up to 14 were gainfully employed, five of the seven individuals who were

21

earning their livings being employed on field work, the other two working as a general servant and a nursemaid respectively.

Finally we come to the children, representing roughly a third of the age range, who were neither at school, nor working, but were simply at home. The great majority were girls — there were only nine boys among the total of firty-five children in this position — and no doubt they were kept busy helping their mothers in the house and performing some of the tasks already described in relation to the truants from school. They must also have supervised the younger children. If those aged up to 4 years old are included, there were, during term time, no fewer than 131 boys and girls neither working nor at school in Elmdon, and the streets must have been full of children turned out of the 'two up, two down' cottages by harrassed mothers, to play out of doors. Indeed this might well have been one of the most noticeable differences with 1964, when there were only sixty-one children aged 14 and under in the whole village,[27] and when the streets on a weekday in term-time were almost deserted.

The housewives

The average number of occupants of each dwelling in Elmdon in 1861 was 4.5 persons, against a national average of 5.26; and if servants, visitors and lodgers are excluded, the average number of kin living in each household was only 4.2 persons. However, it can be seen from table 6 that there were still forty households containing anything from five to eleven related members.

Only two of the eighty-seven married women were in regular paid employment, one being a dressmaker and the other, whose husband was not living in Elmdon, a general servant, but the wives and mothers who stayed at home had a multitude of tasks to perform. If they were agricultural labourers' wives, they would expect not only to make their own bread, but also to go gleaning at harvest time in order to acquire a year's supply of flour. One old man who was a child in the last decade of the nineteenth century remembered the women walking home from the harvest fields with their gleanings in bundles on their heads 'like those Jews in the Bible when they carried their water pots'. The wheat then had to be threshed with a flail, and the grain carried to the

22

Table 6
Household size, excluding servants, visitors, and lodgers not known to be
kin of household head, Elmdon village, 1861

no. of household members	no. of households	no. of individuals	Percentage of all households
1	7 (i)	7	6
2	26	52	23
3	20	60	17
4	22	88	19
5	9	45	8
6	10	60	9
7	8	56	7
8	7	56	6
9	4	36	3
10	1	10	1
11	1	11	1
	115	481	100

Average household size: 4.2 persons

(i) Includes one 'household' formed by a man who, according to the census, 'slept in an outhouse'.

Source: 1861 census

Wenden Lofts mill to be ground. The bread, when baked, was crusty and had excellent keeping qualities. Men would take it to the fields for their lunch, and eat it topped with a lump of fat pork 'under the thumb'. The heat from the thumb would melt the pork and the fat would trickle down into the bread.

Beer was another staple commodity, and many wives would brew it in the barrels called 'niners' because they held nine gallons at a time. Then there were clothes to be washed, dried, starched and ironed, and the mending to be done, since on such low wages a rigid economy had to be practised. Perhaps most demanding of all, water had to be fetched, either from a well or from a communal pump in the street. Like the children, housewives would also take on occasional outdoor work, such as gathering acorns or picking stones from the fields. Small wonder that the census report of 1861 recognised their contribution to society in the words 'These women are sometimes returned as of no occupation. But the occupation of wife and mother and housewife is the most important in the country, as will be immediately apparent if it be assumed for a moment to be suppressed.'[28]

Single women and widows not in regular paid employment

The Victorian stereotype of a middle-aged spinster sitting quietly at home and possibly indulging in good works was not entirely absent from Elmdon in 1861, since the two sisters of the Rev. Collin could be said to fall into this category. But there were no other representatives of the species. Apart from the Misses Collin, only eleven unmarried girls and women of 15 and over were living at home. Four of these, aged 15 or 16, belonged to big families and were probably too busy helping their mothers to be spared from home; two were housekeeping for bachelor brothers, both farmers; one suffered from fits; two middle-aged women were living on parish allowance; one was visiting friends; and for only one, the 27-year-old daughter of a blacksmith, is there no obvious explanation of her apparent idleness.

None of the fourteen widows without occupation was under 57 years of age, and nine of them were classified either as paupers or as being on parish relief, as were five of the six retired men in the village.

The community as a whole

As we saw earlier, Elmdon in 1861 was neither a completely closed village, as it might have been had the Squire owned it entirely, nor a wholly open one in which there was no large land-owner. But there can be no doubt at all that it was an extremely self-contained community. Among the root causes of this self-sufficiency were the facts that the local farms were the basis of the village's economy, and that there was no town near enough to provide Elmdon's population with day work as an alternative to agriculture, as will be seen in the next chapter.

Incomers

The degree to which Elmdon lived within itself is demonstrated in table 7, which shows that nearly three-quarters of its total population had been born within the parish. If we look only at the males in the population, the figure is even higher, rising to just over eight out of every ten inhabitants.

24

Table 7
Population by place of birth, Elmdon village, 1861

| | born Elmdon[(i)] | | born elsewhere | | total |
	no.	%	no.	%	no.
Males	203	81	47	19	250
Females	175	65	95	35	270
All	378	73	142	27	520

(i) 'Elmdon' here covers the parish, not only the village since the 1861 census does not distinguish between Elmdon and Duddenhoe End as a birthplace.

Source: 1861 census

Table 8
Immigrants in Elmdon, 1861

Those with family connections

Women, including widows, who had married Elmdon men	44	
Men married to Elmdon women	3	
Children with one or both parents born in Elmdon	20	
Wives accompanying immigrant husbands	12	
Widows who had probably accompanied immigrant husbands	4	
Children accompanying immigrant parents	9	
Miscellaneous family connections - e.g. living with a sibling, cousin, uncle or aunt, adult child, or visiting at the time of the census	20	112

Those coming to Elmdon to work

Males

Clergy	2		
Craftsmen and tradesmen	8		
Workers in private households	3		
Farmers	1		
Farm bailiffs	1		
Shepherds/cowmen	2		
Agricultural labourers	3	20	

Females

School teachers	1		
Shop assistants	1		
Servants	8	10	30
		all:	142

Sources: 1861 census; Elmdon parish registers

What brought the 27 per cent born outside Elmdon parish to live in the village? Further analysis of the 142 incomers is set out in table 8. This shows that no fewer than 112 people, or over three-quarters of the total immigrants, came to the village because of family connections. Some came to marry an Elmdoner; in some cases women who had married into Elmdon went back to their own village to have their first-born child, who thus appears from the census to be an incomer, though living in Elmdon for all but the first week or two of life; some children were born to Elmdon parents during a temporary spell of work outside the village; some were staying with relatives or friends; and some were dependants of what may be termed true migrants, who came to earn a living and for whom no family connection has been traced. Only thirty people fell into this last category, and of these only three were agricultural labourers, as opposed to specialised farm workers such as shepherd or cowman. Of these three, one was a 14-year-old boy from the next door parish of Strethall, lodging with another agricultural labourer, and another was a widower from Arkesden, also on Elmdon's parish boundary, who again lodged with a farm worker. It is possible that both these immigrants could have had a family link with their landlords, though none has been proved. Certainly neither had been present in 1851 and both had gone by 1871. There was only one case of an immigrant agricultural labourer who was also a household head, and who had thus become established in Elmdon. This man was called Peter Reeves, and even in his case we know that his father lived in Wenden Lofts at some time, and may have worked on a Lofts Hall estate farm. This almost total pre-emption of agricultural labourers' jobs by those with Elmdon connections, of which more will be said later, is reminiscent of a present-day closed shop policy, though whether this was operated by the Squire, the farmers, the workers themselves, or a combination of all three is a matter for debate.

Like Peter Reeves, the majority of immigrants did not have to move far when they came to Elmdon. Table 9 shows that only a quarter of them came from outside a ten-mile radius of the village, and most (60 per cent) came from within five miles.

Table 9
Immigrant population by distance of birthplace from Elmdon village, 1861

up to 5 miles		5—10 miles		10—20 miles		over 20 miles		not known[i]		total
no.	%	no.	%	no.	%	no.	%	no.	%	no.
85	60	22	15	11	8	16	11	8	6	142

(i) Includes three unidentified birthplaces in Suffolk.

Source: 1861 census

Table 10
Elmdon village marriages, 1861[i]

Elmdon-Elmdon marriages		husband b. Elmdon, wife b. outside		wife b. Elmdon husband b. outside		both born outside		total
no.	%	no.	%	no.	%	no.	%	no.
33	38	38	44	3	4	12	14	86

(i) Although there were 87 married women in Elmdon in 1861, their spouses were present in 86 cases.

Source: 1861 census

Marriage was the most important cause of entry for women. Table 10 shows that thirty-eight women in 1861 had come to Elmdon for this reason, and that three men from outside had married Elmdon girls and settled in their wives' place of birth. However in 38 per cent of the eighty-six marriages concerned, both husband and wife were Elmdon-born, thus reinforcing the kinship network within the village.

Household structure

In 1861, as today, most families in Elmdon lived either as a married couple without children, or as parents, or a single parent, with children. Table 11 shows that nearly three-quarters of the households in Elmdon were simple family households of this kind. There were only two cases of multiple family households, in which two related 'simple families' were living together. But once elderly parents were widowed, they were rarely left on their own if they were female, and never if they were male. Either they were given a home by a married son or daughter, as happened in six cases, or perhaps a grandchild would go to live with them. Table 11 shows that only three widows (out of a total of twenty-four) were living alone, but even this is a little misleading, since one of them had a son living nearby while another was Sarah Smoothy, landlord of the Wilkes Arms. At the time of the census in 1861 she was putting up four lodgers, so she had plenty of company. In general, family arrangements in Elmdon in the mid-nineteenth century were such that even the poorest seemed to escape the workhouse. In 1861, only four people born in the parish were among the inmates of the Saffron Walden Union, and three of them had been gone from the village for at least twenty years, if not longer. The fourth, an

27

epileptic who was incapable of employment, had been looked after by his parents in Duddenhoe End until they died.[29]

As table 12 shows, there were nineteen individuals, not known to be related to the household head, who were described as lodgers in the census, but here again, any impression of an influx of people from outside would be very misleading. All but four of the nineteen were Elmdon-born, the exceptions being the two agricultural labourers already referred to, together with a cowman and a bricklayer. The great majority of the Elmdon-born lodgers were either widowers, with or without children, or single men, and if indeed they had no kinship link with the household in which they lodged, they may well have been taken in out of a desire on the household head's part to help in a time of difficulty.

The impression of the Elmdon community in 1861, then, is of a close-knit society, which looked to the village itself to provide

Table 11
Household structure,[(i)] *Elmdon village, 1861*

	without servants	with servants	no.	total %
1. Solitaries (a) widowed	3	–	7	6
(b) single	3	1		
2. No family (a) co-resident siblings	–	2	8	7
(b) other co-resident relatives	5	1		
3. Simple family households				
(a) married couples, alone	13	1	85	74
(b) married couples with children	55	2		
(c) widowers with child(ren)	2	–		
(d) widows with child(ren)	11	1		
4. Extended family households				
(a) extended upwards	6	–		
(b) extended downwards				
(1) nephews and nieces	–	–		
(2) grandchild(ren)	3	–	13	11
(c) extended laterally				
(1) brothers	2	–		
(2) other kinsmen	1	–		
(d) combinations of (a) (b) or (c)	–	1		
5; Multiple family households, secondary unit down	2	–	2	2
6. Indeterminate	–	–	–	–
Totals	106	9	115	100

(i) Excluding visitors, and lodgers not known to be kin.

Source: 1861 census

28

Table 12
*Households which included servants, lodgers not known to be kin, or visitors,
Elmdon village, 1861*

size of related household group	servants	visitors	lodgers	total household size
11	1	—	—	12
7 (i)	—	—	2	9
6	2	1	—	9
6	—	1	—	7
5	—	—	1	6
5	—	2	—	7
4	—	—	3	7
4	—	—	1	5
4	—	—	4	8
4	2	—	—	6
3	—	1	—	4
3	3	—	—	6
3	—	—	1	4
2	—	—	2	4
2	1	—	—	3
2	1	—	—	3
2	1	—	—	3
2	1	—	—	3
1	—	—	1	2
1	3	—	—	4
1 (i)	—	—	4	5

Totals		size of related household group	servants	visitors	lodgers	total household size
	Persons	78	15	5	19	117
	Households	21	9	4	9	21

(i) Both these households were headed by publicans.

Source: 1861 census

work, friends and often marriage partners. How far did it differ
from the community which existed in the 1960s, and what were
the forces responsible for change? It is suggested that the answers
to these questions may be found in transport, employment, marriage
and family size, and housing, and it is in these directions that we
shall be looking in the following chapters.

2

Links with the world outside

Even today, to drive the fourteen miles from Cambridge to Elmdon is an agreeable experience. Admittedly the A10 road out of Cambridge may be unpleasantly crowded, with local traffic and long-distance juggernauts jockeying for position as soon as the city boundary has been passed, but some five miles out from the town centre a turning leads into a quiet B-road running across flat, green countryside, to the village of Fowlmere, and from then on the roads leading to Elmdon are little more than lanes. There is only one busy highway to cross before beginning the long, gentle climb up the slopes of the chalk ridge on which Elmdon stands, and that is the main road linking the trunk routes from London to Ely and Norwich respectively.

The approaches from Elmdon's other neighbouring towns are little different. Royston, on the A10, is some nine miles away to the west, and Saffron Walden, Elmdon's natural market town, lies about six and a half miles eastwards. The B-road linking these two towns passes south of Elmdon, and those who come upon the village by chance are likely to be Sunday drivers wanting to enjoy the countryside but going nowhere in particular, rather than serious travellers *en route* from one town to another.

Such a driver, though able to avoid towns and traffic, would not find it easy to go far without meeting settlements of some kind. A quick glance at an Ordnance Survey map shows that there are no fewer than twenty-four named villages and hamlets within a five-mile radius of Elmdon. The isolation of that village from the nearest towns — undoubtedly a major factor in saving it from the fate (or depriving it of the opportunity, whichever way you look at it) of becoming a 'development village' — is counterbalanced by its local position as part of a network of small settlements in very similar settings, all well within reach of each other even in the days when walking was the only way to keep up social contacts.

30

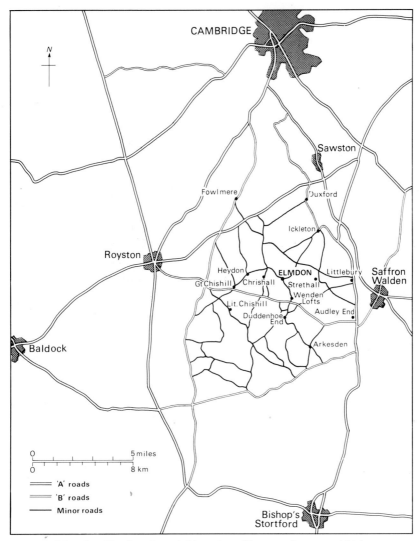

Map 3   Elmdon, its neighbouring villages and towns, 1964

The carriers[1]

Nineteenth-century Elmdon was not of course completely cut off from the larger world. In 1851, for instance, Mr Tinworth was operating the Elmdon-London carrier route. He left his house in the village on Tuesdays, travelled with his cart to the Old Catherine Wheel in Bishopsgate, and returned to Elmdon on Thursdays. At the same time a second Elmdon carrier, Joseph Gamgee, was running weekly services to Royston and Cambridge. But with Mr Tinworth's death that year, the service to London lapsed. It was not replaced, doubtless because by this time the main London-Cambridge railway line had been in operation for nearly ten years, and Audley End, a station on this route, was under five miles from Elmdon.[2]

The carrier service to Cambridge continued up to 1886, running two or three times a week, and a weekly journey was made to Royston until 1908, with a break of eight years from 1874 to 1882. It is surprising that a regular Elmdon-Saffron Walden carrier run did not begin until 1890, since 'Walden', as it is called locally, was Elmdon's nearest town and market centre. The explanation may well be that carriers from neighbouring villages operated such a .service, picking up and putting down Elmdon goods and passengers *en route*. An Elmdon schoolmistress, speaking of the early years of the twentieth century, remembered that a carrier's cart travelling from Heydon to Saffron Walden used to pass through Elmdon. 'If you wanted to travel on it, you hung a red flag from your window and it stopped. Of course, it was uncomfortable. A woman had to sit on top of the parcels and balance there.' As far as she could recollect, it cost 1 shilling to make the journey. At a time when farm wages were around 12 shillings a week, this charge must have made travel by the cart a luxury out of reach of most agricultural labourer's wives. Moreover a walker could make faster progress than the cart. The carrier service was therefore probably only used when the passenger had a heavy load to carry or a considerable distance to cover.

Whatever the reason for the late introduction of an Elmdon-Saffron Walden carrier service, there is no doubt that Saffron Walden was a busy route centre, and Elmdon people who walked or rode there could then make connections with the rest of Essex. As early as 1851, there were coach services each weekday from Haverhill via Saffron Walden to Audley End station, to Newport station, to London; and to 'Linton, Thurlow, Clare, the Bumpsteads and all places adjacent'. Finchingfield and Braintree were visited on Saturdays, and omnibuses met all Audley End trains, both incoming and outgoing.

Although it was 1933 before an Elmdon carrier failed to be listed in Kelly's Directory for Essex, it looks as if a decline in the business set in during the last quarter of the nineteenth century, a time marked by agricultural depression. From 1878 the carriers are listed as having dual occupations, indicating that they could no longer make their livings from the transport trade alone. Henry Burgess in 1878 was a beer retailer as well as a carrier. Edward Jeffery from 1890 to 1914 was also licensee of the Wilkes Arms, and George Hopwood had additional work as a butcher and a beer retailer.

Mr Weeden was the last carrier listed for Elmdon, and he linked the old, slow age of horsedrawn carts with the new era of fast motor transport. In 1929 he was operating a service to Saffron Walden on Tuesday and Saturday, but this was by a motor vehicle. Older people in the village remember using his van, fitted up with wooden trestle seats, at the cost of 3d a ride. This was the fore-runner of a regular bus service, and with it the need for the carriers vanished.

The early post office

Elmdoners' links with the outside world in the second half of the nineteenth and early twentieth centuries were not limited to the services that the carriers could provide. By 1851 a post office had been established in the village. The grocer and draper, William Crisp, was appointed receiver of the mail, a position which he held for over twenty years. From 1855 to 1866, there was one incoming and one outgoing mail each weekday, via Royston, but by 1870 Sunday deliveries had been added, and the letters now came from Saffron Walden by foot messenger. Mr Crisp still dealt only with mail — for money orders Elmdoners had to go to Great Chesterford or Saffron Walden — but by 1874, when Mrs Crisp had taken over her husband's position after his death, money orders and post-office savings were administered in Elmdon post office. By 1882, telegraph offices were open in Great Chesterford and Saffron Walden; by 1890, under the Crisps' daughter, Mrs Elizabeth Wabon, the Elmdon post office was designated an Annuity and

Insurance Office, and nine years later a telegraph office had been opened at Heydon, three miles away.

The Crisps' association with the village post office ended in 1906. For fifty-five years or more, over two generations, their shop had been the centre for the distribution of Elmdon's mail. Now, a new sub-postmaster was appointed. He was Henry Brand, a blacksmith, whose wife, Emma, had her own job as a beer retailer. By the same year, 1906, parcel post had been added to the services available, and telegrams could be received and sent from Elmdon itself. This advantage was said to have been gained for the village by Sir James Bailey, the wealthy hotelier and financier who at the time was tenant of Lofts Hall. It seems that he was a gambling man, who found it quite impractical to send a messenger to Heydon every time he wanted to place a bet with his bookmaker, and as a result of his representations, telegraph facilities were installed in Elmdon.

By 1908, Elmdon was receiving two posts a day. Henry Brand continued as sub-postmaster until 1925, when he died after a bicycle accident. Today the post office is again associated with the village shop, and is a centre for village news and notices, as well as for communication with the rest of the world.

Private transport before the motor-car

While the poorer people in the village may have depended on the services of the carriers, or the use of their own legs, the better-off had more choice. We know that at least eleven blacksmiths and five wheelwrights worked in Elmdon at different times between 1841 and 1871[3] and no doubt they serviced both horses and vehicles for private use as well as for farm work, though there seems to have been no saddler in the village. The Squire kept his carriage, and his coachman occupied one of the lodges of Lofts Hall. Later, Sir James Bailey, who was thought to bear a close resemblance to King Edward VII, is remembered as passing through the village in a smart equipage, drawn by four horses, and driven by a coachman in a cockaded hat. The tenant farmers and some of the tradesmen had traps, as well as riding horses; so had the retired police inspector who lived in Elmdon. A local butcher used to be seen going about his business in a pony-cart, with a hunting dog loping along underneath it, from which position it would make an occasional foray across the open, rolling plough

34

lands to catch a hare for the pot. Old people living in Elmdon in 1964 remembered that two pony-traps and a four-wheeler were available for hire from the King's Head. One old lady recalled that as a girl, working in service in Streatham, she used to visit her sick brother once a fortnight in Elmdon, travelling by train from Liverpool Street to Audley End for 3s 6½d return, and then taking a pony-trap the rest of the way. An Elmdon commuter, the forerunner of many more to come, travelled daily to London as early as the 1920s. He drove to Audley End station in a pony-trap, took the train to work and returned home in the evenings. The doctor visited the village in a dog-cart or even, in really wintry weather, in a sleigh.

A great step forward in personal mobility came with the advent of the bicycle. Penny-farthings were introduced in 1871 and quickly became popular, though the safety bicycle, with two wheels of equal dimensions and a chain, did not become fully established until 1885, while the Dunlop pneumatic tyre was invented three years later.[4] Bicycles were not at first for the working poor; they were expensive to buy. On the other hand, maintenance costs were low, and gradually their use spread.[5] The assistant schoolmistress in Elmdon was one of the first to ride a bicycle there, an event which she dated at 1897. She did not go so far as to wear bloomers when riding her machine, but donned a special skirt, with flaps. One old man remembered riding a penny-farthing the fourteen miles from Cambridge to Elmdon and another recollected bicycling on the flint-stone road to Saffron Walden for a night out and constantly having to mend punctures by the light of an acetylene lamp. Indeed, the unmetalled roads were often so stiffly rutted in dry weather and muddy in wet, that neither bicycling nor indeed walking were always easy. Nevertheless, some Elmdon women made a weekly visit to Cambridge and back by bicycle, while for men the mobility which the bicycle gave opened up possibilities of employment some distance outside Elmdon itself.

For most Elmdoners of those days, though, walking remained the normal means of getting about, and considerable distances were covered without the journeys being considered at all out of the way. One man for a while worked in Fowlmere, while continuing to live in Elmdon. He would leave his cottage at about four in the morning and by the light of a lantern walk the five miles to his work in order to get there in time to feed the farm animals. After a full day's work, he walked home again, arriving late in the evening. Many women walked to Saffron Walden, over six miles away, for their weekly marketing. One woman remembers pushing a perambulator containing her children there and back, in order to buy them shoes, and another recalls that she herself was sometimes pushed by her mother in a pram, with another child, all the way from Puckeridge to Elmdon to see her grandmother, a distance of some fifteen miles. They would stay the night in Elmdon, and then return to Puckeridge next day, the children still riding in the pram. The aversion to walking which so many Elmdoners seem to feel today may well stem from such feats in the past. As one of the older generation said, 'When you had to walk to Walden to shop, you never walked for pleasure.'

Nevertheless, it was walking that enabled Elmdoners to keep in touch with those living in the numerous villages and hamlets of the neighbourhood. While town-visiting may have been rare, contact with family and friends within a five-mile radius was always possible, and young women coming to live in Elmdon on marriage from villages within this range, or young teenage girls arriving for their first 'living-in' place on a local farm, were not completely cut off from their own families.

Motor transport

1929–45

We have already seen that the last of the carriers, Mr Weeden, was also the first of the motor-bus operators to include Elmdon on his routes, and the period during which he ran his buses was one of transition between the old, personal service for goods and passengers provided by the Elmdon carriers, and the more rigid, impersonal way of running things used by the much larger organisation, without close local connections at managerial level, which is in charge of public transport in the area today. Although Mr Weeden never lived in Elmdon, his home was only a mile-and-a-half away in Chrishall when he started up his bus service around 1929, and he knew most people in the village.

The early days of the buses were difficult. The first vehicle was a 14-seater, and ran from Heydon through Chrishall and Elmdon to Saffron Walden, on the same roads as the old carrier's cart, for a cost of 9d return, but expansion soon brought routes linking Elmdon with Cambridge, Royston, Bishops Stortford, and once a

Mothers' Union outing in the 14-seater

week with London. These services were not daily ones, and so could
not be used by those wanting steady work outside the village;
rather they were for housewives wanting to shop in the towns, and
for men attending market, just as the earlier carriers' journeys had
been.   At first it was difficult to persuade passengers onto the
buses, and even the comparatively low fares were too high for
many prospective users, though many women would take a single
fare, and walk back the other way.   But the buses also took parcels,
which the staff would put off at their destinations, and farmers
would send crates of eggs or live chickens for delivery at the
market.   On one memorable journey the bus trundled back from
Saffron Walden with two calves as passengers in the rear.   For a
time, so few people used the London route that Mr Weeden was
only able to keep it going by taking produce with him which he
sold on a street market stall between the arrival of the bus in the
morning and the return journey in the afternoon.   But gradually
more and more people used his vehicles.   The personal nature of
the service remained, and it was Mr Weeden's boast that he and his
men never left a passenger behind.   During the Second World War,
he once drove one of the 32-seater buses from Cambridge in the
blackout with 82 passengers aboard, some sitting on others' laps,

37

some in the racks, and some even in the boot at the back. But everyone got home.

By 1945, when the business was sold to Premier Travel Ltd, the number of vehicles had increased to fourteen, and the new means of transport had become an accepted part of Elmdon life.

1945 to the present day

It was not until a year or two after Premier Travel Ltd had taken over the bus service that Elmdoners were able to use public transport to get to work outside the village. By 1947, however, daily services had started, and early buses were put on which allowed people in the villages to reach Cambridge, Saffron Walden or Royston in time for work. For a while, these early buses were packed with people, but the number of passengers declined when work buses were introduced to take employees to the Spicers factories at Sawston, some seven or eight miles from Elmdon. The firm had first come to Sawston in 1914, when it bought the existing paper mill there together with 650 acres of land, and the business had expanded steadily over the years until by 1966 the factory and warehouse accommodation in the district covered almost a quarter of a million square feet.[6] After the Second World War, expansion reached the point where new sources of labour had to be tapped. By providing free transport to and from work, the firm was able to attract many employees from the surrounding villages, and Elmdoners were no exception. A number of Elmdon men who had previously been agricultural labourers left the farms for the factory, using the transport provided, and they were joined by many Elmdon school-leavers, both boys and girls. Workers at Spicers from Elmdon and Chrishall alone virtually filled one bus each day, and as their numbers increased so the number of users of the early buses on the scheduled services declined, until by 1974 the early morning service to Cambridge was kept going almost entirely by children travelling in to the city to school. Although other factories, for instance Pye's of Cambridge and Ciba-Geigy of Duxford, operated similar work buses, none of their routes touched Elmdon, and so the majority of Elmdon factory workers continued to go to Spicers. But the higher wages paid raised the standard of living of many Elmdon families, and enabled wage earners to buy cars, so that those who wished to leave Spicers for other work were able to do so, being able to

38

Ciba-Geigy, 1979

transport themselves to their new work place. Today, in spite of the increased cost of petrol, there is a growing tendency even for Spicers' workers from Elmdon to use their own cars instead of the convenient work bus.

The scheduled bus services also helped Elmdon women to work outside the village. In the 1940s and 50s, a number of girls went into Saffron Walden by bus to work as shop assistants, or in the laundries. At fruit or vegetable picking times, Elmdon women were able to follow a traditional occupation outside the parish boundaries, for quite often enough women wished to go in one large party to justify hiring a bus to carry them — for instance to Nuthampstead to pick strawberries for the Chivers jam factory at Histon, near Cambridge. Today women still go picking, but the tendency is for individuals to make the best financial arrangements they can for themselves, instead of combining in a group. As a result, several employers each send a car to pick up two or three women, instead of one farmer being able to employ a whole bus load.

Just as native-born Elmdoners have been able to find work outside the village as a result of improved transport facilities, so others have been drawn to live in the village, because of the freedom of movement given to them by the motor car. At first they came to retire, or to buy a week-end cottage, but soon a number of men and women working in London found it possible to travel there daily, using their cars to get to and from Audley End station, and taking advantage of the excellent train service into the heart of the City. By 1964, at least ten individuals were commuting in this way.

Pleasure, as well as work, makes its demands on transport. Before motor travel came in, most Elmdoners had to find their amusements within walking distance. The older people still remember parties of young men and women, with linked arms, singing as they stepped out along the lane to a dance at Duddenhoe End two-and-a-half miles away, a distance which no young Elmdoner nowadays would dream of going on foot. For young children, the most exciting event of the year might be a ride in a farm cart to Royston to collect the winter supply of coal, and although the round trip covered only eighteen miles, it would take the whole day. But with the buses, all this changed. For years Premier Travel Ltd provided a coach for the annual Elmdon church outing to Clacton on very favourable terms, for the affair had become a tradition, starting in Mr Weeden's day; another popular excursion was a visit to London at Christmas time to see the decorations. During the 1950s, the weekly London service was heavily patronised, but even so the bus company found it profitable to run special coaches to Barkers' sale in Kensington, or to Bedford for shopping, or to Wembley to watch the Norwich speedway races. In 1964, a group party for a holiday in Ostend was arranged, and ten Elmdoners joined it. On a less ambitious scale, the provision of scheduled buses leaving Cambridge at 11 p.m. on Wednesdays and 10.45 p.m. on Saturdays meant that villagers without cars could enjoy evening entertainment in the town. Similar arrangements for 'picture' buses existed on the Saffron Walden route. The Evergreen Club arranged outings, such as a visit to Windsor, and now takes the 'over 60s' by private cars once a week to Saffron Walden to shop and look around, although this laudable activity has had the effect of emptying the buses still further and thus reducing the services available to the dwindling number of younger people who have no cars or motor bicycles of their own.

Not all Elmdoners took advantage of these facilities. As late as 1964, there remained an elderly couple who had never taken a holiday together out of the village, though the wife did admit that some thirty years earlier she had spent three days with her sister in Haddenham in the Fens; and the old gentleman had once visited

40

London when he went for the day to watch a test match against the West Indies at Lords.

In Elmdon as in the rest of the country, car-ownership has spread until almost all wage-earning families possess their own vehicle. In some cases the main use of the car is to travel to work, but it is also important in providing a means of keeping in touch with members of the family who have moved to nearby villages, some of which would only a few years ago have been considered to be in easy walking range. 'We see Bob now and again at Chishill [three-and-a-half miles away] but we haven't got a motor-car, or we'd go more often' said one couple. But a few of the older generation still use their bicycles, if their children cannot give them a lift in their cars.

Just as the adult Elmdoner's standards of transport changed with the advent of the motor vehicle, so did the children's. Young people used to walk to Elmdon school from as far away as Strethall (two-and-a-half miles) and Chrishall Grange (nearly four miles), but when the school in Duddenhoe End closed, the children were carried the two-and-a-half miles to Elmdon school by bus, and later in two taxis. With the closing of Elmdon school itself in 1973, children now go by bus to the big new primary school at Chrishall, and at the age of 11 they are taken daily to Saffron Walden. The picture is very different from the days when the clever son of an Elmdon villager was unable to go on to school in Saffron Walden because of his parents' inability to get him there and back.

Motor transport not only allowed Elmdoners to leave the village more easily, it also brought the outside world to Elmdon, as we have seen in the cases of the week-enders and commuters. Native-born Elmdoners found an increasing number of services coming to their doors. A fish-and-chip van visited the village regularly from 1932, and its recent discontinuation has been a great blow to many housewives in the village. In the 1960s, deliveries were made from Saffron Walden grocery stores, and a travelling butcher called, as well as the baker and milkman. Even expectant mothers were catered for, with the arrival of a mobile clinic twice a month, while the doctor held a twice-weekly surgery in the kitchen of one of the village houses, the parlour being used as a waiting room by the patients. Some of these services remain today, but the tendency in the 1970s has been towards a reduction rather than an expansion in this field.

41

Attitudes to transport

Elmdoners in the 1960s did not always appreciate their apparently greatly increased facilities for travel. From the comments made in interviews, some of them hardly seemed to recognise that such facilities existed. One elderly lady did not think that people got out of the village any more than they used to do; a younger woman complained that transport was so difficult in Elmdon — the services were bad and her little boy had never been on a train (though Audley End station remains four and three-quarter miles away, just as it was in 1851). A keen cinema-goer said that it took half a day to get out of Elmdon and back just to see one film through. But those who complained were indeed those who had benefited least from the new opportunities — the old, and the housewife with children to look after. The latter's husband might well have a car, but she could not use it during the working week. For these categories, increased mobility for their neighbours through the use of private cars meant less ease of movement for themselves; as the numbers using the buses declined, the services were reduced, and the fares raised. For them, a journey far outside Elmdon was still something of an event, and their contacts remained with the nearby villages and the market town, rather than with any other urban centre.

3

Landownership in Elmdon, 1739-1930

In 1894, Enoch Greenhill left Elmdon school. He was a bright 9-year-old, and had just passed Standard IV, two years earlier than most children, so he was allowed to leave before the usual age of 11. He went straight to work on Elmdon Bury Farm for 5d a day, working a six-day week. 'You had to in those days', he said, many years later, as he remembered the beginning of his life as a wage earner, leading the horses over the chalky fields.

Enoch differed from most other boys in Elmdon only in the age at which he started work. The farms were the main source of employment for Elmdon men and boys right up to the end of the Second World War, when the daily work buses to Saffron Walden, Royston and Cambridge were introduced. If the farmers did badly in a time of agricultural depression, and so had to turn off some of their men, or if new methods of farming reduced the number of workers needed, then Elmdoners could not expect to find alternative work while still living in the village, and emigration was inevitable.

A knowledge of the agricultural history of Elmdon is thus a necessary part of any study of social change from the mid-nineteenth century to the 1960s, and central to such a history is the development of the Lofts Hall estate. Because many of the features of agriculture in Elmdon in 1861 cannot be fully understood without some knowledge of previous events, let us look at the growth of the estate from its purchase by Nathaniel Wilkes in 1739 to the point where its owner became the most important land holder in the parishes of Wenden Lofts and Elmdon.

The Lofts Hall estate

1739–1829

Although Nathaniel Wilkes came from London to buy the Lofts

Hall estate in 1739, he was not a complete townsman, for his paternal grandfather was a yeoman farmer living in Albrighton, Shropshire, and three of his uncles remained there. The Wilkes family history will be related at greater length in chapter 7; here, it is sufficient to say that Nathaniel's father, John, left the farm to join his brother Israel in a very successful malt-distilling business in Spitalfields, London, and this was the source of the money which enabled Nathaniel, at the age of 32, to take up the life of a country squire. It was money derived from the London property, too, which allowed Nathaniel's sons and grandson to expand the Lofts Hall estate, and to alter and enlarge the Hall itself. The succeeding generations of Lofts Hall Wilkes are set out in figure 1.

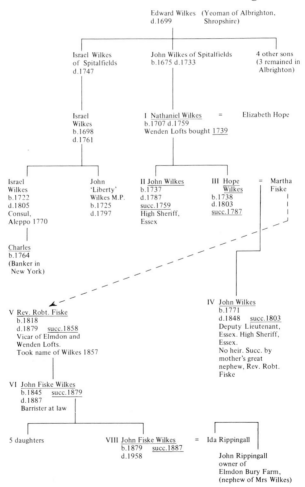

Fig. 1   Wilkes family tree (skeleton)

44

We do not know how much land Nathaniel bought in 1739, and the first mention of the size of the estate comes in 1790, when Nathaniel's younger son, Hope, who had recently inherited the property, had it surveyed. The survey[1] showed that the estate at that time was comparatively modest, amounting to only 1,052 acres in the parishes of Wenden Lofts, Elmdon and Chrishall, with a further 485 acres in Chishill. As figure 2 shows, the Chishill property was some distance away from the rest of the estate, and it seems always to have been treated as a separate unit. For this reason, it will not be considered in detail here.

The 1790 survey listed the tenancies, acreages and type of holding on the estate, and its findings are summarised in table 13. From this list, and from figure 2, two things become clear. First, much the greater part of the Lofts Hall estate in 1790 lay in Wenden Lofts, with an extension into Chrishall, and in the southern part of Elmdon parish. The Wilkes territory in and around Elmdon village in the northern part of the parish amounted only to 83 acres, well under a tenth of the whole estate. Second, this difference between north and south was repeated in the types of farm held. All the farms in Wenden Lofts and the southern half of

Table 13
The Lofts Hall estate in Elmdon, Wenden Lofts and Chrishall parishes, 1790

			acres
Lofts Hall farm (Wenden Lofts)	boundaries fully enclosed		208
Pond Street Farm (Elmdon and Wenden Lofts)	enclosed open field	94 acres 57 acres	151
Chiswick Hall farm (Chrishall and Wenden Lofts)	enclosed open field	151 acres 68 acres	219
Duddenhoe End farm (Elmdon and Wenden Lofts)	enclosed open field	140 acres 19 acres	159
Cosh Farm (Elmdon)	boundaries fully enclosed		115
Breens Millar's tenancy, Chrishall	mostly open field		95
Elizabeth Brand's tenancy, Elmdon	enclosed open field	5 acres 59 acres	64
Samuel Jackson's tenancy, Elmdon	open field		19
Woodlands, etc			22
			1,052

Source: Survey of the Lofts Hall estate 1790

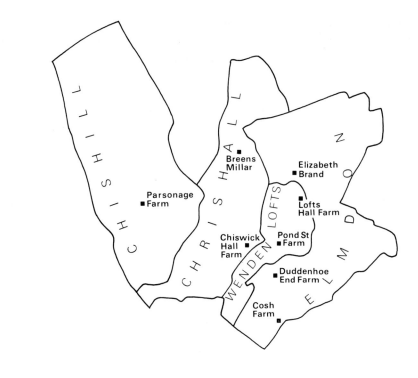

CHISHILL

CHRISHILL

CHRISHILL

WENDEN LOFTS

ELMDON

N

■ Breens
Millar

Elizabeth
■ Brand

Parsonage
■ Farm

■ Lofts
Hall Farm

Chiswick
Hall ■
Farm

Pond St
■ Farm

■ Duddenhoe
End Farm

Cosh
Farm
■

| 0 | miles | 2 |
| 0 | km | 3 |

Fig. 2 Lofts Hall estate farmsteads, 1790

46

Elmdon parish were more than half enclosed, or fully enclosed. In the north, the only enclosed land was the five acres covered by Elizabeth Brand's house, yards and home pastures, which seem to have been the homestead later known as Hill Farm. The remainder of the estate land round Elmdon village lay in the open fields.

We see, then, that the open field system of farming was still operating to some extent in Elmdon and Wenden Lofts in 1790, as it had been since before the Domesday Book was compiled in 1086. In that year the lord of the manor, Roger de Sumeri, lived on Elmdon Bury hill, with twenty-six villeins, or tenants, each of whom had rights to some 30 acres of arable land in the open fields. In return for these rights, they paid their lord dues of money and produce, and worked for him on his own farm land. There were also fifteen bordars, or smaller tenants. Some of these had rights to about 5 acres of land, and probably did paid work in addition, in order to make a living; while others were craftsmen, or specialised farm workers such as the shepherds or swine-herds who looked after the lord's sheep and pigs. Altogether, Elmdon's population probably amounted to about 200 souls at this time.[2]

To support this population, crops were grown on the common fields outside the settlement. An individual peasant could not hope to acquire either the equipment or enough draught animals to work the land alone, and so groups of tenants pooled their resources to form plough teams. Elmdon had ten of these teams in 1086, and each tenant was allocated strips of land in the open fields in proportion to the number of oxen he supplied to his team. As more land was opened up, so new strips were allocated, and holdings became more and more dispersed. This scattering of holdings was accentuated as time passed, for rights to the strips could be passed on by inheritance or by sale, though at each change of ownership a payment had to be made to the lord of the manor. There were also communal rights in meadow land, which was in short supply in Elmdon; and in woodland, which provided feed for swine, as well as being a source of firewood and building timber.

Views differ[3] as to how the common rules of sowing, harvesting and fallowing grew up on these strip lands, or open fields, but with the land divided into so many small, unfenced parcels belonging to different owners but worked by communal ploughing teams, it was in everyone's interest to have an agreed farming programme. As farming methods became more advanced, however, the system proved increasingly inefficient. Individual strip-holders could not use their own initiative but had to abide by the common rules. For example, a man could not experiment with winter crops, such as turnips, when these were being introduced elsewhere, because all the open-field strips had to be left fallow from the end of the grain harvest until the spring sowing, so that cattle and sheep could graze freely over them.

In many other parts of England, enclosure had been achieved much earlier, simply by agreement between the open-field strip-holders. Elmdon and Wenden Lofts, however, lay in the area of north-west Essex and southern Cambridgeshire where enclosure came late, largely because the chalk hills were suited to arable farming, and arable farming in turn could be contained by the open field system more easily than other types of agriculture. Even so, by 1790 it was clear that in Elmdon and Wenden Lofts, too, the old ways were breaking down, and considerable areas in the south of the Lofts Hall estate were already out of the open-field system, forming separate fenced or hedged units which could be farmed according to the wishes of the individual owner or tenant, without seeking the agreement of a body of other cultivators.

Unfortunately, we do not know who the individual holders of land in Elmdon's open fields were in 1790, but it is clear that Hope Wilkes owned only a small proportion of its total area. By 1824, however, the position had changed. Perhaps some of the strip-holders had sold their rights when corn prices fell dramatically at the end of the Napoleonic War — a time when many small farmers throughout the country were bankrupted -- or perhaps the buying out of the smaller farmers by the local landowners had been a steady and continuing process. Be that as it may, maps of the 1,966 acres of open fields in Elmdon and Wenden Lofts, drawn just before the Enclosure Act of 1824,[5] show that the strip-holdings throughout the parishes were shared by only twenty-eight individuals, and that thirteen of these were members of the gentry, who between them held well over 90 per cent of the area. John Wilkes, Hope's son, was the largest holder, and the only one in this group who was resident in either of the parishes. Most of the other gentry held land in the open fields of Elmdon parish only as extensions of their larger properties in neighbouring parishes, and some, like the Earl of Shannon, lived far away and may never even have visited their Elmdon holdings.

48

The remaining fifteen holders lived and worked in the two parishes. Only one, John Hayden, was as well off in terms of land holding in the open fields as the villeins of the Domesday period with their 30 acres, for he held 30 strips in Lee Field, Mill Field and Daws Field, as well as some enclosed land near Duddenhoe End hamlet. Three other yeoman farmers owned smaller numbers of open-field strips, as well as some enclosed fields. Eleven individuals remained whose land holding, as opposed to their cottage gardens and orchards, lay wholly in the open fields, and of these, five held no more than one strip each. Only two of them, Thomas Smith with sixteen strips and Mrs Chapman with thirteen, could be supposed to rely on their open-field holdings for a major part of their livelihoods.

It is clear that for many years the principal landowners of the parishes, and especially the Wilkes family, had been buying up rights to open-field strips from the descendants of the yeoman farmers who had worked the open fields in past generations. In fact, an unofficial form of enclosure had been taking place within the system. Figure 3, illustrating land holding in Mill Shot, part of Mill Field just south of Elmdon village, shows what had been happening throughout the open fields. John Wilkes had acquired sufficient adjacent strips to form quite large consolidated areas, and so to a lesser extent had Miss Hadsley. The only Elmdon villager to retain any strips in the shot was Mrs Chapman, who had inherited them from her husband. One can see how irritating it must have been to John Wilkes, or to his tenant farmer, not to be able to treat Mill Shot as an independent unit, and equally one sympathises with any desire Mrs Chapman may have had to hold on to her open-field land and the rights which had gone with it for so many generations. North of the village in Elmdon Field, where the Lofts Hall estate had never been so strongly represented as in the south, consolidation had not gone so far, as figure 4 shows. The largest single area which the estate had been able to acquire in Valley Shot was only four strips wide, and successful farming of the shot must have required close cooperation among the owners.

By 1824, the principal landowners concerned had agreed that it was time to bring the open-field system to an end. A private Enclosure Act was therefore laid before Parliament 'for inclosing lands in the Parishes of Wenden Lofts and Elmdon in the County of Essex and for extinguishing the Tithes in the said Parishes'. The

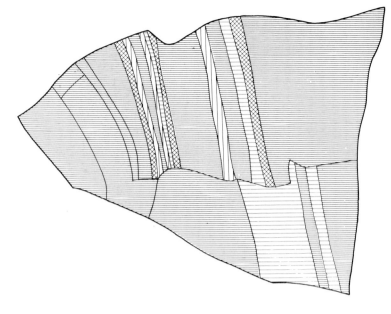

Land belonging to
John Wilkes
Miss Hadsley
A. Mayling
Mrs Chapman

Fig. 3 Pre-enclosure land holdings in Mill Shot, Mill Field

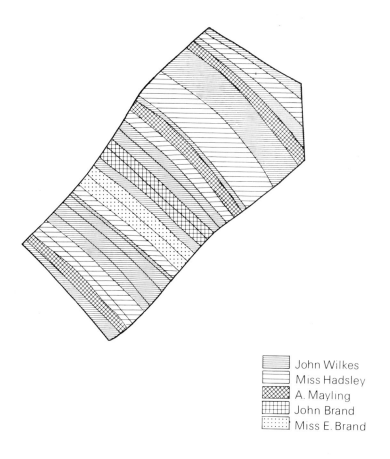

John Wilkes
Miss Hadsley
A. Mayling
John Brand
Miss E. Brand

Fig. 4 Pre-enclosure land holdings in Valley Shot, Elmdon Field

Act was passed,[6] and Parliament appointed commissioners to supervise the allotment of open-field land. It took five years to work out the new division of land, under which each open-field landholder received a consolidated area equivalent in size to the total area of his scattered holdings in the open fields. The buying out of the villagers, and dealings in land, went on even during this time, which was marked nationally by continuing agricultural depression; and when the Award was made in 1829,[7] the number of the gentry who held open-field land had been reduced from thirteen in 1824 to ten; and the yeomen and villagers from fifteen to seven. Mrs Chapman, for instance, had died and her rights had been bought from her executors by Miss Hadsley, while John Wilkes had bought Thomas Smith's holdings, and some of the Hayden property. But when it was all done, the Lofts Hall estate emerged with roughly 249 of the 258 acres awarded in Wenden Lofts, and with some 990 acres, or more than half, of the 1,708 acres allotted in the parish of Elmdon.

There was one more set of people who were affected by the Enclosure Act. These were the occupants of certain cottages who were legally entitled to graze their livestock on the common land, and they held other privileges such as the right to use or sell turf, gorse or brushwood taken from the commons. When these rights were extinguished by the Enclosure Act, the holders were entitled to compensation, and in Elmdon they were given allotments of half an acre or so each, running side by side southward from the Ickleton Road, where today the Hollow Road council houses stand. Seven villagers who were living in Elmdon cottages with rights of common, but who had no land in the open fields, were compensated in this way.

Let us for the moment leave aside not only these cottagers, but also those absentee landlords who had total holdings of less than 85 acres each in Elmdon or Wenden Lofts parishes, and those to whom allotments had been made *ex officio*, such as the clergy and the trustees of the grammar school. Table 14 lists the holdings of the four principal landowners in 1829 after the Award had been made, and shows that John Wilkes, with his 2,488 acres, was far and away the largest, the size of the estate having more than doubled since 1790. The other three landowners, Lieut. General Raymond, the Hadsley family, and Miss Sarah Jane Maling, only held 948 acres between them and none of them lived in Wenden Lofts or Elmdon.

52

Table 14
Principal landowners, Elmdon and Wenden Lofts parishes, 1829

	allotment in 1829 acres	land already enclosed acres	total holding acres
John Wilkes	1,239	1,249	2,488
Lieut. General Raymond	166	237	403
The Hadsley family	206	125	331
Miss Sarah Jane Maling	214	—	214
	1,825	1,611	3,436

Source: The Elmdon and Wenden Lofts Enclosure Award, 1829

By 1829, the Wilkes family had become the most important landed family in the two parishes. They had achieved this position by a gradual process of buying up land as it became available, over a period of nearly forty years, so that the actual Enclosure Act and Award regularised a *fait accompli* rather than acting as an instrument to dispossess a large number of smallholders dependent on their open-field strips for their living. The descendants of the yeomen farmers of pre-enclosure days and other villagers who still owned land, whether open-field or enclosed, did so on a very small scale indeed, as table 15 shows. John Hayden, who had already sold much of his property to the Lofts Hall estate, heads the list with a total holding of 17 acres. It is unlikely that any of those

Table 15
Small landowners, Elmdon and Wenden Lofts parishes, 1829

	allotment in 1829 acres	land already enclosed acres	total holding acres
John Hayden	4	13	17
John Graves	—	13	13
Thomas Wisby	2	8	10
Debden Wright	—	9	9
*John Brand	8	—	8
*W.G. & J. Gibson	8	—	8
*James Ward	—	8	8
*Robert Jarvis	3	2	5
Joseph Buck	2	2	4
*John Cane	—	1	1
*Elisha Jeffery	—	1	1
	27	57	84

*Holdings in Elmdon village

Source: The Elmdon and Wenden Lofts Enclosure Award, 1829

holding less than 10 acres could have lived entirely off their land. Indeed, as far as those who received allotments in and around Elmdon village are concerned, we know for certain that most of them did not. John Brand's main occupation was as a blacksmith, and he owned his own forge. The Gibsons, who had bought their strip land in 1821 when the estate of the widowed Mrs Hoy was sold at auction, also purchased the King's Head public house[8]. James Ward had additional income from the rents of six cottages which he owned in the village; John Cane was a wheelwright; Robert Jarvis, a butcher, had bought his land some time between 1824 and 1829, probably for grazing for his cattle; and although Elisha Jeffery's occupation in 1829 is not known, he would have been hard put to it even to subsist on one acre of land.

1829–60

The landowners, smallholders and cottagers experienced varying fortunes after the enclosure had been completed. To find out how they fared, let us look at what happened to them during the period from 1829 to 1860, when the next major survey of the Lofts Hall estate was made for its new owner, the Rev. Robert Fiske Wilkes.[9]

Landowners

The Lofts Hall estate. Nine years after the reallocation of land in 1829, the Lofts Hall estate spent £6,700 on buying the 253-acre farm known as Rockells, on the southern borders of Elmdon parish.[10] After this, however, expansion on the scale that had been taking place over the previous forty-eight years ceased,[11] and John Wilkes settled down to the task of reorganising his property. The Enclosure Award gave him the opportunity to create new farms out of the consolidated areas which he received in place of his former scattered open-field holdings, particularly in the north of Elmdon parish on the old Elmdon and Mill Fields, and by 1860 there were ten estate farms in Wenden Lofts and Elmdon parishes, compared with five in 1790. By far the largest of the new farms was Elmdon Bury, taking its name from the old manor, which covered 700 acres. Its seventeen arable fields included two which were more than 100 acres each, clear evidence that they lay on the site of one of the old open fields.[12]

54

The Wilkes family had not confined their attentions to increasing their property in Wenden Lofts and Elmdon alone. The expansion there had gone hand in hand with enlargement of estate lands in the next-door parish of Chrishall, where enclosure had taken place in 1806, and the Chrishall property in 1860 was roughly two-and-a-half times the size it had been in 1790. Table 16 gives a list of all the estate farms in Elmdon, Wenden Lofts and Chrishall in 1860, showing that the Rev. Robert Wilkes owned 3,251 acres of farm land in the three parishes. He was also the owner of woods, some smaller holdings outside the farms, and various cottages and houses covering a further 531 acres, bringing his total property to 3,782 acres. His separate estate in Chishill had also grown, and now contained 851 acres. Although the Wilkes were not the major landowners in Chishill or Chrishall, in Wenden Lofts and Elmdon parishes they held pride of place.

Table 16
Lofts Hall estate farms, 1860

Wenden Lofts and Elmdon		
farm	*acreage*	*acreage*
Elmdon Bury	702	
Church	209	
Hill (Elizabeth Brand's tenancy in 1790)	107	
Home (Lofts Hall farm in 1790)	163	
Hope + part Rockells	476	
Pond Street	205	
Duddenhoe End	234	
Rockells	344	
Cosh	109	
Duddenhoe Grange	217	
	2,766	2,766
Chrishall		
Chiswick Hall	350	
Gentleman's (Breens Millar's tenancy in 1790)	135	
	485	485
Total farm acreage, 1860		3,251

Source: Survey of the Lofts Hall estate, 1860

Other landowners. In spite of the spread of the Lofts Hall estate, there still remained some property in Elmdon parish which was outside its control. The three landowners listed in table 14 who received allocations of 200 acres or more through the Enclosure Award of 1829 also set up farms on their new, consolidated holdings. Baker's Farm, on the edge of Elmdon village, grew out of the Hadsley property; Elmdon Lee, away on the boundary between Elmdon and Littlebury, was created by General Raymond; and Poplars Farm was set up on Miss Maling's allotment of land on the north-east boundary of the parish.[13]   Like the Lofts Hall estate farms, these three holdings were at first all tenanted, though as none of the landowners lived in Elmdon, the farmers may have had more freedom of action than those who leased their land from the Wilkes. But in 1858, James Hayden, the sitting tenant, bought Baker's Farm[14] and became the first farmer in the parish to be an owner-occupier.

The large landowners, then, and especially the Wilkes family, came well out of the enclosure. Their holdings were rationalised, and they could expect higher rents from their tenants, for the new farms were easier to work than the old, scattered strips, and therefore more profitable, both to the farmer and the landowner. Furthermore, they now had complete control over the use to be made of their land, as they were freed from all the restrictions inherent in the working of the common fields.

The smallholders

As we shall see, the fortunes of the smaller landholders after the enclosure were mixed. Like the large landowners, those who received small allocations were compelled under the Enclosure Act to fence or hedge their allotments. The cost of this obligatory fencing fell particularly heavily on the man who had only owned a limited amount of open-field land, for in general the smaller the allotment made, the greater the costs of fencing in proportion to the total value of the property. Indeed, this may have been why some of those who only owned one or two strips in the open fields sold out to the large landowners before the Award was made. How far did the smallholders listed in table 15 succeed in maintaining their holdings in the more competitive age of large-scale enclosed farming which now began in Elmdon and Wenden Lofts? By 1860, John Hayden, the Gibsons and Joseph Buck or their heirs had not succumbed to pressure from the larger landowners. Although they and their families do not seem to have lived in the parish, they apparently retained their holdings, which were shown on the map accompanying the 1860 survey as still being in their possession. It is also certain that the Wilkes family had not yet acquired the property of John Graves or Debden Wright, though it is not possible to state categorically that these smallholders or their heirs retained the land themselves, since it lay in an area shown on the 1860 map as belonging to 'divers owners'.

The land originally belonging to Thomas Wisby, John Brand and Robert Jarvis, on the other hand, had been sold to the Lofts Hall estate before 1860. In the case of Wisby and Brand, it is possible that the transactions were made on the understanding that the land should be leased back to them, or their heirs, for in 1851 the widowed Mary Wisby, helped by her son George, was in charge of 20 acres[15] and as late as 1860 George was renting from the estate the same ten acres which had been allotted to Thomas Wisby by the Enclosure Award thirty-one years earlier. Similarly, in 1860 John Brand was paying £22 0s 0d a year to rent the 10 acres south of the Ickleton Road allotted to his father. Alas, the estate surveyor noted that Brand had 'allowed his arable allotment to become disgracefully foul', and it is probable that his lease was not renewed, for while in 1851 he was described in the census as 'blacksmith and farmer of ten acres', in 1861 his occupation was recorded only as 'blacksmith'. It looks as if George Wisby lost his tenancy at the same time, for he was no longer living in Elmdon parish in 1861. Of the three remaining smallholdings, James Ward's eight acres had been incorporated into Baker's Farm by 1860; Elisha Jeffery's plot, which was a garden rather than a separate field, had been sold along with his cottage to the Lofts Hall estate; and John Cane's house, workshop and garden had passed to Ann Cane, who was living there with her wheelwright husband in 1861.

These smallholders, then, fell into two classes. First were those, largely living outside Elmdon, whose property there was a supplement to other forms of income, and who had retained their holdings, presumably as a form of investment. Second, a smaller group, living and working in Elmdon itself, sold out to the large landowners. Of these, George Wisby was probably the least fortunate, for he seems to have had no trade other than agriculture to fall back on once his days as a tenant smallholder were over.

There was, however, a third group of smallholders in Elmdon

Table 17
Holdings of 5—99 acres in Elmdon and Wenden Lofts in 1851 and 1861

	1851 acres	1861 acres
Elizabeth Dean	94	—
George Clark	70	—
Nathan Bailey	50	27
Charles Letchfield	45	—
James Letchfield	36	—
James and Ann Jeffery	30	26
George Ratcher	—	60
George Nottage (miller)	—	27
Mary Wisby	20	—
John Brand	10	—
Sarah Smoothy (Wilkes Arms)	9	(Probably) 9
Ann Morris	6	—
	370	149

Source: 1851 and 1861 censuses

and Wenden Lofts, who had owned no land in 1829. The creation of the major farms after the Enclosure Award did not mean that landowners entirely ceased to let smaller areas. Table 17 lists these other holdings between 5 and 100 acres, which were being worked in 1851 and 1861. Although evidence is not available in every case, it is likely that the great majority were tenanted and not owner-occupied. It is clear that there was a considerable reduction in their numbers between 1851 and 1861, and that the acreage let to small farmers fell by more than half during the decade. One reason for this may have been that the ten years in question fell within the period of 'high farming', when agriculture was prosperous and profitable, so that the larger tenant farmers were eager for more land. This they could only obtain at the expense of the smallholders, or of each other. Another reason may have been the general reorganisation of the estate's affairs by Robert Fiske Wilkes when he came into the property in 1858. Whatever the cause, the effects were severe, and it is this group of smallholders who seem to have suffered most, being reduced from farmers, albeit small ones, to the working classes. Elizabeth Dean's son and son-in-law, for example, who had run her 94-acre farm for her in 1851 as a family affair, were both agricultural labourers by 1861. So was James Letchfield, while Charles Letchfield had left Elmdon altogether.

The cottagers

One more group of property holders remain whose position declined between 1829 and 1860. As we saw earlier, at the time of the Enclosure Award seven villagers owned cottages with rights of common; but the Award also listed sixteen cottages without such rights which were owned, not by the major landowners or small-scale speculators, but by the cottagers themselves. By 1860, four of the better cottages and five of the smaller dwellings had been absorbed into the Lofts Hall estate. Probably the cost of repairs and the obligatory payment of the corn rent, which had replaced the tithes and which in 1829 worked out at around one penny for each perch of land covered by a cottage and its garden,[16] had influenced those who sold to the Wilkes family. By 1860 the estate owned thirty-nine tenements which were let to Elmdon villagers, compared to about seventeen in 1829, and the point had been reached at which, as we saw in chapter 1, the Lofts Hall estate controlled roughly half the farmland and house property in the northern half of Elmdon parish.

1860–1922

The Lofts Hall estate

When Robert Wilkes came into his inheritance in 1858, British agriculture was enjoying the best years it had known since the Napoleonic wars. True, the estate had not been managed as well as it should have been over the preceding ten years. The surveyor who prepared the 1860 report noted that buildings had not been efficiently repaired in the past, and found it necessary to recommend a reduction in the rents charged to the estate farmers, at a time when elsewhere agriculture was at the height of its prosperity. But by 1867 matters had righted themselves. From that year the farms were again let on seven-year leases at their full value,[17] bringing in well over £6,000 per annum in rents, and all looked set fair.

Within eight years, there had been a fundamental change. From 1875 to 1884, and again from 1891 to 1899, agriculture moved into a state of deep depression.[18] The Lofts Hall estate had additional troubles to contend with. Robert Wilkes, who had taken a lasting interest in his property and his parishioners, died in 1879 and was succeeded by his son, John. While his father had lived all his adult life in Elmdon or Wenden Lofts, John's case was different. Instead of following his father, grandfather, great-grandfather and great-great-grandfather into the church, he became a barrister, living outside Elmdon after he qualified until he came into the property. His first two children were born in Surrey, and he did not take up residence in Lofts Hall until 1882.[19] His reign there was brief. His wife, Lucy, died in 1885 at the early age of thirty-five, and he himself was dead two years later, leaving a son, John, aged eight, and five young daughters, to be brought up by their aunt, first at Lofts Hall and then, from about 1894, in Saffron Walden.

The estate therefore had to face the second trough of the great agricultural depression with an owner who was a minor. It was in

Table 18*
Lofts Hall Estate, Elmdon, Wenden Lofts, Chrishall and Chishill. Total rents received from farms and cottages, 1888–1919

year	£
1888	4,186
1889	3,971
1890	4,313 - includes shooting income
1891	4,120 ,, ,, ,,
1892	3,650 ,, ,, ,,
1893	2,476 ,, ,, ,,
1894	3,710 ,, ,, ,,
1895	3,139 ,, ,, ,,
1900–1	2,899 - includes rent from lease of Lofts Hall
1901–2	3,201 ,, ,, ,, ,, ,, ,,
1902–3	3,475 ,, ,, ,, ,, ,, ,,
1903–4	3,227 ,, ,, ,, ,, ,, ,,
1904–5	3,332 ,, ,, ,, ,, ,, ,,
1905–6	3,362 ,, ,, ,,, ,, ,, ,,
1907	3,559 ,, ,, ,, ,, ,, ,,
1908	3,830 ,, ,, ,, ,, ,, ,,
1909	3,866 ,, ,, ,, ,, ,, ,,
1910	3,944 ,, ,, ,, ,, ,, ,,
1911	3,772 ,, ,, ,, ,, ,, ,,
1912	3,788 ,, ,, ,, ,, ,, ,,
1912–13	3,807 - timber excluded. Shooting in hand excluded and let privately, apart from Lofts Hall
1913–14	3,802 - Chishill property sold Sept. 1914. Rents reduced by £642 p.a. from that date
1914–15	3,622
1915–16	3,293
1916–17	4,102
1917–18	4,305
1918–19	4,167

*Table prepared by David Woodhill

Source: Lofts Hall estate cash accounts

60

fact administered by young John Wilkes's uncle, Mr Collin, a solicitor of Saffron Walden, until the heir reached his majority.

Perhaps because the estate was in the hands of a 'regent' who was also a member of the legal profession, meticulous accounts were kept from 1888 onwards.[20] The rent rolls, summarised in table 18, show the overall downward trend of the estate's income between 1888 and the turn of the century, as times grew hard and farm rents had to be reduced. The rise in 1890 came not from improved farm rentals, but from including the receipts obtained by letting the shooting. This may well have been fairly lucrative, for the area had always been well known for its sporting amenities. As early as 1768, Rockell's Wood near Duddenhoe End was known as 'the joy of fox-hunters',[21] while in 1819, John Wilkes had been so determined to safeguard his game that he had set up spring guns in Chrishall woods to deter would-be poachers. Three young men (including one of the Brand family) had nevertheless entered the wood to gather hazelnuts, and in doing so had set the guns off. So many pellets entered the legs of one of them, Ilot by name, that they could not all be extracted. He was awarded £50 damages against John Wilkes at Essex Summer Assize, but this judgement was reversed on appeal, on the ground that 'no imputation could possibly be cast on Mr Wilkes, for he was only doing what every man of property had been in the habit of doing . . .'[22] By the end of the nineteenth century such extreme methods against poaching had long since been illegal, but the number of game does not seem to have noticeably diminished as a result. Mr Arthur Blyth, who leased the Elmdon shooting rights in 1899–1900, reported a record bag comprising 4,389 partridges, 3,275 pheasants, 1,652 hares, 2,781 rabbits, 12 woodcock, 48 pigeons, and 38 creatures labelled 'various', making a total of 12,195 for the season.[23]

A second move towards retrenchment came in 1896, with the letting of part of Lofts Hall to a preparatory school, although the resultant income was not included in the rental accounts until 1900. When the school moved out, Sir James Bailey, who has been mentioned in earlier chapters, took out a lease and lived in the Hall. Stories are still remembered about the parties he gave. He died in 1910, and for one who lived in Wenden Lofts for only five years, he seems to have made a deep impression, probably because his way of life and his social contacts were those of the fashionable world, while the local residents were used to seeing

Lofts Hall inhabited by country squires, with clerical connections.

From the expiry of Sir James Bailey's lease, the Hall was let to one tenant or another right up to its sale in 1927. John Wilkes, or Jack Wilkes as he was known, never returned to live there. When he had finished his education at Harrow and Cambridge, he attended a course in estate management in Westmorland, and then, in 1906, took over the house and farm at Elmdon Bury, where he lived for the next twenty years, except for a break for war service.

The farm's livestock and cropping books[24] provide a detailed picture of how Elmdon Bury was run when Jack Wilkes and his farm manager took it over. By 1906, wheat prices were slowly recovering from the depression marking the closing years of the nineteenth century, but even so, foreign imports were still providing keen competition, and farmers in the Essex uplands had learnt to diversify. In the farming year running from September 1907 to September 1908, Elmdon Bury was carrying cattle, sheep, pigs and poultry. The number of beasts bought and sold are set out in table 19, from which it can be seen that the gross profit on livestock for the year came to £1,343 1s 10d. Most of the trade in

Table 19
Elmdon Bury farm livestock account, September 1907 - September 1908

	bought			sold			gross profit		
	no. of beasts	*price* £	s d	*no. of beasts*	*price* £	s d	£	s	d
Cattle	41	520 10	0	50	760 1	9	239	11	9
Sheep	100	242 10	0	421	1,015 14	7	773	4	7
Pigs	1	3 0	0	136	230 18	10	227	18	10
	142	766 0	0	607	2,006 15	2	1,240	15	2
Poultry	to the value of £8 2s 6d was bought; and eggs and birds to the value of £110 9s 2d were sold making a gross profit of						102	6	8
					Total gross profit		£1,343 1s 10d		

Source: Elmdon Bury livestock and cropping book

bullocks and sheep was done with two major dealers, Britton, who was the Elmdon butcher, and Cheffins, but the accounts show that where pigs and poultry were concerned, Elmdon villagers were also customers of the farm. Store pigs were sold to Frank Hammond, Thomas Greenhill, John Gamgee and other farm workers at prices ranging from £1 0s 0d to £1 5s 0d each. Fattened and slaughtered, such a pig would play an important part in the domestic economy of its owner. Alice Gamgee bought quantities of eggs at 2s 4d a score, presumably to keep the customers of her small egg business supplied when her own hens were not laying. Edward Jeffery, licensee of the Wilkes Arms, is recorded as buying 'an old hen' for 1s 9d which did not augur well for those dining at the inn. A 10 lb turkey was sold to George Gamgee for 8s 4d. Even Miss Wilkes, probably the Squire's aunt, figures in the list, buying a pullet for 3 shillings.

Table 20
Elmdon Bury cropping account, 1907

	acreage sown	average yield per acre quarters	bushels	gross receipts £	s	d
Wheat	145	3	6	883	6	5
Oats - winter	21	5	2	104	6	0
spring	17.5	6	7	111	8	6
Barley	116.5	4	4	769	6	6
Beans	30	3	3	155	1	9
Beans and peas	20	4	4	136	10	—
Peas	10	4	2	65	18	—
Totals:	360	—	—	2,225	17	2

Source: Elmdon Bury livestock and cropping book

In spite of diversification, the cropping account for the same year, summarised in table 20, shows that Elmdon Bury was still making a greater gross profit from arable farming than from the livestock side of the business. Receipts from the sale of crops totalled £2,225 17s 2d, with wheat bringing in the most money, closely followed by barley. Winter and spring oats, beans and peas were the other cash crops. A year later, the cropping book shows that the farm was growing fodder crops such as swedes, mangolds, clover, lucerne and coleseed to support its livestock. The gross profits for cattle, sheep and pigs had risen to £1,799 15s 6d and the acreage under crops for sale from 360 to 427 acres.

As table 18 shows, the rents received from the rest of the estate also improved slowly but steadily in the first decade of the twentieth century, although it was not until 1917–18 that they exceeded those brought in thirty years earlier in 1888, and they were still far below the £6,000 or more received during 1867. However, the Chishill property had been sold in 1913–14, and from that year onwards the total rental income had been reduced by the £642 per annum which Chishill farm and various cottages in that parish had brought in.

It should perhaps be emphasised here that the figures of rents received, set out in table 18, take no account of expenditure made by the estate, and do not represent net income to the estate's owner. From 1914 to 1919, for instance, the total receipts, including rents, for the estate were £19,655, but the outgoings over the same five-year period came to £10,771, so that the net income was £8,884, or an average of approximately £1,775 per annum.

Other landowners

The three Elmdon farms which lay outside the Lofts Hall estate also experienced changes between 1860 and 1922. Baker's Farm was up for sale twice after the Haydens left it. In 1872 it was bought by Sidney Kent, and a new farmhouse was erected in 1883. Four years later, Edwin Goode bought the property, by now called Elmdon Lodge, and ran his steam-engine contracting business from it. He stayed on in the house for a while after his retirement, but sold the farm to the Fison family in 1920.[25] Poplars Farm came on the market about a year earlier, and was bought by the sitting tenant, Thomas Wood, who had originally come from Great Chishill in 1908 to work as farm bailiff. It thus became the second farm in Elmdon to be owner-occupied. But the third farm, Elmdon Lee, which carried with it not only the title of Lord of the Manor of Leebury, but also a large and elegant farmhouse bearing some similarity to that of Elmdon Bury, was bought by Jack Wilkes in 1920, for £5,500.[26] The size of the farm at the time of the sale is not recorded, but it can be estimated at around 350 to 400 acres. This in fact was the main transaction which increased the size of the Lofts Hall estate in Elmdon, Wenden Lofts and Chrishall from 3,782 acres in 1860 to 4,187 acres in 1927, when it was sold. Even the number of cottages on the estate had gone up by only a few in the sixty-seven years since the survey made for Jack Wilkes' grandfather, Robert, in 1860; for in that year the estate had thirty-nine tenants in Elmdon village, while in 1927 the number had only risen to forty-three.[27]

The end of the Lofts Hall estate

By 1922, agriculture had lurched into yet another depression. An attempt was made to dispose of the estate in that year, but no

64

buyers could be found and it had to be withdrawn from sale. In 1926 Jack Wilkes left Elmdon for Wiltshire, where he took a job with a land agency firm. In October 1927, the whole estate was sold to E. C. Fairweather, a speculator, who within a month had arranged for the firm of Jackson Stops to offer the property by auction in 112 separate lots.[28] As an illustration of declining land values, while Rockells Farm was bought in 1838 at around £26 10s 0d an acre, in 1927 Freewood Farm fetched only £7 an acre at auction.[29]

Mr Fairweather's speculation does not seem to have been a particularly successful one, for after the auction nearly a third of the estate remained unsold. By 1930, however, this remnant had been bought by another speculator, H. Morris Wheeler. It was he who removed from Lofts Hall the panelling which ended in the Hearst collection in America. He held what was left of the estate for only a short time, however. On 30 September 1930[30] the remaining 1,233 acres covering six farms in Duddenhoe End and Wenden Lofts, and thirty-seven cottages, were sold by auction to a number of individuals and the disintegration of the Lofts Hall estate was complete.

4

The men on the land, 1860-1930

The Lofts Hall estate tenant farmers

We have seen how the Wilkes family steadily increased their land
holding in Elmdon, Wenden Lofts and Chrishall, and how John
Wilkes created new farms from the land he received from the
Enclosure Award of 1829. But to own an estate was not necessarily
to farm it. Up to 1906, at least, the Wilkes seemed content with
the power and prestige brought by landownership, and showed no
signs of emulating Viscount Townshend, more familiarly known as
'Turnip' Townshend, and the great Coke of Holkham Hall in
Norfolk, who farmed part of their estates themselves and led the
way in agricultural innovation. Nevertheless, they needed some
economic return on the capital they had invested in the estate, and
this they obtained by renting their farms to tenants.

There were eleven tenant farmers on the Lofts Hall estate when
the 1860 survey[1] was carried out, one of whom, James Rolfe,
leased two farms. The birthplaces of these men show that the
Wilkes family had not gone far afield to find their tenants. Seven
of them had been born in Elmdon or Chrishall, and the other four
had come either from the neighbouring parishes of Arkesden and
Langley, or from Great Chesterford only five miles away. But if
we investigate their backgrounds a little further, we find a remarkable web of family connections, which are set out diagrammatically
in figure 5. James Rolfe, who leased Hope and Home Farms in
Wenden Lofts, was the cousin of John Rolfe up at Elmdon Bury.
John Rolfe's second wife and Moses Prime's second wife, at
Duddenhoe End Farm, were sisters. Moses Prime's father-in-law
through his first wife was James Hayden at Church Farm. James
Hayden's son Edward was married to Martha Pigg, the daughter of
James Pigg at Gentleman's Farm. Martha Pigg was therefore
sister-in-law to Thomas Hayden, Edward's brother, at Pond Street
Farm. Thomas Hayden's sister was mother of young John Brand

66

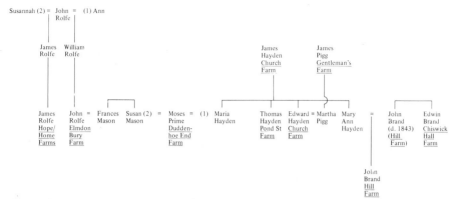

Fig. 5 Farming families' interrelationships, Lofts Hall estate,
1860

at Hill Farm, and John Brand was nephew on his father's side of
Edwin Brand at Chiswick Hall Farm. The only three estate farmers
in 1860 to be outside this tight little kin-linked group all lived in
the south of Elmdon parish, centred on Duddenhoe End. They
were William Barnard at the Cosh, John Nottage at Rockells, and
Joseph Pilgrim at Duddenhoe Grange. Joseph came from Great
Chesterford, but he too had a family link with Elmdon in that his
brother, Robert, had been personal servant to the Wilkes family
for over twenty years, while John Nottage's son, George, rented
the Lofts mill from the estate.

More will be said about these farming families, their social
connections and their place in village affairs, in later chapters.
Here we are concerned chiefly with their relationship to the land,
and with the length of time they remained associated with the
Lofts Hall estate.

It would be a mistake to assume from the intricate relationships
which had grown up between them by 1860 that the farmers born
in Elmdon or Chrishall were all direct descendants of yeomen who
had lived in the two parishes from time immemorial. True, there
had been Piggs in Chrishall for many generations, just as there had
been Brands in Elmdon from the time the parish records began in
1618, and probably earlier. But though John Rolfe was born in
Elmdon, his father, like James Rolfe's father, was an Arkesden
man; the Haydens did not arrive in Wenden Lofts or Elmdon until
well into the second half of the eighteenth century; and the Primes
came even later. The Brands, in fact, are the only family that can
be surely linked to the Lofts Hall estate as far back as 1790, when
Hope Wilkes's survey was made.

67

Hill Farm, 1979

As we saw in the last chapter (table 13), Miss Elizabeth Brand was then the tenant of 64 acres of estate land, most of which consisted of strips in Elmdon Field, which she farmed from the homestead later known as Hill Farm. She lived to be 88 years old, and when she died in 1841 she left the bulk of her personal estate to her great-nephew, John Brand.[2] This great-nephew (not the same John Brand, blacksmith and farmer, who was mentioned in the last chapter) tenanted Hill Farm in his turn and, probably because the farm was small by Elmdon standards, being only just over 100 acres, also retained the shop in the High Street which he rented before taking over the farm tenancy. Unfortunately he did not share his great-aunt's robust constitution, for he died only two years after her at the early age of 36, leaving an 8-year-old son, also called John, and two daughters. That, one might think, would be the end of the Brands' connection with Hill Farm. But the 1851 census shows us that young John's maternal uncle, Edward Hayden, had taken over the tenancy, and by 1860 John Brand himself, now a grown man of 26 years of age, was leasing both Hill Farm and the shop, like his father before him. We do not know exactly how these arrangements came about, or who suggested them, but in their effects, as far as succession was concerned, they were akin to those which an owner-occupier

68

might make, willing his farm and shop to his son but leaving a relative in charge until the heir reached his majority.

Nor was that the end of the story. When Edward Hayden left Hill Farm and his nephew John took it over, Edward joined his father, James Hayden, at Church Farm, which was a larger unit of just over 200 acres. The old man retired, and Edward became the tenant, but by a strange coincidence he himself died in 1862 at a comparatively young age, leaving a number of daughters and one 8-year-old son. John Brand then left Hill Farm and moved to Church Farm in his uncle's place. It would be nice to be able to say that he looked after Church Farm for his orphaned cousin as his uncle Edward had looked after Hill Farm for him, but such was not the case, for the Hayden children had left Elmdon by the time of the 1871 census, and John Brand remained at Church Farm until his own death in 1883. His widow retained the tenancy for another thirty years or more, and was followed by her son, William Arthur, who some time in the first quarter of the twentieth century also took over Hill Farm again. He was tenant of both farms at their sale in 1927, whereupon he retired to Cambridge, thus ending

Table 21
Continuity of farming tenancies, Lofts Hall estate, 1841–1922

Farm	1841	1860	1887	1922
Church	James Hayden [i]	Unchanged	Mrs M.J. Brand [ii]	William A. Brand
Elmdon Bury	John Rolfe	Unchanged	Charles Rolfe	In hand
Hill	John Brand Sr	John Brand Jr	Joseph Burton	William A. Brand
Home	Not known	James Rolfe	Not known	In hand
Hope	James Rolfe	Unchanged	Francis Rolfe	Mrs E.A. & B.W. Smith
Pond Street	Thomas Hayden	Unchanged	Henry Rolfe	G.W. Mallows
Cosh	William Barnard	Unchanged	Moses Prime	E.H. Smith
Duddenhoe End	Jacob Prime	Moses Prime	Unchanged	Oswald Prime
Duddenhoe Grange	Not known	Joseph Pilgrim	W. Maynard	E.H. Smith
Rockells	Not known	John Nottage	James Nottage	W.P. Cowell
Chiswick Hall	Not known	Edwin Brand	Charles Smith [iii]	H.A. Grover
Gentleman's	Not known	James Pigg	Thomas Pigg	Charles Pigg

(i) James Hayden's son Edward held the tenancy in 1861. (ii) Edward Hayden's niece by marriage. (iii) Not related to 1922 tenants of the same name.

Sources: 1841 census. Lofts Hall estate survey, 1860. Lofts Hall estate cash accounts, 1887. Sale catalogue of the Lofts Hall estate, 1922.

69

a family association with the Lofts Hall estate which had lasted at least 137 years, and covered four different generations.

The Brands may have been tenants of the estate over more generations than any other farming family, but it was by no means exceptional for a son to follow his father as an estate tenant. When the first attempt to sell the estate was made in 1922, Oswald Prime was the third generation of his family to tenant Duddenhoe End Farm, as was Charlie Pigg at Gentleman's Farm in Chrishall. John Rolfe at Elmdon Bury was succeeded by his son Charles, and it is very likely that he had been preceded by his father, who we know was also a farmer in Elmdon. Other families where one generation followed another as estate tenants were the James Rolfes; the Church Farm Haydens and the Nottages, as can be seen from table 21. There was even a case of a son-in-law taking over as tenant from a man who had two daughters but no son of his own. This happened at Hill Farm, after John Brand had left it in the 1860s. He was replaced by Joseph Burton, who in turn was followed by Robert Burgess, husband of Burton's daughter Mary, before William Arthur Brand finally took over. The recently proposed Bill to enable the children of tenant farmers to retain the tenancies after their parents' death or retirement would hardly have been necessary on the Lofts Hall estate in the second half of the nineteenth century.

Tenancies were not automatically renewed, however. Joseph Pilgrim's tenure of Duddenhoe Grange is a case in point. The surveyor in 1860 noted that cultivation on that farm was 'the worst on the estate and bears evidence of a want of capital'. He recommended that the tenant should not be allowed to re-lease the farm unless he could prove that he had adequate capital of his own. Poor Pilgrim evidently failed to satisfy this condition, and by 1861 the farm was out of his hands. He found himself a smaller farm, of only 59 acres, in Clavering and was installed there the year after he left Elmdon. In other cases, it was the tenant who decided to leave the estate. Edwin Brand of Chiswick Hall Farm, for instance, removed himself to a farm at Kimpton in Hertfordshire. As Kimpton was the seat of Lord Dacre, then the principal landowner in Chrishall, it seems likely that he transferred to one of Lord Dacre's farms, possibly through a contact with the latter's bailiff in Chrishall.

The evidence, then, shows that although tenancies of the Lofts Hall estate were likely to pass from one generation of kin to another, this was not always the case. What caused the various owners of the estate to decide on which tenants should be offered new leases, usually running for a seven-year term, and which not, and what made established tenants leave? Were the landowners motivated solely by a desire for the highest rents they could get, or did other factors come into play?

The remarks of an elderly Chrishall farmer, whose father had been a tenant, throw some light on the general attitude of landowners in the district during the late nineteenth and early twentieth centuries. He stated that provided a farmer 'behaved himself', the landlord would leave him in possession, and his son after him. 'Bad behaviour', bad enough to justify turning the tenant out when his lease expired, would cover really poor farming, but more commonly it would involve some kind of interference with the landowner's game, such as shooting a troublesome fox or bagging a pheasant. But if the tenant avoided these pitfalls, and paid his rent, the landlord would leave him to go along much as he pleased.

Looked at against this background, the farmers' continuity of tenure on the Lofts Hall estate seems to fit in with the practice of other local landowners of the time. There must always have been some differences due to the personal characteristics and preferences of individual landowners, however. For example, it seems safe to say that either John Wilkes or his widow was influenced by their servant, Robert Pilgrim, to lease Duddenhoe Grange farm to Robert's brother, Joseph, for all his want of capital, but it seems that Robert Fiske Wilkes, their successor, was not so easily persuaded. He certainly took the opportunity to remove Joseph from the farm as we have seen.

There is also the question of the tenants' influence over the Squire of the time. Once within the system, it was easy to suggest that a vacant tenancy should be allocated to a younger son, or a nephew or son-in-law. On the Squire's side, it would be natural to think first of the tenants he already dealt with, and knew to be reliable. The 1860 survey tells us that Thomas Hayden at Pond Street Farm had given in his notice as from Michaelmas of that year, and the surveyor suggests that a new, smaller farm should be created from the old one 'either for James Rolfe or his son', while the rest of the land should be added to existing farms tenanted by Rolfe, Prime and Edwin Brand, with 15 acres going to George Nottage, the Lofts miller, 'to help him find more constant employment for himself and his horses than he is now able to do at times

71

when he cannot work his Mill'. But whether the intricate kinship network of the estate farmers, so evident in 1860, arose because the tenants persuaded the Squire to give leases to their relations; or whether the Squire preferred to take on new tenants with whom he was already acquainted through their relationship with existing tenants; or indeed whether the estate tenants as a whole felt such group solidarity that inter-marriage resulted almost as a matter of course, are questions to which no clear-cut answers can be given.

Pressure of outside events also played its part in relations between landlord and tenant. As we saw in the previous chapter, the Enclosure Act of 1824 had the effect of causing small land-owners to sell out to the Lofts Hall estate, some of whom subsequently rented back their former holdings. The same thing may well have happened with the Hayden family. The John Hayden who sold much of his land to John Wilkes around the time of the Enclosure Award of 1829 was the older brother of the James Hayden tenanting Church Farm in 1860, and Thomas Hayden at Pond Street was his nephew.

During the prosperous period of high farming, the landowner could afford to look on his estate as a social as well as an economic unit, for he was able to charge rents which gave him a good return on the capital invested, while still allowing the tenant farmer to make a satisfactory living. But with the two great agricultural depressions which overshadowed the last twenty-five years of the nineteenth century, the situation changed radically. The corn-growing areas were particularly badly affected, and many tenants of long standing were ruined when landowners failed to reduce their rents. On the Lofts Hall estate, as table 18 in chapter 3 has shown, rents were in fact lowered, and most of the tenants managed to weather the storm and survive into the twentieth century, though the standard of living of the Wilkes family was considerably reduced. The estate cash accounts for 1887–1900[3] show that in 1899, Charles Rolfe was paying £375 a year rent for Elmdon Bury, where thirty-nine years earlier his father was finding £1,040.[4] The rent of Church Farm had gone down from £315 in 1860 to £145; and the rents of the other farms had all been dramatically reduced. In spite of this, Thomas Pigg at Gentleman's Farm was shown as being £300 in arrears at the end of 1899. Yet Thomas's son, Charlie, was still tenant of Gentleman's Farm in 1922,[5] and the only known case of a Lofts Hall estate tenant

72

leaving because he considered the rent too high was that of Charles Rolfe. The story goes that in 1906 he asked the Squire to reduce his rent on Freewood Farm, then part of Elmdon Bury, because it lay on heavy boulder clay soil which was hard to work. The Squire agreed to reduce the rent a little, but Rolfe was not satisfied and asked for a further reduction, whereupon the Squire decided that enough was enough, and took the farm over himself. It was not a case of a hard-hearted landowner evicting a tenant of long standing and leaving him penniless, however, for Charles Rolfe was said to have made a considerable sum of money through a lucky investment on the Stock Exchange, and he retired in good order to a large house in Saffron Walden.

As we saw in the last chapter, the agricultural difficulties experienced in the 1920s finally brought the Lofts Hall estate down, and the tenant farmers with it. Oswald Prime and William Arthur Brand, both well over 60, retired away from Elmdon. Charlie Pigg at Gentleman's Farm and John Brand, William Arthur's son, who might have been expected to take on Hill or Church Farms, failed before 1927 and left the district. William Cowell left Elmdon Lee, and neither of his sons took on the tenancy, although one of them rented Old Rockells for a time. Indeed none of the tenants actually in occupation at the time of the sales in 1927 and 1930 bought their farms, even though prices were at rock bottom. With the sale of the estate, the association of a group of farming families with the land in Elmdon, Wenden Lofts and Chrishall largely came to an end, although, as we shall see in the next chapter, one or two attempts were made to retain the old links.

The farmers outside the Lofts hall Estate

At first sight, the three Elmdon farmers who were outside the Lofts Hall estate in 1861 differed markedly from those within it. None of them had been born in Elmdon, Wenden Lofts or Chrishall, and although Miss Perry at Poplars came from the adjoining parish of Strethall, the other two had both been born in villages between eight or nine miles away. This pattern of the farms being occupied by people coming in from outside continued throughout the period under consideration, and none of the individuals named in table 22 were Elmdon-born. Nor did any web of kinship link the occupants of one farm with those of the other two. Nevertheless,

Table 22
The continuity of farming families outside the Lofts Hall estate, 1841–1922

Farm	1841	1861	1899	1922
Baker's/Elmdon Lodge	William Hayden tenant	James Hayden owner-occupier	Edwin Goode owner-occupier	The Fison Bros. owner-occupier
Poplars	George Wilford tenant	Rebecca Perry tenant[i]	W.C. Emson tenant	Thomas Wood owner-occupier
Elmdon Lee[ii]	Not known	Charles Mickley tenant	W.P. Cowell tenant	Unchanged

(i) Niece of George Wilford. (ii) Elmdon Lee became part of the Lofts Hall estate in 1920.

Sources: 1841 and 1861 censuses. *Kelly's Directory of Essex, Hertfordshire and Middlesex, 1899.* Sales catalogues, Baker's Farm/Elmdon Lodge. Title deeds, Poplars Farm. Sales catalogue, Lofts Hall estate, 1922.

there were certain resemblances between the farmers on the estate and those outside it.

In the first place, up to 1858 all three farms were tenanted. As we have already seen, Baker's Farm was bought by the sitting tenant in that year, while Poplars was taken over by an owner-occupier in about 1919. The Lee, however, remained tenanted throughout the period, ownership changing from a landowner outside Elmdon to the Lofts Hall estate in 1920.[6]

Second, there was some continuity of tenure while the farmers were still tenants, as table 22 shows. James Hayden at Baker's Farm in 1860 was the son of William Hayden, the tenant in 1841, though neither of them was related to the other Haydens at Church Farm and Pond Street; they came from a long-established family in Henham. Rebecca Perry, too, was related to her predecessor, being George Wilford's niece. She may also have been related in some degree to the Rolfe family at Elmdon Bury, for John's son Charles had 'Wilford' for his second name. Miss Perry had an unpleasant scandal to face in 1849. Nehemiah Perry, almost certainly a relative of hers and possibly her brother, was then living at Strethall Old Hall, and was married to a woman of gypsy blood, but he incurred the emnity of her kinsfolk by discarding her after two or three years. One night a group of gypsies broke into the Hall with intent to rob, and Nehemiah, standing on the stairs, shot and killed the leader of the gang as he advanced. This was bad enough, but he then proceeded to display the body in the belfry of Strethall Church and what is more, charged an admission fee for people to come and see it. Two of the dead man's accomplices were given light sentences for attempted burglary, but Nehemiah himself was never brought to trial, as he was considered

to have acted in self-defence.[7]   The story of the murder, which
took place nearly 130 years ago, is clearly remembered in the
district even now, and is described as if it had happened yesterday.
However, the unfortunate affair seems to have made no difference
to Miss Perry's 'inheritance' of the Poplars tenancy, which she
retained until her death in 1875.

There was an Elmdon connection, too, in the case of William
Cowell.   He was the nephew of a butcher living in Elmdon in the
1860s, and set up in the trade for himself before finally becoming
a farmer.

The farmers outside the Lofts Hall estate, therefore, each with a
different landlord to deal with in the days when they were tenants,
were not inter-related in the way that the Lofts Hall estate tenants
were.   The tendency towards separation as isolated family units
was increased by the fact that both James Hayden and Rebecca
Perry remained single, thus reducing the opportunities of linking
one family with another through children's marriages.

The farm workers

Whether the farms belonged to the Squire, to other landed gentry,
or to an owner-occupier, the land still needed to be ploughed, the
crops sown and harvested, the ricks built, the stock and horses
cared for.   As we saw in chapter 1, these and other tasks on the
farms occupied no fewer than 114 men and boys of Elmdon village
in 1861.

The picture which emerges from an analysis of these men's
origins is one of remarkable homogeneity.   Table 23(a) shows that
ninety-nine of them, or 87 per cent, were Elmdon-born; and
further examination of the fifteen whose birthplace was outside
Elmdon reveals that five were children of Elmdon men who were
temporarily working elsewhere when their sons were born, or
whose wives had gone back to their home villages to have their
first child.   In another three cases, the apparent 'outsider' had
close kin in the village.   Joseph Gamgee, for example, was born in
Cambridge, while his widowed mother with whom he was living in
1861 came from Therfield.   But in fact his father, Stephen, was
an Elmdon man who had emigrated to Cambridge to work as a
coal porter.   When Stephen died in his middle 30s, his widow and
children found a home in the village, probably encouraged by
Stephen's relations.

75

Table 23
(a) *Birthplace of all farm workers, Elmdon village, 1861*

| born in Elmdon parish | | 5 miles | | born within a radius of: | | | | | | total |
| | | | | 5—10 miles | | 10—20 miles | | over 20 miles | | |
no.	%	no.	%	no.	%	no.	%	no.	%	no.
99	87	12	11	—	—	3	3	—	—	114

(b) *Birthplaces of fathers[i] whose sons were farm workers, Elmdon village, 1861*

| born in Elmdon parish | | 5 miles | | born within a radius of: | | | | | | total |
| | | | | 5—10 miles | | 10—20 miles | | over 20 miles | | |
no.	%	no.	%	no.	%	no.	%	no.	%	no.
37	86	5	12	—	—	1	2	—	—	43

(i) The birthplaces of 39 fathers are not known. The number of fathers is not the same as the total number of farm workers, since one father may have had more than one son in the work force.

(c) *Occupations of fathers[ii] whose work differed from that of their son(s) in the farm work force in Elmdon village, 1861.*

Father's occupation	no. of fathers	son(s) occupation
Farm bailiff	2	Agricultural labourer
Thatcher	1	,, ,,
Carpenter	2	,, ,,
Carrier	1	,, ,,
Coal porter	1	,, ,,
Blacksmith	1	,, ,,
Total	8	

(ii) The occupations of the fathers were known in 54 cases only. In the remaining 46 known cases, or 85% of all known cases, the father's occupation was identical with that of his son(s).

(d) *Birthplace of wives of the 54 married farm workers in Elmdon village, 1861*

| born in Elmdon parish | | 0—5 miles | | | born within a radius of: | | | | | | total |
| | | | | | 5—10 miles | | 10—20 miles | | over 20 miles | | |
no.	%		no.	no.	%	no.	%	no.	%	no.	%	no.
27	50	Ickleton 6		26	48	1	2	—	—	—	—	54
		Littlebury 5										
		Chrishall 3										
		Gt Chishill 2										
		Saffron Walden 2										
		8 other villages 8										

Source: 1851 and 1861 censuses.

76

As we saw in chapter 1, only three of the remaining seven who were born outside Elmdon were ordinary agricultural labourers. Three others were specialist farm workers, and the fourth was the son of Miss Perry's farm bailiff, who had come to Elmdon with his father. Five of the seven had gone again before ten years had passed. The younger ones, like Thomas Camp, the cowman from Littlebury, were probably gaining work experience outside their own villages before they were encumbered with wives and families, just as a few Elmdon boys worked in surrounding villages for some years before returning to a job and a tied cottage attached to one of the Elmdon farms.

There was nothing new in this tendency for Elmdon men and boys to fill the great majority of the available jobs on the land. We know the birthplaces of forty-three men whose sons were farm workers in 1861, and table 23(b) shows that 86 per cent of them were Elmdon-born, almost exactly matching the 87 per cent given in table 23(a) for all farm workers. In both cases, only 2 or 3 per cent had been born more than ten miles away from the village. Then, in the same way that tenant farmers' sons suceeded their fathers on the farms, so the land workers' sons followed in their fathers' footsteps. If a boy's father was a shepherd, then it was almost certain that he would start his working life learning to be a shepherd himself, just as agricultural labourers' sons became labourers in their turn. The occupations of fifty-four fathers of members of the 1861 farm work force are known, and only in eight cases did the sons follow a different line of work. These exceptions are set out in table 23(c), from which it can be seen that all these sons were agricultural labourers, although five of the fathers were not directly employed in agriculture, one being a blacksmith, another a carrier, a third a coal porter, and a fourth and fifth, carpenters.

The impression that, for the farm worker, Elmdon was at the centre of a small world encompassing only the villages and hamlets within a radius of five miles or so is reinforced if we look at where the men's wives came from. Fifty-four of the agricultural workers in 1861 were married men, and of these, exactly half had chosen wives born within Elmdon parish. All but one of the other twenty-seven wives had been born within five miles of Elmdon and, as table 23(d) shows, more than half of them came from the three villages of Ickleton, Littlebury and Chrishall. The intricate web of relationships resulting from this pattern of marriage is a subject in itself, and is covered by Marilyn Strathern's companion book on Elmdon, *Kinship at the core.*

In 1861, then, the typical middle-aged farm worker in Elmdon would have been born in the village, like his father before him, with an even chance that he and his wife would have known each other since early childhood, and a near certainty that even if she had not been born in Elmdon itself, her parents' home would have been within walking distance.

The census of 1871 gives us some idea of what happened to the agricultural work force of 1861. In the intervening decade, eleven had died, thirty-five had left, and sixty-eight were still in Elmdon. But table 24 shows that, as one might expect, it was largely the young men who had gone. Nearly seven out of every ten emigrants

Table 24
The migration pattern of Elmdon village farm workers, 1861–1871[i], by age

| | 0–9 | | 10–19 | | 20–29 | | 30–39 | | 40–49 | | 50+ | | total | |
	no.	%	no.	%	no.	%	no.	%	no.	%	no.	%	no.	%
Dying	—	—	—	—	2	9.5	—	—	2	12.0	7	32.0	11	10.0
Leaving	—	—	23	59	5	24.0	2	16.5	2	12.0	3	13.5	35	30.5
Staying	3	100	16	41	14	66.5	10	83.5	13	76.0	12	54.5	68	59.5
Totals	3	100	39	100	21	100	12	100	17	100	22	100	114	100

age group in 1861, in years

(i) Two pages of the 1871 census for Elmdon are missing, due to miscopying by the enumerator. The abstract of totals at the beginning of the census shows that 13 males and 11 females were listed on the missing pages. It is therefore possible that a few labourers shown as emigrating were present in the village in 1871.

Source: 1861 and 1871 censuses.

had been between ten and nineteen years old in 1861. It seems, therefore, that although virtually all Elmdon boys were given their chance to learn how to become a land worker when they left school, as we saw in chapter 1, the majority of them had to find work elsewhere once they had passed through what was in all but name their apprenticeship period. However, if a boy was picked for a man's job where he grew up, he had a reasonable prospect of staying on in the village for the rest of his working life.

Not quite all the farm workers of 1861 who remained in Elmdon ten years later were still at their old jobs, however. Six of them had made a change. A young shepherd had become a combined farm labourer and butcher's man; three others had left agriculture for private service as gardeners or grooms. Another had made the jump from labourer to blacksmith, even though his father had

78

been a labourer too; and a sixth had won promotion within agriculture, becoming a farm bailiff. The other sixty-two workers, or 91 per cent, were all employed in the same capacity as in 1861, and the general pattern of the son following his father continued.

The material amassed in the full censuses is not yet available for 1881 and later years, under the rule which prohibits publication of detailed information on named individuals for a hundred years after its collection. From then on, therefore, it is rather more difficult to trace in detail the pattern of life of Elmdon's farm workers. There are ways, however, in which at least an indication of what happened can be given.

Table 25 names the families containing farm workers whose children were baptised in Elmdon Church for each decade from 1861 to 1930, and also shows how many individual fathers were included in each family group during successive ten-year periods. There were twenty-eight such family groups in 1861 whose members had children in later decades, and nearly seventy years later, eight of these families still contained farm workers whose wives were bearing children in the village.

The table also gives some idea of the extent to which incoming families were successful in establishing themselves in Elmdon. The two new groups, Goode and Mustill, named in the baptismal register between 1861 and 1870 do not seem to have lasted long, for no births to anyone of either name were recorded after that decade. But some of the families first mentioned in later decades

Table 25
Families containing farm workers, Elmdon village, 1861–1930

		Numbers of agricultural workers shown as fathers in the Elmdon baptismal register, 1861–1930						
		1861–70	1871–80	1881–90	1891–1900	1901–10	1911–20	1921–30
Families	Baker	—	—	1	—	—	—	—
represented	Barker	1	—	1	1	—	—	—
in Elmdon	Bird	1	1	1	1	—	—	—
in 1861	Button	1	—	—	—	—	—	—
	Challis	1	1	2	2	1	—	—
	Clements	1	1	—	—	—	—	—
	Dellar	3	1	—	—	—	—	—
	Elcock	—	1	—	—	—	—	—
	Flack	1	—	1	—	—	—	—
	Gamgee	2	2	2	2	—	—	1
	Greenhill	—	—	1	1	—	1	1
	Hammond	1	4	3	4	3	4	5

79

Harvey	1	—	1	—	1	—	1
Hayes	4	5	3	1	4	4	1
Hoy	—	—	2	2	—	2	1
Jeffery	2	2	5	2	1	—	1
Kirby	2	2	2	1	1	—	-
Loveday	1	—	—	—	—	—	-
Miller	1	—	—	—	—	—	-
Morris	—	—	1	1	—	—	-
Negus	1	—	—	—	—	—	-
Prime	—	—	1	1	—	—	-
Reeves	2	2	2	3	3	—	2
Tinworth	1	—	—	—	—	—	-
Waller	2	2	—	—	—	—	-
Waters	2	1	1	1	1	—	-
Wright	1	—	—	—	—	—	-
Young	2	2	1	—	—	—	-

Families first named in the baptismal register between

1861 and 1870	Goode	1	—	—	—	—	—	—
	Mustill	1	—	—	—	—	—	—
1871 and 1880	Hagger*		1	—	—	—	—	—
	Andrews*		1	1	—	—	—	—
	Beans		1	1	1	1	1	—
	Drury		1	1	—	—	—	—
	Fordham		1	—	—	—	—	—
1881 and 1890	Cowell*			1	—	1	—	—
	Dyer*			2	1	—	1	—
	Adams			1	1	—	—	—
	Pledger			1	1	1	—	—
	Watts			1	—	—	—	—
1891 and 1900	Wilson				1	1	1	—
1901 and 1910	Burgess					1	1	—
	Baynes					2	—	—
	Creek					1	—	—
	Clark					2	1	2
	Chapman					1	—	—
	Potterill					1	—	1
	Rush					1	—	—
1911 and 1920	Bard						1	1
	Cook						1	—
	Neeves						1	—
1921 and 1930	Fox							1
	Law*							1
	Starling							2
	Hammond*(i)							1
Total no. of fathers		36	32	40	28	28	19	22

*Duddenhoe End families who came up to Elmdon
(i) Not related to 1861 Hammonds

Source: Elmdon baptismal registers, 1861–1930

80

seem to have settled for considerably longer periods. How did they manage to integrate themselves into the apparently closed community which has just been described?

Six families, those marked with an asterisk in table 25, had come up to Elmdon from Duddenhoe End. We do not know how the village people felt about the occupants of the hamlet in the last quarter of the nineteenth century, although their attitudes at a later period are discussed in Marilyn Strathern's book. But apart from any general inter-community feeling, the Duddenhoe Enders shared a squire and a parson with the Elmdon villagers. They had almost certainly worked on Lofts Hall estate farms when living in the hamlet, so that their transfer to the main village may have occurred through recommendation by one estate farmer to another, or through the Squire speaking for them to one of his tenants. To that extent their arrival would have been in the nature of a *fait accompli* as far as the Elmdoners were concerned. In other families, marriage to an Elmdon woman helped to establish an incomer. Alfred Potterill from Chrishall, for example, married the widow Jane Hammond, who was connected to two of the most prolific families of farm workers in Elmdon, through her first marriage to Bob Hammond, and by her birth as Jane Hayes. The Clark boys, who first fathered children in the first decade of the twentieth century, had come into the village as children themselves, with their parents. Their father was a blacksmith, and craftsmen seem always to have been more mobile than agricultural labourers; the boys grew up in Elmdon and presumably were accepted at least as near-Elmdoners themselves. One of them indeed married a Hammond girl. It must be added, though, that in some cases we do not know why certain families appeared in Elmdon, and the ease of their assimilation or its reverse can only be a matter for conjecture.

Table 25 may also be used to give some indication of how the agricultural work force fluctuated in size from 1861 to 1930. The figures given at the bottom of the table for the numbers of individual farm workers whose children were baptised in succeeding decades do not of course show us the total farm labour force, since the young, the old, the unmarried and those whose wives did not bear children are all excluded. Nevertheless, over the period, these numbers do represent most of the members of one important group within the labour force, namely married men in the prime of life, and one would expect the decennial totals to reflect the

81

influence of major external events, such as the agricultural depressions and the First World War, which influenced all farm workers in the country. Table 26 shows that, however rough and ready the comparison of this Elmdon group with agricultural workers in England and Wales as a whole may be, the decrease between 1871 and 1930 of 39 per cent in the Elmdon group and 30.7 per cent for agricultural workers in England and Wales is roughly comparable, bearing in mind that a particular small group in Elmdon is being set against the whole national agricultural work force. The considerably greater decrease in Elmdon during the decade covering the First World War is easily understandable since the Elmdon group consisted entirely of men of an age to do military service, while the figure for England and Wales included both young boys and old men whose age would disqualify them from serving in the Armed Forces. But the 25 per cent increase in the Elmdon group between 1881 and 1890, when the agricultural depression was at its height and there was a decrease of 10.3 per cent nationally, demands an explanation.

Table 26
Changes in numbers of agricultural workers, 1871–1931

| | England and Wales | | | Elmdon village agricultural workers whose children were baptised in Elmdon | |
| *years* | *agricultural workers* | | *years* | | |
	no.	*% increase or decrease*		*no.*	*% increase or decrease*
1871	962,348		1861–70	36	
1881	870,798	9.5 decrease	1871–80	32	11 decrease
1891	780,707	10.3 decrease	1881–90	40	*25 increase*
1901	620,986	20.5 decrease	1891–1900	28	30 decrease
1911	643,117	*3.6 increase*	1901–10	28	no change
1921	558,854	13.1 decrease	1911–20	19	32 decrease
1931	472,789	15.4 decrease	1921–30	22	16 decrease
Overall changes,					
1871–1931		30.7 decrease	1871–1930		39 decrease

Sources: Lord Ernle, *English farming, past and present*, appendix VI tables I and II. For the period 1871–1911, the figures refer to England and Wales, agricultural workers of all classes on farms; and from 1921–31, England and Wales, agricultural labourers, farm servants, and agricultural machine, tractor drivers, attendants. Elmdon baptismal registers, 1861–1930.

The reason for this increase in the number of married farm workers in Elmdon at such an unlikely period probably lies in the establishment of a steam-engine contracting business in the village, run by Edwin Goode from Elmdon Lodge Farm. To a small village,

82

the opportunities for work which this enterprise offered must have come as a godsend, for they were additional to the usual quota of farm jobs on the six farms in and around Elmdon, all of which continued production even in the worst of the depression, and so had to be staffed, even if by a reduced work force. Few farmers in Elmdon village used the steam ploughs, which were very heavy, weighing from 12 to 15 tons apiece, and which did best on difficult, intractable soils, but Mr Goode and his men worked within a thirty-mile radius of the village, carrying out deep ploughing, deep cultivating, and mole-draining operations. The men would leave Elmdon at five in the morning on Mondays, and often not return until the following Saturday, living in a caravan on the site of their work. They travelled into Cambridgeshire, Bedfordshire, and Hertfordshire, as well as covering north-west Essex. Sometimes their foreman would visit likely farms and arrange contracts with them, and sometimes Mr Goode himself would come out on his motor bicycle and make the arrangements.

One of the men who used to work on these machines recalled ploughing fallow land on warm, dry days. 'The dust! I couldn't see where I was going, there was so much dust. I'd often come home looking like a miller.' Two steam engines made up one set, and each set employed two drivers, one steerer, one man who carted water, another who carried coal and stoked the engines, and a cookboy, whose duty it was to prepare food for the men's dinner and to carry out other odd jobs, such as walking before the engines with a warning flag as they rolled ponderously through the narrow lanes on their way to the next farm. Mr Goode maintained three or four sets of steam engines, and employment was therefore given to at least fifteen men and three boys at a time when farm work was becoming scarcer.

In the winter, the engines would be used to provide power for threshing, which required a nine-man team, saw-milling, and clearing out ponds, and on occasion they would be hired by the council for roadworks. The men who formed the teams no longer described themselves as agricultural labourers when they registered the births of their children, but as engineers. They were proud of themselves and their machines, which they helped to overhaul during the winter re-fit. One man claimed that he even took part in building two of them, while another earned the nickname of 'Shiner', as he was always polishing up the brasswork on his engine. When Mr Goode took his business to Royston, and Elmdon Lodge was sold as a working farm after the First World War, some of the men switched over to work on similar engines for the local council, rather than taking up ordinary farm jobs again.

Although the steam engines gave extra jobs to Elmdoners when they were first introduced, they nevertheless represented the beginning of the mechanisation which in future was steadily to reduce the number of men required for land work. The engines were not used for harvesting, but mechanical reapers and binders were well-established in Elmdon by the middle of the First World War and had replaced the old mowing teams, sometimes twenty-one men strong, which had previously reaped the crops. Most of the old men in Elmdon in 1964 had been too young to join the teams, but they could remember watching them, and listening to the tales their fathers told about them, and all agreed that the long line of men rhythmically sweeping their scythes through the corn 'used to look real pretty'. But one of them had taken his place in such a team behind his father, and looked back on this work with considerable satisfaction. As he remarked, 'They were handy people, that time of day.'

The mowing teams were organised by the farm employees, and they made a special contract with the farmer for whom they usually worked to bring in the harvest for him, in return for wages which were above the normal. Each field was visited in turn, and beans and peas were scythed down as well as wheat, oats and barley. Every team elected the two men who were best mowers to be 'Lord and Lady'. They led the line, and the Lord acted as fore-man, but orders were still taken daily from the farmer himself. The work was hard, and discipline is said to have been strict. Any man not reporting for work on Monday in a clean smock and trousers would be fined. Compensation, apart from the higher wages earned, came from issues of home-brewed beer for 'elevenses and fours', carried up to the fields in barrels hanging from a yoke. A man's wife or young children also carried his meals up to him, where he worked.

When all the effort was over, the gathering-in of the harvest was celebrated by a procession of loaded wagons, decorated with green branches. One man remembered as a boy being tossed up to ride on top of a wagon, and being too sleepy to protest. A further celebration came with the horkey dinner given by the Squire to all his estate tenants on the Michaelmas rent day. Each man would eat a pound of beef and mutton at the feast, washed down with

84

Lunch in the fields

three pints of beer. The Lofts Hall estate account books show the item 'Cash paid for dinner given to cottage tenant, 3 shillings' against the rent received.[8]

The mechanical reapers and binders which replaced the mowing teams were horse-drawn, and horses retained their importance in agriculture right into the 1930s. As table 27 shows, the number of

Table 27
Horses used solely for agriculture, England, 1871—1931

year	no.	% increase or decrease
1871	733,257	
1881	772,087	5.3 increase
1891	796,869	3.2 increase
1901	843,624	5.9 increase
1911	843,632	no change
1921	822,739	2.5 decrease
1931	666,538	19.0 decrease
Overall change, 1871—1931		9.1 decrease

Source: Ernle, *English farming, past and present*, appendix VIII, table III.

farm horses in England decreased overall by only 9 per cent between 1871 and 1931. Horsekeepers therefore continued to be necessary members of the agricultural work force throughout the period we are considering. At one time Elmdon Bury kept something like forty horses, and it took one man to look after five or

85

six of them in the stables. Sheep were also kept, and created a considerable amount of work, for they were not allowed to graze freely, but were hurdled on to the arable land after the harvest and had to be regularly fed. Cleaning and chopping up turnips specially grown for their feed was a laborious business, often undertaken by the boys who were learning their jobs.

The shepherds were not only experts at looking after their sheep but some of them also acted as shearers. One such man, who was living in Elmdon in 1964, had looked after the sheep on a nearby farm in the next parish. He could remember how one day, when he was half way through shearing a sheep, it kicked him and ran away down the lane to Strethall, scattering wool all over the place. He ran after it, and came upon a tramp who in a state of great excitement told him that an animal looking like a lion had come rushing past. The sheep was finally caught, but the shearer had to spend hours collecting up the wool before his employer came home from market. The fleece was worth 7½d a pound weight, and none of it could be wasted. This same shepherd was also asked to use his skill on shearing an aged donkey, but he arranged a special price of 2s 6d for this job, since, as he said, the 3d paid for shearing a sheep was really not enough. Quite why the unfortunate animal needed to be shorn is not clear, since as soon as its coat had been cut off, it had to be wrapped in sacks to keep it warm.

The price of 3d for shearing a sheep was in line with the wages paid to other farm workers. The shepherd in question reckoned to be able to shear seventeen sheep in an afternoon, so he would have finished shearing his flock of 700 sheep in about six or seven weeks, earning £8 1s 6d in the process. If this payment was over and above his normal weekly wage, it was considerably more than the extra £5 or so which the ordinary farm worker earned in the early twentieth century for five weeks of harvest work, but then a shepherd was a skilled man and came at the head of the hierarchy of specialist farm workers, being followed by the horse-keepers, cowmen and pigmen in that order.

Wages for farm workers remained low through almost the whole of the period we are now considering. Table 28 gives the average weekly wage for ordinary agricultural labourers in Essex from 1860 to 1926, and from the recollections of retired farm workers in 1964, the payments received by Elmdon men were very similar. The prosperity of the high farming period was slow to be reflected

Table 28
Average weekly wages of ordinary agricultural labourers in Essex, 1860–1926

year	1860	1869–70	1872	1882	1892	1898	1910	1920	1926
Weekly wages	11s 3d	11s 4d	15s 9d	12s 6d	11s 6d	12s 0d	13s 9d	£2 6s 0d	£1 10s 0d
% increase or decrease	–	0.7 +	39 +	21 –	8 –	4 +	15 +	235 +	35 –

Source: Ernle, *English farming, past and present*, appendix IX.

in the men's pay, and when a substantial rise of 39 per cent did come in 1872, it was short-lived. Ten years later, the country was in the grip of the depression and wages were on their way down again, though as prices fell faster than agricultural wages, the labourers' standard of living was in fact higher than it had been twenty years earlier.[9] The cash level of wages in 1872 was not surpassed until after the First World War. There was, incidentally, no recollection in Elmdon of the abnormally high figure of £2 6s 0d a week shown as being paid in 1920, possibly because many of the men surviving into the 1960s had been serving in the armed forces, and may not have been demobilised in time to profit from the temporarily higher wages of farm workers.

Boys started work at 2s 6d a week in the late nineteenth and early twentieth centuries, and by 1914 the figure had only gone up 6d, to 3s a week. On some farms, at least, the jump to a man's wages came not at a set age, but when the boy in question had developed a man's strength. On Elmdon Bury, the test was the lifting of a sack of beans up the steps near the old barn.

It was difficult for the men and their families to manage on such low pay. Prices were, of course, also low. Milk so creamy that it could be churned into butter cost 1½d a pint, while a can of skimmed milk could be had for only ½d. Before the First World War, beer was 1d a pint, and ten cigarettes cost 3d. Even so, there was unanimous agreement amongst those who could remember these days that it was a very hard struggle indeed to make ends meet. Most cottages had reasonable gardens, and on Elmdon Bury Farm the men were allotted 30 roods of land each on which to grow their own potatoes, so that families could be self-supporting in vegetables, though this meant hard work in the time left after a day's work on the land. Henry Clark used to have his boys out digging the garden at night, by the light of a lantern hung in the old plum tree, which probably accounts for his winning the prize offered by the Squire for the best garden, no less than four times.

Gleaning by the women, described in chapter 1, went on throughout the period, and helped to provide the family's bread supply. Beans were also gleaned, for a payment of 1d for every 100 beans collected. Piglets were bought, and reared until fat enough to be slaughtered and salted down. Men now freely admit to having poached to supplement their diet, and some claim to have had meat every day. Boys would keep goats, not always very profitably since others would steal up and milk them when their owners were elsewhere. Nothing was wasted. The shepherd used to save the tails cut from the lambs, and these were cooked, presumably as oxtail is, and the meat turned into puddings.

Women earned extra money when they could. For stone-picking, they were paid 1 shilling for a heap, and they received a similar sum for doing a day's washing, though dinner and tea were provided as well. But even with all these shifts, some men found that they needed to earn money over and above their wages. With no formal training, they turned their hands to many things, providing small services within the village. One man gained a regular clientele as a hair cutter and five or six men would be seen waiting their turn outside his house on a Sunday afternoon. Others mended shoes, made and sold sheep hurdles, or caught moles.

Arrangements were made within the village to provide a modicum of help in times of sickness. There was a branch of the Foresters Club, which used to meet at the Wilkes Arms where it held its annual dinner, and which acted as a mutual benefit society, and a rival Slate Club, with its headquarters at the King's Head. In exchange for weekly payments into the clubs, sick pay of 8 shillings a week could be drawn for the first four weeks of an illness, after which the benefit dropped to 4 shillings a week. Any surplus funds at the end of the year were shared out amongst members at Christmas time. Clothing clubs and coal clubs were also organised in Elmdon, Chrishall and Duddenhoe End and were supported by subscriptions from the Squire. When, however, the Elmdon farm workers looked outside the village for help during the First World War and tried to join the National Union of Agricultural Workers, it was a different matter. The Squire is said to have been outraged, and to have threatened to dismiss the branch Secretary from his farm job if he did not resign his Union post. The Union group in Elmdon virtually disintegrated, and the secretaryship of the local branch was not again held by an Elmdoner until after the Lofts Hall estate had been sold up.

88

Earlier in this chapter, we saw in what a small world the Elmdon farm worker of 1861 lived, and how closely knit his community was. This picture changed little during the seventy-odd years which elapsed before the final disintegration of the Lofts Hall estate in 1930.

In many ways, the period was one of transition. Steam engines came in, mechanical reapers and binders replaced the old mowing teams, and jobs grew scarcer, but horses continued to provide the main motive power on the farms and a great deal of intensive labour was still needed. Agriculture went through the two depressions of the late nineteenth century and a further one in the early 1920s, while the Elmdon farms suffered the additional uncertainties caused by the various attempts to sell the Lofts Hall estate over the eight years from 1922 to 1930, but even so, farm work still offered the best chance of a job to boys who wanted to stay in the village. As we saw in chapter 2, the village carrier was using a primitive form of motor bus to operate his twice-weekly service to Saffron Walden in 1930, but it was still impossible for most people to travel daily out of Elmdon to work by public transport. So agriculture remained the mainstay of Elmdon's economy, as it had done for centuries.

How far the pattern of life of the farm workers changed over the period, it is more difficult to say. Table 25, covering those farm workers who had children baptised in Elmdon between 1861 and 1930, shows that of the twenty-two families whom we positivly know to have been in Elmdon in 1930, thirteen were already established in the village sixty-nine years earlier. We have insufficient evidence relating to the other nine families who came in at different times after 1861 to provide statistical material for comparison with the farm workers of 1861, about whom we know so much through the details of the census. But as a result of an earlier study, published under the title of *Some Elmdon Families*,[10] we do know a considerable amount about six family groups, namely the Gamgees, the Greenhills, the Hammonds, the Hayes, the Hoys and the Reeves. From the detailed genealogies and life histories collected for these families, it has been possible to draw up tables to see how far they, and some of their kin, differed from the farm workers of Elmdon in 1861.

These six families, of course, were among those which had survived in the village throughout the period, and one would expect them to be more conservative in their ways, perhaps, than newcomers might be. But comparison of tables 29 (a) to (d) with tables 23 (a) to (d) shows an astonishing similarity. In 1861, 87 per cent of all farm workers were born in Elmdon; in 1930 89 per cent of farm workers in the six families had been born in Elmdon. In 1861, 86 per cent of the fathers of farm workers whose birthplace was known, had been born in the village, compared with 89 per cent of the six families' fathers in 1930; in 1861, 85 per cent of the fathers had been farm workers themselves; in 1930, 86 per cent. Finally, 50 per cent of the married farm workers' wives in

Table 29
Elmdon village farmworkers belonging to the Gamgee, Greenhill, Hammond, Hayes, Hoy, Bard, Wilson and Reeves families, 1930

(a) *Birthplaces*

born in Elmdon parish		0—5 miles		5—10 miles		born within a radius of: 10—20 miles		over 20 miles		not known		total
no.	%	no.	%	no.	%	no.	%	no.	%	no.	%	no.
24	89	1	4	—	—	—	—	1	4	1	4	27

(b) *Birthplaces of fathers, where known*[i]

born in Elmdon parish		0—5 miles		5—10 miles		born within a radius of: 10—20 miles		over 20 miles ·		total
no.	%	no.	%	no.	%	no.	%	no.	%	no.
17	89	2	11	—	—	—	—	—	—	19

(i) The birthplace of three fathers was not known

(c) *Occupations of fathers*[ii] *whose work differed from that of their son or sons, Elmdon village, 1930*

same occupation as son(s)		different occupation from son(s)		total
no.	%	no.	%	no.
18	86	3	14	21

(ii) The occupation of one father was not known

(d) *Birthplaces of wives*[iii], *1930*

born in Elmdon parish		0—5 miles		5—10 miles		born within a radius of: 10—20 miles		over 20 miles		total
no.	%	no.	%	no.	%	no.	%	no.	%	no.
14	56	9	36	—	—	1	4	1	4	25

(iii) 25 of the sample of 27 men were married

Source: *Some Elmdon Families*

90

1861 had been born in Elmdon, compared with 56 per cent of the wives of farm workers in the six families in 1930. In this group, at least, patterns of marriage, occupation and dwelling place seem hardly to have changed at all. What evidence there is of greater geographical mobility comes from the wives rather than the husbands, since the two married women in 1930 who came from more than ten miles away had arrived in the village to work in service, and their future husbands had not had to move outside Elmdon to meet them.

In other ways, too, continuity was shown throughout the period. In some cases, we know that son followed father, not only in his occupation, but on the same farm, and though unfortunately we are not in a position to assess statistically whether or not this was normal practice, it was certainly held to be so by some of the men who could remember the early days. What we do know is that farm workers continued to teach the boys their jobs, as they themselves had been taught when they were young. The cookboy on the steam engine spent his lunch hours learning to be a steerer, and so gradually progressed to full driver. The newcomer to the mowing team, known as a 'colt', had to learn how to sharpen his scythe correctly, and if he failed, he would be knocked down by an older man and beaten on his feet until he shouted 'Beer, beer'. He was then expected to pay 2s 6d to provide the team with drink, and indeed, this process was more like an initiation ceremony than a serious attempt at training. But as one elderly worker in 1964 said, the older men looked on it as their job to pass on their specialised knowledge of the land to the young, and 'to give them a box over the ear if they didn't do as they was told'.

In many ways, then, the Elmdon farm worker's life continued on much the same lines as it had in the past, right up to 1930. How far this was to continue into the future will be discussed in the next chapter.

5

Farms, farmers and farm workers, 1930-1964

Owners and tenants

The last two chapters have shown how the Lofts Hall estate and its tenant farmers dominated Elmdon's pattern of agriculture up to the sale of 1927. At that time, only two of the farms we were considering were owner-occupied; the remaining thirteen were either tenanted, or 'in hand' awaiting a purchaser. The families of some of the tenants had been associated with the estate for three or more generations, and kinship connections had grown up among them. Yet fewer than forty years later, all the fifteen farms were owner-occupied, and of the eight farmers included in the Elmdon Survey, carried out in 1964[1], none was connected by marriage; only one had his birthplace within five miles of the village, and the others were born as far away as the Fens, Norfolk, Edgware, London and even the United States. We learned in the last chapter that none of the tenants in occupation in 1922 bought the farm they were actually tenanting at the time of the sale. It might be thought, then, that Elmdon's farms immediately fell into the hands of strangers, and that the whole pattern of landownership changed at once.

In reality, the changeover was protracted. In the first place, tenancies did not disappear overnight when Jack Wilkes sold the estate in 1927 to a property speculator. This individual clearly wanted to realise on his new asset as quickly as possible for, as we saw earlier, he put the estate up for sale by auction within a matter of months. However, only a few of the farms were sold, and a little later the remainder of the estate was bought by a second speculator. He too found that sales hung fire, and for a time he was obliged to keep the land he had bought in some sort of order while waiting for buyers. This he did either by putting a responsible farm worker on to a farm as a kind of caretaker, a role filled by Ted Gamgee on Hill Farm, or by leasing properties

92

on a temporary basis, as he did at Elmdon Bury. Chiswick Hall Farm in Chrishall was bought as an investment by William Cowell, formerly tenant at Elmdon Lee. He let the property for some years before he finally sold it, and he never farmed there himself. The Home Farm attached to Lofts Hall was let from 1934 to 1952, and Elmdon Bury Farm was tenanted right up until 1960.

Secondly, three people found that a total break with the past was not to their liking. As we saw in chapter 3, in 1926 Jack Wilkes left Elmdon Bury, which had been his home for twenty years, to take up a job with a land agency firm in Wiltshire. At this time he married Miss Ida Rippingall. But some time in the mid-1930s, he decided to return to Elmdon. He was able to buy back the Bury, and he and his wife lived there up until his death in 1958. He let the farm land and the tenancy was continued by his widow for a further two years. In 1960, however, she made over the farm (and later, Elmdon Bury house), to her nephew, Major Rippingall, so that in 1964 there was still a connection of the Wilkes family who owned land in Elmdon, even if on a reduced scale. The question of how far Jack Wilkes retained his status as Squire, while holding only one farm instead of an estate, is discussed in the Introduction.

Jack Wilkes was not the only person who preferred to come back to part of the old Lofts Hall estate instead of making a clean break. In the last chapter, we learned that Charlie Pigg at Gentleman's Farm, failed during the early 1920s, and left the district. The 1927 sale, however, gave his son, Martin, the chance to return to the land which his family had farmed for generations. He bought Gentleman's Farm, in partnership with Mrs Westwood, and stayed there until the Second World War, when the farm was sold and the Piggs' connection with it finally ceased.

One member of the Smith family, who had been in Hope Farm in Wenden Lofts, belonging to the Lofts Hall estate, since the turn of the century, also managed to acquire a farm in the parish. Mrs Smith, the tenant of Hope Farm, had three sons and a daughter. At different times the boys tenanted the Cosh, Duddenhoe Grange farm, and even Elmdon Lee for a short period, but it was neither they nor their mother who actually bought a farm, but their sister Nellie. She acquired Lower Pond Street, then covering some 140 acres, and was still living there in 1964.

The sales of 1927 and 1930, then, did not result in a complete influx of strangers on to Elmdon's farms, since the Squire himself and members of two of his old tenant families managed to buy land, and so provided a measure of continuity between the old system and the modern era.   Newcomers of course there were, particularly on the Duddenhoe End farms.   Lofts Hall and the Home Farm which went with it were also bought by a newcomer in 1928, and sold again in 1934 to a London stockbroker and his wife, Mr and Mrs Graham Watson.   But Church Farm, right in Elmdon village, which had been reduced to some 70 acres by the time of the sales, was eventually bought by the Elmdon butcher, George Arnold, while Freewood and Hill Farms were sold to Thomas Wood of Poplars Farm, who had been living in the parish for twenty years or more.   Indeed, as table 30 shows, in spite of all the upheaval resulting from rapid changes in ownership of the estate, by the middle of the 1930s only one of the old Lofts Hall estate farms in and around Elmdon was owned by a man without close Elmdon connections, and that was Elmdon Lee.

Table 30
Ownership of former Lofts Hall estate farms, Elmdon village, 1938

Elmdon Bury	John Wilkes, former owner of the Lofts Hall estate
Church Farm	George Arnold, former Elmdon butcher
Hill Farm, including Freewood	Thomas Wood, tenant/owner of Poplars Farm since *c.* 1908
Elmdon Lee	Albert Duke. No known connection with Elmdon, although Dukes were farming in Gt. Chishill from the late nineteenth century

Source: Elmdon survey notebooks

Continuity on Elmdon farms was not only provided by the former Squire and some of his old tenants.   The two owner-occupied farms were not affected by the estate sales, although, as we shall see, their owners managed to increase their land holdings during the next two decades by a mixture of ownership and tenancies.

Thomas Wood had come to Poplars Farm from Great Chishill around 1908 to work as farm bailiff for William Emson, who was renting the property from its London-based landlord.   Some years later, Wood bought the freehold and, as we have seen, at the 1927 sale he increased his property by buying Freewood Farm, by then separated from Elmdon Bury and covering some 240 acres.   Later he took advantage of the extremely low land prices caused by the depressed agricultural conditions of the 1930s to purchase the adjoining Hill Farm, and some 350 acres of Elmdon Bury Farm lying to the east of the Ickleton Road. He and his wife went to live in Hill farmhouse, leaving Poplars to be occupied and farmed by their son, George Wood. By the mid-1930s, father and son between them owned and farmed nearly 900 acres.

There was no more land for sale in Elmdon village at that time, but as we have seen, a few tenancies were still available. In 1934, the young Wood leased Home Farm from the Graham Watsons of Lofts Hall, thus bringing the family holdings up to about 1,050 acres — a considerably larger amount of land than any father—son group of Lofts Hall estate tenants had held in the past.

This period of maximum expansion was not to last long. The agricultural depression which had allowed Thomas Wood to buy land cheaply, unfortunately also worked against profitability and made difficult the acquisition of capital which could be ploughed back into the business. At all events, in 1938 Thomas Wood sold Freewood Farm. Four years later, Hill Farm and the land formerly belonging to Elmdon Bury were also sold. George Wood remained at Poplars and continued to rent Home Farm until 1944, but the lease was not then renewed, so that he found himself, like his father in the 1920s, farming only the 240 acres of Poplars Farm. He was still there at the time of the 1964 Survey, 56 years after his father came to the property.

The second family of owner-occupiers in Elmdon before the Lofts Hall estate sale were the Fisons. Frederick Fison was a Fenland farmer who bought Elmdon Lodge farm from the steam-engine contractor, Edwin Goode, around 1920. Three of his four sons came with him, and when their father retired, they continued to run the 300-acre holding. Like the Woods, they expanded by adding tenancies to the land they owned, and also like the Woods they found their total farming acreage decreasing again as leases were not renewed. Their first expansion came when they rented Elmdon Bury from Jack Wilkes during the Second World War. By this time Elmdon Bury had been reduced by sale to 350 acres, but even so, the tenancy raised their total holdings to 650 acres. Four years later, they were granted the Home Farm lease, so that they were farming 800 acres. Again, this situation did not last very long. In 1952, they gave up Home Farm, and Mrs Graham Watson took it over herself, with the help of a manager. In 1960, after Jack Wilkes's death, they relinquished Elmdon Bury to its new owner, Major Rippingall, so that by the time of the 1964 Survey, their land holding had dropped from 800 acres at its peak to the 300 acres which their father had bought in 1920. In one sense, the custom of the old days was followed in that not only Jack Wilkes but also the newcomers at Lofts Hall let their farms to men who were already established in Elmdon; in another, change was evidenced by the comparatively short space of time that the tenancies lasted, as agriculture grew increasingly profitable and the advantages to landlords of farming their own land became more apparent.

Both the Fisons and the Woods were traditional farmers in the sense that they came of farming stock, and had learned their business through practical experience while growing up on the land. But when Thomas Wood sold Hill Farm to Frank Cross, the way was opened to a measure of change.

Frank Cross came from a family with a long tradition of farming, too, and he had always wanted to be a farmer himself. In order to acquire the necessary capital, however, he became an estate agent, auctioneer and builder in Edgware. By 1929, he was in a position to buy a house in the country, and when he saw Pigots farmhouse in Elmdon advertised, with 13 acres of land, he bought it. He found it in a state of disrepair, but he had a feeling for old houses and after its purchase he spent much time and care restoring it, while continuing to run his firm in Edgware. With the purchase of some 240 acres from Thomas Wood in 1938 he realised his ambition to become a farmer himself. Four years later, he bought a further 465 acres from the Woods. His son Jack, who spent a good deal of his boyhood in Elmdon although he was born in Edgware, read for an agricultural degree at Cambridge University and was later appointed as Assistant to the Farm Economist there. When his father became seriously ill after the war, he came home to take over the 700 acres or so of the family property, which he was still farming at the time of the 1964 Survey. In 1965, he extended his property still further eastwards by buying the 400-acre Strethall Hall Farm, and in 1969 he bought Poplars Farm when George Wood retired, thereby increasing his land holding to over 1,300 acres. This made him by far the largest landowner in Elmdon village, although he was rivalled in Duddenhoe End by the Duke family, who over the years had bought not only Elmdon Lee but also Hope and Upper Pond Street Farms, amounting in all to more than 1,000 acres. Farming on this scale allows the owner to

96

be fully employed in organising and marketing, so that he becomes a manager, comparable with his opposite number in industry,[2] as opposed to the owners of smaller properties who are closely involved in the practical, day-to-day work of the farm.

Jack Cross was the first farmer in Elmdon whom we know to have had a formal agricultural training, and as we shall see later, he made certain innovations, particularly in relation to the employment of specialised labour. It was not long, however, before a second farmer of this kind arrived in the village. Church Farm was sold in 1952 to Geoffrey Turner, a Londoner by birth, who had taken an agricultural course and who came to Elmdon from a farm in Worcestershire.

Yet another kind of farmer was represented by Mrs Graham Watson, the American-born wife of the new owner of Lofts Hall. Starting by farming the parkland around the Hall as part of her war effort, she amalgamated this with the Home Farm when the Fisons' lease was given up in 1952, and from then on she ran the 200-acre unit herself, with the help of a manager who combined his work for her with running his own apple orchards some twenty-five miles away. This situation continued until the late 1960s, when the Graham Watsons sold the Hall and Home Farm to Major and Mrs Philipson, the present owners, who use it as a stud farm.

The latest recruit to farming in Elmdon at the time of the 1964 survey was Mrs Wilkes' nephew, Major Rippingall, at Elmdon Bury, who came to the farm directly from his service in the army, and who had no previous experience as a farmer, although his father had been a landowner in Norfolk.

The period from 1930 to 1964, then, saw the final transition from the system of farm tenancies to owner-occupation. The sale of the Lofts Hall estate did not result in an immediate changeover, although it gave it considerable impetus, and thirty years were to pass before the last farm tenancy in Elmdon village was relinquished.

The period also saw a move away from farming families of a traditional kind familiar to Elmdon land workers for generations, to a new kind of employer. Although neither the Fison family nor the Woods had been born in Elmdon, they both followed naturally in the line of farmers such as the Haydens and Primes who came into Elmdon in the last half of the eighteenth and first half of the nineteenth centuries. Both had gained their knowledge of farming by years of practical experience, and as far as farming methods were concerned, it was an experience which they held in common

97

with their Elmdon-born farm workers. With the advent of two farmers who had received formal agricultural training, even though one of them came from a long farming line, and two more who were venturing into farming for the first time, the range of farming employers was broadened and the way opened for innovations and changes in the farms themselves.

Changes in agriculture

The shift from farm tenancies to owner-occupation, following the sale of the Lofts Hall estate, reflected in part the massive change in agriculture which took place during the same period. Farming had been an unprofitable business from the end of the First World War, but from 1929 to 1933 an intense depression made the farmers' lot even less enviable, with crop prices falling by nearly a third, and livestock doing little better.[3] It was no wonder that the estate farms proved so hard to sell, and that they finally went for such very small sums. Chiswick Hall Farm is said to have cost William Cowell only £4 10s 0d an acre, a figure which is hard to believe today. Although the worst was over by 1933 and profits began to improve slowly up to 1939, there was still no great demand for land, and it is unlikely that the Woods and the Fisons had many rivals for the farms, whether owned or tenanted, which they acquired during this time.

With the outbreak of war, all this changed. Farmers and their workers suddenly became key figures in the fight for national survival. Official agricultural policy called for grain production, both for human and animal consumption, and the farmers of the major grain-producing area in which Elmdon lay found that prices for their crops were raised, to ensure that farming should be profitable. Indeed, farming incomes trebled during the war years, showing a rate of increase that was probably higher than that enjoyed by any other section of the community.[4] Nor were farm hands altogether left out of this greater prosperity. Agriculture became a reserved occupation, and land workers were exempted from military service. Because men were compelled to stay on the land, it was felt that their wages should be raised, and in the decade from 1936/7 to 1946/7, the average minimum wage for farm workers rose by 147 per cent, while the cost of living over the same period increased by only 65 per cent.[5]

The government's support for agriculture continued when the

98

war was over, and by 1961/2, direct and indirect aid to agriculture represented eight-tenths of net farm income.[6] Farming continued to be a profitable enterprise, land prices rose steadily, and in the thirty years from 1939, the value of agricultural land with vacant possession increased eight times.[7] The whole position looked very different from the situation facing Jack Wilkes in the 1920s when he decided to sell his estate. (Had it remained intact, it would have been worth over £3,000,000 by the mid-1970s.) Farm workers' wages continued to rise faster than the cost of living. The only people closely connected with the land who found themselves no better off in terms of income, as opposed to capital appreciation, were the landlords, since rent restrictions were in force. For this reason, it became much more profitable for a landowner to farm his land himself than to let it, and when leases fell in they were often not renewed. In Elmdon, as we have seen, this happened when Mrs Graham Watson of Lofts Hall took over the Home Farm in 1952, and later, when Major Rippingall as owner-occupier replaced the Fisons who had been tenants at Elmdon Bury. As a result, by 1964 farm tenancies in Elmdon parish had disappeared.

Arable farming continued to predominate in and around Elmdon, as it had done since the time of the enclosure, but naturally enough, some changes did occur. When the Fison family, for instance, bought Elmdon Lodge in 1920, they found that there was no dairy herd near the village, and so they bought fifteen Shorthorns with them. This provided a real service, and the villagers used to queue up at the dairy with cans and jugs to fetch their own milk. When the Second World War started, the Fisons gave up the herd, partly because of shortage of labour, and partly because of the government's directive that cereal-growing should take precedence over livestock. The gap was filled by Mrs Graham Watson at Lofts Hall, who as part of her war effort used the 43 acres of park to pasture dairy cattle, supplying local people by means of a milk round. After the war, when Jack Cross came to Hill and Freewood farms during his father's illness, he started up a herd of pedigree Jersey cattle, in response to the big demand for milk, obtaining his first beasts from his uncle. This herd, incidentally, has now become one of the largest in the country.

Another change introduced by the Fisons was the growing of sugar beet. They first planted it in 1926, and were soon allocating 50 acres to its cultivation. Sheep, on the other hand, had almost

99

disappeared from Elmdon by 1964. In the past, they had played an important role in fertilising the land, but since they were folded on to the fields and had to be fed, rather than grazing freely, they needed a good deal of labour. The Fisons gave up their flock at the beginning of the war, and by 1964 the only farmer in Elmdon to carry any sheep on his land was George Wood at Poplars Farm.

Once the war was over, government policy moved from encouraging the maximum production of crops, to emphasising livestock and animal produce. Because of world-wide food shortages, which meant that large grain crops were still of vital importance, it was some years before this policy could be brought fully into effect, but its influence on Elmdon farmers in the 1950s was clearly marked. When Geoffrey Turner bought the 70-acre Church Farm, he farmed it intensively with pigs, beef cattle and poultry. Mrs Graham Watson too, specialised in pigs when she and her manager took over the Home Farm, combining them with arable farming. The Fisons had always kept beef cattle and pigs, and they continued to do so. There was only one exception to this trend towards livestock production, and that was on Elmdon Bury, when Major Rippingall took possession of it in 1960. He decided to concentrate on cropping his land, which lay on the light, easily worked soils of the old Elmdon field of pre-enclosure days, and apart from a flock of turkeys, livestock ceased to be kept on this farm.

While there were no great changes in the kind of crops produced in Elmdon from 1930 onwards, the means by which the crops were grown underwent a revolution during the period. This was, of course, due to mechanisation. The 667,000 horses for agricultural use in England and Wales in 1931 had been reduced to 19,000 by 1965,[8] and in Elmdon they had disappeared entirely. The Fisons, Crosses and Woods still kept some work horses up to and during the Second World War, and Robert Fison used to shoe his himself, using the experience he had gained in the Horse Artillery during the First World War, but the first tractor appeared on an Elmdon farm in 1930, and from then on, in accordance with the national trends set out in table 31, more and more tractors were used, displacing first the steam ploughs, and finally the horses themselves. Many tractors were imported during the Second World War from the United States under Lend-Lease, as part of the effort to increase cereal production. The Fisons were said to be the first farmers in the district to be allocated a combine harvester, imported from Canada. After the war, some of the stables no longer needed

100

for horses were converted into piggeries, with the addition of innovations such as infra-red lighting for the raising of piglets, or used for other stock. Nor were tractors and combines the only new mechanical aids. Milking machines, sugar beet harvesters, and corn driers all helped to take some of the drudgery out of farm work, but at the same time steadily reduced the number of jobs available on the farms during the 1950s and 60s.

Table 31
Agricultural machinery in the United Kingdom

year	tractors	combines
1942	101,500	940
1948	231,283	4,969
1954	392,709	21,117
1958	430,805	39,890
1963	417,300	55,060

Source: *A century of agricultural statistics, Great Britain, 1866–1966*, Ministry of Agriculture, Fisheries and Food, (1968) table 30.

Table 32
Numbers of full-time agricultural workers in England and Wales, 1931–64

year	number (thousands)	% increase or decrease
1931	616	—
1939	511	17.0 −
1945	616[(i)]	20.5 +
1951	554	10.1 −
1961	384	30.7 −
1964	333	13.3 −
overall decrease	283	45.9 −

(i) Includes Women's Land Army and Prisoners of War.

Source: *A century of agricultural statistics, Great Britain, 1866–1966*, MAFF, table 26.

As table 32 shows, the numbers of full-time agricultural workers in England and Wales fell by almost 46 per cent between 1931 and 1964, and there is no evidence to suggest that this general trend was reversed in Elmdon. Indeed, if we look at the numbers of agricultural workers whose children were baptised in Elmdon church for each decade from 1931 onwards (given in table 33), and compare the totals with those for the period 1861–1930 set out in table 25 (p.79), we see that the numbers of individuals in this group dropped from twenty-two in the period 1921–30 to

Table 33
Families containing farm workers, Elmdon village 1931—1964

| Family | present by | Numbers of agricultural workers shown as fathers in the Elmdon baptismal register | | | |
		1931—40	1941—50	1951—60	1961—4
Hammond (I)	1861	1	1	—	—
Hayes	1861	—	2	—	—
Hoy	1861	—	1	—	—
Reeves	1861	—	—	2	—
Dyer	1881—90	—	—	3	—
Wilson	1881—1900	2	1	—	—
Clark	1901—10	1	—	—	—
Potterill	1901—10	—	1	—	—
Hammond (II)	1921—30	1	—	1	—
Law	1921—31	1	1	—	—
Starr	—	1	1	—	1
Andrews	—	—	1	1	—
Flack	—	—	1	—	—
Gray	—	—	1	—	—
Galloway	—	—	1	—	—
Badcock	—	—	—	1	—
Felstead	—	—	—	1	—
Wallage	—	—	—	1	1
Walsh	—	—	—	1	—
Hiles	—	—	—	—	1
Homer	—	—	—	—	1
Rance	—	—	—	—	1
Total no. of fathers		7	12	11	5

Source: Elmdon baptismal registers

only seven in the decade 1931—40. Such small numbers, taken from only one section of the whole agricultural work force, cannot give a completely accurate picture. They do suggest, however, either that there was a marked exodus from the land in Elmdon following the sale of the Lofts Hall estate, during the depression years, or that the work force was an aging one and was not being reinforced by younger workers whose wives were of child-bearing age. It is noteworthy that only one new name, Starr, appears among the farm workers mentioned in the baptismal register between 1931 and 1940. Its owner came from the next-door parish of Strethall, and married into one of Elmdon's old families of farm workers, the Hayes.

With the war, farm workers were suddenly in demand again. The need was met in part by prisoners of war, and Italian and Austrian prisoners were employed on Elmdon farms. One or two of the former even stayed in the district after their comrades were repatriated. The Women's Land Army was also represented, and two of its members remained in the village after hostilities ended.

One married an Elmdoner whom she met on the farm, and the other, helped by her former employer, took over the Carrier public house, where she and her husband were still living in 1964.

The rise in the number of farm jobs was only temporary, however. After the war, mechanisation continued to reduce the amount of hand labour needed on the farms, and so the number of jobs available fell steadily. But now there was a difference, in that fewer men were ready to fill the vacancies that came up. It was not that farm wages did not rise. As table 34 shows, the average weekly earnings of agricultural labourers went up by 131 per cent, from £5 9s 9½d (£5.49) in 1949 to £12 13s 8d (£12.68) in 1964. However, during the same period, wages paid to manual workers in manufacturing industry increased even faster, so that a farm worker in 1964 would see himself as being £6 0s 0d a week worse off than his contemporary in a factory, and what is more, working four hours a week longer in order to earn his smaller pay packet, although he did not have to spend as long on travelling to and from work as did those Elmdoners employed outside the village.

Table 34
Relative earnings of agricultural workers and manual workers in manufacturing industry, 1949–1964

| | Average weekly earnings (£ p) | | Average hours worked | |
year	agric.	industry	agric.	industry
1949	5.49	7.25	51.1	46.5
1954	7.34	10.26	51.2	48.2
1959	9.99	14.21	52.1	48.2
1964	12.68	18.68	51.2	46.9

Source: Howard Newby, *The Deferential Worker*, 1977, p. 172

Even if he occupied a tied cottage at a nominal rent, the money saved did not make up for this large cash differential. Industrial workers had been better paid than men on the land for many years, but up to the end of the Second World War, Elmdoners who wanted to go on living in the village had little choice but to accept farm work. As we saw in chapter 2, all this changed with the introduction of work buses from 1946 onwards. School-leavers now had the chance to work in the factories of Sawston and Duxford, and young men who had thought themselves lucky to find a job on the land when they left school were in a position to leave the farms. By 1964 there were nine men living in Elmdon who had once been agricultural workers but who had either changed over to factory work, or gone on the buses, while a tenth had acquired a job as a maintenance man.

The desire to earn more money seems to have been the main motive driving men from agriculture. 'I'd be on the land now if the money was the same' said one, while another who left an Elmdon farm for council roadwork in the depression years explained his move by saying 'I got a few more bob from the council. They were harder times then. You had to go where the most money was.' But this particular man came back to agriculture in the late 1940s, when farm wages had risen, finding the increased standard of living of a post-war farm worker sufficient for his needs, even if it was not as high as that which a factory worker might enjoy. As his wife said, 'Before the war, Fred used to bring home a pound of cream biscuits on a Friday night, and that was a luxury in those days. Now we go shopping and we don't know what type of biscuit to buy'. The same man's son left the land for factory work during the early 1960s, but he too found that he really preferred to work on a farm and he returned to agriculture within a year or two.

Men who came back to work on the farms, once they had left them, were the exception rather than the rule, and in contrast with the depression years, the farmers found themselves faced with a shortage of local labour. It was no longer easy to attract school-leavers, and by 1964 only three boys under 21 were at work full-time on Elmdon farms. More and more the farmers had to rely on the men who had found themselves too old or too settled to take advantage of the new work opportunities which came with improved transport facilities. When Major Rippingall took over at Elmdon Bury in 1960, he found that none of the five men working there was under 50, while two of the men were over 60.

Nor were part-time and casual workers so easy to find as they had been. Many older farm workers still took on extra jobs outside their working hours, but part-time gardening was their favourite occupation. The only man known to continue the old job of picking stones from the fields had an ulterior motive, since he had been a building worker for some years before becoming a farm worker, and he wanted the flints to make a wall. The days of the local mowing teams were long past, and even in the 1930s the Fisons had used travelling Irish workers to help with the harvest; but at that time schoolboys would hope to find paid work on the farms during their holidays, and women were still employed on

104

many casual tasks. One Elmdon resident, incidentally, was noted for gleaning the harvest fields as late as the 1940s. Twenty years later, Elmdon women were still making up work-parties in the summer, but they specialised in fruit and pea-picking, and in the skilled job of pruning, and much of their work was done on farms outside the village. Boys still helped out occasionally in emergencies — the 14-year-old son of one farm worker took over the tractor of another worker who had left a farm during a very busy spell, and the work of 'that little ole boy' was greeted approvingly by the other men — but the numbers of Elmdon boys prepared to help regularly in the holidays or after school steadily declined, and by 1964 the practice seems to have ceased. Wives' and children's visits to the farms were reduced to bringing up tea to the men in summer, or coming to look at the animals, and just before Elmdon primary school closed in 1973, the schoolmaster found that most of the children did not know the difference between barley and wheat.

With this drying up of the local supply, farmers had to look elsewhere for at least some of their labour. Jack Cross went outside Elmdon for all his specialist workers, since Elmdon men were not used to working with dairy cattle. At the time of the Survey, his three cowmen had come from as far away as Harlow, Glossop and Co. Durham. His stockman was from Castle Camps in Suffolk, and his farm foreman, whose status was rather that of a farm manager, came from Farnham, near Bishops Stortford. Mrs Graham Watson even introduced a Spanish farm worker on to the Home Farm, though this was a special case in that she heard of him through the Spanish couple who helped her in the house. Four years later, two farms were employing visiting Australians to help first with the grain harvest, and later the sugarbeet lifting.

One of the results of this shortage of labour was that jobs changed hands more frequently. No longer did a farm worker feel that at all costs he must hold on to the job he had, and other factors could come into play. For instance, the wife of one man who was born locally but who changed his farm job several times within the neighbourhood, said that her husband had moved from some jobs because he was not really happy in them, while in others their tied cottage was isolated and the children were too far away from school, which in winter could only be reached by walking along muddy tracks. The employment of farm workers from outside the district also increased the turnover rate. Of the seven

105

individuals listed in table 33 as becoming fathers in Elmdon between 1951 and 1964, only two were still in the parish by 1965, and one of these had a previous connection with the village, having spent most of his childhood there.

Farm workers, 1964

The changes which have been described were reflected in Elmdon's agricultural work force of 1964. First, although the area of land to be farmed remained much the same, the numbers of farm workers, including farm foremen, living in and near the village had dropped from 114 in 1861 to thirty-six[9] in 1964, or by 68 per cent, reflecting the enormous effect of mechanisation. Also, the farm workers were drawn from a wider area than in the old days, as table 35 (a) shows. While nearly nine out of every ten agricultural labourers in 1861 had been born in Elmdon, just over a hundred years later the proportion had dropped to nearly six out of ten; and while no farm workers in 1861 had been born more than twenty miles from Elmdon, 14 per cent of the agricultural work force in 1964 had come from places beyond that radius.

Table 35
(a) *Birthplace of all male farm workers living in Elmdon, 1861 and 1964*

| | born in Elmdon parish | | born within a radius of: | | | | | | | | | | total |
| | | | 0—5 miles | | 5—10 miles | | 10—20 miles | | over 20 miles | | not known | | |
	no.	%	no.	%	no.	%	no.	%	no.	%	no.	%	no.
1861	99	87	12	11	–	–	3	3	–	–	–	–	114
1964	21	58	7	19	1	3	1	3	5	14	1	3	36

(b) *Birthplace of wives of married farm workers, Elmdon 1961 and 1964*

| | born in Elmdon parish | | born within a radius of: | | | | | | | | total |
| | | | 0—5 miles | | 5—10 miles | | 10—20 miles | | over 20 miles | | |
	no.	%	no.	%	no.	%	no.	%	no.	%	no.
1861	27	50	26	48	1	2	–	–	–	–	54
1964	6	27	3	14	–	–	3	14	10	45	22

Source: 1861 census, and Elmdon survey, 1964.

However, the 1964 figure of 58 per cent for farm workers born in Elmdon was still a high one. In Suffolk in 1972, for instance, only about a third of a sample of 233 farm workers were working in the

106

parish in which they were born.[10] Moreover, in Elmdon in 1964 three of the fifteen workers born outside the village had in fact moved there as children with their parents, and had been living in Elmdon when they started work. If we look only at the twelve men who came in as adults, we find that all those born more than five miles away were working for the same farmer, Jack Cross. On Elmdon Bury, Church Farm, Poplars and Elmdon Lodge, all the workers but one were born Elmdoners. The exception was a man coming from a nearby village who had married an Elmdon girl. Therefore, on all but the largest farm in Elmdon, where concentration on dairy cattle created special conditions, the old habit of employing local men was still continuing in 1964, and the employers using this labour included not only the two traditional farmers, but one of the college-trained farmers and a newcomer.

Another apparent area of change is illustrated by table 35 (b), which shows the birthplace of the wives of farm workers living in Elmdon. Between 1861 and 1964, the proportion of Elmdon-born wives dropped by nearly half, while the percentage of those coming from within five miles was over two-thirds lower. To counterbalance this, more than half the wives in 1964 came from over ten miles away, though none had done so in 1861. It would be wrong, however, to infer from this that as travel became easier, Elmdon men moved further out of the village to find their wives. If we look at the thirteen wives who were born more than ten miles from Elmdon, we find that six of them were married when they came to the village, accompanying their immigrant farm-worker husbands. Six of the remaining seven, all married to Elmdon-born men, were already living in Elmdon when they met their future husbands, either because they had come to work as household helps, or because they had been brought by their parents or first husband. Only one Elmdon-born farm worker had gone outside the parish himself to find a spouse, and that was a man who joined the army in the Second World War and met his future wife near the army camp where he was stationed.

A major area of change between 1861 and 1964 lay in the age of the farm workers. As table 36 shows, while the proportion of men aged 21-60 remained much the same, there was a very marked shift from the employment of young workers in 1861 to old workers in 1964. In that year, nearly a third of all farm workers were 61 years old or over, and only 8 per cent were under 21, while a hundred years earlier, the position was reversed, since 7 per cent were 61 or over, and just over a third were under 21. With the drying up of the large pool of experienced young Elmdon farm workers on which farmers in the past could draw to fill their adult vacancies, it was inevitable that in the 1960s more workers should be brought in from outside as the old men retired.

Table 36
Ages of male farm workers, Elmdon village, 1861 and 1964

	under 21		21–60		61 +		total
	no.	%	no.	%	no.	%	no.
1861	43	38	63	55	8	7	114
1964	3	8	22	61	11	31	36

Source: 1861 census, and Elmdon survey, 1964.

When some of these immigrant farm workers came into the village in the late 1950s and 60s, they differed from the Elmdon-born men not only in their place of origin, but because they had no agricultural background at all when they took up farm work. All but two of the Elmdon-born workers had fathers who had been agricultural labourers themselves, and all of them had close relatives working on the land. However, Jack Cross's outside employees in 1964 included one man whose father was a school teacher, and whose wife had worked in a tailoring factory, but who nevertheless decided that he would do farm work. Another who felt the same way was the son of two Londoners, though admittedly he had an Elmdon contact through a cousin of his in the village. A third, brought up in Manchester, had worked on the railways and in repair shops before he took part in a government training scheme to become a farm worker. These men were in agriculture because they wanted to be, and not because lack of other employment or years of tradition had pushed them in that direction, as may well have been the case with some of the Elmdon-born farm workers in the past. Even Elmdoners themselves now had a choice. One of the young men brought up in the village estimated that he had had at least fifteen jobs outside agriculture in the years between leaving school and settling for farm work, which he felt offered more variety than other work he had tried.

By 1964, then, the agricultural labour force in Elmdon was showing a split between locally born men who were descended from generations of farm workers, and incomers, some of whom had no previous connection with farm life. Elmdon men usually stayed for many years on the same farm, where they often had

108

close kin connections with their fellow workers. On Elmdon Lodge, for example two of the four workers in 1964 were brothers, who had started at the farm when their uncle was working there, while a father and son filled the two jobs on Poplars Farm. But kinship links spread far wider than this. One of the most noticeable features of the 1964 group of Elmdon-born farm workers was their connection with the six families, going back to 1861 or earlier, which were described in the last chapter. Of the twenty-one Elmdon-born farm workers in 1964, only three were not members of these six families, either by birth or through marriage. In contrast, the incomers in the 1960s generally found their jobs in Elmdon by answering advertisements in farming papers, and would quite likely move out of the village fairly soon. Half the men born more than five miles away had left again by 1972. Without family links in the area, they had nothing to hold them to a rather isolated village if they heard of another job with better facilities elsewhere.

6
Non-farming occupations

In 1861 Harriet Toysbee, the young woman who had come from Islington to teach in Elmdon village school, was living in a cottage on Cross Hill with a 10-year-old cousin to keep her company. After spending her day in the new brick and slate schoolhouse with its two classrooms, which from the outside looked not dissimilar to a branchline railway station of the same period, she would return home and set about her housekeeping.

Although Elmdon may have seemed a backwater to Harriet after town life, it nevertheless could provide her with all but the most exceptional things she might want to buy, as we saw in chapter 1. She could purchase groceries, bread and meat, and buy materials for her clothes, which she could make up herself or send out to a dressmaker, without walking more than a few hundred yards from her cottage. If she needed to visit Royston or Cambridge, the carrier's cart passed her door. Should she so wish, she could have her home cleaned for her by one of the many young girls ready to do domestic work. While it was most unlikely that she would frequent any of the public houses or beer-shops, she must often have heard the noise as customers spilled out of the King's Head close to her cottage.

Who were the men and women providing these and other services? Were they Elmdoners of long standing, like so many of the farm workers, or had they come into the village as strangers, as herself had done?

Elmdoners and immigrants at work[1]

Table 37 shows at once that there was a marked difference between those working outside agriculture, and those on the land. As we have already seen, the farm workers formed a homogeneous group with nearly nine out of every ten men being born in Elmdon

110

parish, but just over half the men and women providing Elmdon with its shops and services had come in from outside, and of these immigrants, only about a third were born within five miles of the village. Even in 1861, it is possible to imagine those born and brought up in Elmdon commenting on the appearance of new faces and remarking on how things were changing, just as they were doing in 1964. An important difference in 1861, however, was that the incomers had arrived not only to live in Elmdon, but to work there as well, and in general there was no question of their using the village simply as a dormitory.

Table 37
Birthplace of all males and females employed outside agriculture, compared with male agricultural workers, Elmdon village, 1861

| | born in Elmdon parish | | born within a radius of: | | | | | | | | | | total |
| | | | 0–5 miles | | 5–10 miles | | 10–20 miles | | over 20 miles | | not known | | |
	no.	%	no.	%	no.	%	no.	%	no.	%	no.	%	no.
Male agricultural workers[i]	99	87	12	11	–	–	3	3	–	–	–	–	114
All workers, other occupations[ii]	42	48	18	20	9	10	5	6	9	10	5	6	88

(i) Excludes farmers   (ii) Includes a shopkeeper who was also a farmer

Source: 1861 census

If we look more closely at the jobs held by immigrants and those of the Elmdoners, we see that certain kinds of work were more likely to be done by incomers, while other occupations seemed to be the preserve of those born in the parish. Table 38 shows that, with the exception of domestic servants, the majority of incomers did not migrate to Elmdon to take up lower-paid work. Jobs in this category were largely filled by Elmdoners themselves. For example, the bricklayers' labourers and the carriers were all born in the village. So were the thatchers, three out of the five carpenters, and all but two of the eleven bricklayers, one of the exceptions being a relative of the firm's owner, the widowed Naomi Greenhill, and the other a worker who was probably employed only temporarily in the village since he was putting up at the King's Head. Much of the work for the thatchers, carpenters and bricklayers would have been provided by the Lofts Hall estate,

111

and by those farmers outside it, and in this respect these craftsmen were in a position very like that of the agricultural workers.

Table 38
Place of birth by occupational grouping, Elmdon village, 1861

| | born in Elmdon parish | | born outside | | total |
	no.	%	no.	%	no.
Group i	—	—	2	100	2
Group ii	9	32	19	68	28
Group iii	10	37	17	63	27
Group iv	23	74	8	26	31
Total	42	48	46	52	88

Group i: clergy
Group ii: shopkeepers, bakers, butcher, tailors, dressmakers, shoemakers, strawbonnet makers, blacksmiths and wheelwrights, schoolmistress, publicans.
Group iii: those employed in private households.
Group iv: bricklayers, their apprentices and labourers, painter, carpenters, thatchers, carriers, shop and business assistants.

Source: 1861 census.

Whether Elmdoners were able to fill such jobs by somehow excluding outsiders from them; whether the Lofts Hall estate gave preference to local craftsmen; or whether incomers simply did not want this kind of work can only be conjectured. Certainly, none of the occupations included in group iv of table 38 demanded much capital, so they were not out of reach of most Elmdoners on financial grounds. There were plenty of Elmdon boys who would welcome the chance to train as craftsmen, or to work for them, as an alternative to farm labouring. Such chances did not often occur, however, for once a man had established his position as a craftsman, he gave first preference to his relatives when it came to taking on employees. This was a rule which applied to the shopkeepers and tradesmen as well as to craftsmen, and in seven out of every ten cases in which the occupation of the father is known, it was identical to that of the son working outside agriculture in Elmdon in 1861. In three other cases the son held an occupation in the same group in table 38 as his father; in another, the father was a superior worker in private service while his son was a shoemaker; and in the other five cases the fathers were all agricultural labourers whose sons had moved only a very little way up the ladder by becoming bricklayers' labourers, garden labourers or carriers. It was not therefore easy to break out of one type of employment and into another.

112

The craftsmen

The best example of how craftsmen took on members of their own family, and so reinforced the tendency of lower paid jobs to be filled by natives of Elmdon, is provided by the Greenhills. They made a first appearance in Elmdon some years before Nathaniel Wilkes acquired the Lofts Hall estate in 1739, but it was not until the last quarter of the century that they became firmly established in the village. By 1783, the first of the eight children of Richard Greenhill and his Elmdon-born wife had been baptised, but it is only Henry, the third and youngest of their surviving sons, who concerns us here. Born in 1803, Henry, unlike his brothers, spent his life in Elmdon, and in his early days he worked as a labourer, as well as being a bricklayer as his father had been. He must have needed as much work as he could get, for he and his wife had twelve children, ten of whom survived infancy. All the eight boys became bricklayers, and the elder ones doubtless helped to rebuild the church at Wenden Lofts, close to Lofts Hall, in 1845-6. Today, the brickwork they laid can be seen through flaking plaster on the arches supporting the derelict building, now deconsecrated and falling into ruin.

By 1861, however, the trouble which was to destroy the thriving brickwork firm had already made itself felt. In 1856, the elder of the two Greenhill girls died at the early age of 23. Three years later, her brother James, the mainstay of the firm, also died, leaving the business to his wife Naomi, who before her marriage had been the village schoolmistress. All the Greenhill boys who were old enough were already working as bricklayers, or apprentices, and it is possible, though not certain, that to fill the gap left by James's death the firm took on Elmdon's other bricklayer, Edward Negus, an Elmdon boy whose father and two elder brothers were already in the carpentry trade.

Naomi did not live long to carry out her duties as head of the business. She died four years after her husband, leaving four orphaned children under the age of 11. Her death was followed in quick succession by those of her only remaining sister-in-law, her father-in-law and her eldest brother-in-law. Within the space of thirteen years, the Greenhills lost their three senior male workers, and the firm seems never to have recovered. Four of James's six younger brothers went away from Elmdon, and of the two who stayed, one turned to bakery work. Joseph Greenhill and one of his nephews remained in the business, but both of them had died

113

by 1909 and the Greenhills who were left in Elmdon ceased to be associated with the building trade.

This rise and fall of a small business was fairly typical in Elmdon in the last half of the nineteenth century, even if the reasons for decline were not usually so tragic. As we saw in chapter 2, a succession of carriers came and went, often combining their carting work with other jobs, until the need for their services disappeared with the arrival of Fred Weeden's bus service in the 1930s. None of the thatchers and carpenters, or their descendants working at the same craft, was living in Elmdon by the early twentieth century, and there is no evidence to suggest that they were replaced by men in the same line of business working from Elmdon. Indeed, the two carpenters who had come from outside to live in Elmdon in 1861 had gone again by the time of the next census ten years later. Mrs Elizabeth Godfrey, who by 1861 had inherited her late husband's small painting and plumbing business, managed to keep it going until her son James was old enough to take it over, but it only lasted until 1908. Edward Negus, the bricklayer who was probably working for the Greenhills in 1861, carried on in the building trade after the Greenhill's business had closed, and was followed by his son Robert. The latter went to work in London for a while, but then returned to Elmdon, where he remained up to his death in 1952. He is remembered as captain of the bell-ringers as well as for his building work, and he was the last of the craftsmen to live and work in the village. The seven builders, carpenters, painters and timber dealers who lived in Elmdon in 1964 were all employed by outside firms, and left home each day to go to their work.

Domestic service

The tendency for Elmdoners to fill the lesser jobs in the village was repeated in the sphere of domestic service. As we saw in chapter 1, in 1861 the upper echelons of the Lofts Hall staff, both male and female, had all come in from outside, and so had the servants in Elmdon's two clerical households. Elmdon-born girls and women in service in the village in that year were in the main either too young to go right away from home, and were therefore employed in the humblest capacities, or were widows needing to support themselves and their families, who took work where they could find it.

Of course, just as girls from outside came in to fill the higher status domestic posts in Elmdon, so Elmdon girls left the village to find similar jobs elsewhere. Many of them met their future husbands in their new places of work, and the marriage registers from 1861 to 1881 show weddings between Elmdon girls and young men from towns as far afield as Woolwich, Streatham, Croydon, Islington, Westminster and Edinburgh.

Old ladies still living in Elmdon in 1964 remembered London as being the great draw for girls going out into service. One of them took a job there as a nursemaid and recalled enjoying a holiday by the sea with her charges, before she came back to Elmdon to marry a farm worker and settle down. Another went to a house in Streatham as a scullery maid, was promoted to kitchen maid, and worked so hard that when the cook left she was able to take her place. These old ladies looked on domestic service as a good training ground for married life. 'Who's going to marry a girl who can't cook?' asked one, adding 'It's all wrong to live out of tins, and it's too expensive.' Like the older generation of farm workers, they considered that a young person should learn through doing the job and that there was no substitute for experience.

Not all girls got as far as London, of course, and not all jobs carried seaside holidays with them. One girl found herself away in the Fens at Wisbech in her first place, earning only 4 shillings a week, but she felt the separation from Elmdon a little less because her brother was working in the same town.

None of these old ladies resented their days in service, one of them declaring emphatically that she would gladly go back to work again for any of her past employers. This may well be because, when they were young, domestic service offered the best available opportunity to travel and see something of the world outside Elmdon, as well as sometimes leading to better paid jobs as the years went by. The financial position of young women in service also compared quite favourably with that of their brothers working on the land. In 1861, for instance, Mrs Beeton[2] listed the wages of a living-in upper housemaid at £12 0s 0d a year, where no allowance was made for tea, sugar and beer, whereas in the same year, as we have already seen, an agricultural labourer in Essex, who took cash instead of his beer allowance, was earning about £32 10s 0d, including his harvest money. But he had to keep himself and his family in food and clothing out of this, as well as paying about a tenth of his wages in rent, or if he was unmarried

115

and living at home he would be likely to give his mother a large part of his earnings. Many girls out in service must have sent money home to help their families too, but some also managed to save quite considerable sums, which went a long way towards setting up house when the time came to be married. One Elmdon girl had saved £70 by the time she was 20, and this in spite of the expense of coming home from London by train and hired pony trap once a fortnight to help her mother nurse a sick brother. When the Lofts Hall estate was sold up in 1927, with cottages going very cheaply, the only farm worker in Elmdon to acquire his cottage was a man whose sister bought it for him. She was working as a housekeeper in another village, and in fact she bought two cottages, one for him and another for her parents.

Because there were so few other work opportunities open to girls in rural areas, service in private households was adopted by a wide variety of women. In 1861, Miss Perry's companion at Poplars Farm was a farmer's daughter, and the house servants in Elmdon at that time included daughters of a blacksmith, a carpenter, a bricklayer and a farm bailiff as well as girls whose fathers were agricultural labourers. These young women from varying backgrounds were easily absorbed into domestic service, which offered a range of different jobs, from the maid-of-all-work on a farm who might also help in the dairy or barnyard, to the cook in a middle-class suburban household or the servant at the top of the domestic hierarchy in a big house like Lofts Hall. When the elder son of James and Naomi Greenhill died at a comparatively early age, like his parents, the young widow he left behind him, Polly Greenhill, was offered the post of housekeeper at Lofts Hall, thus providing her with a home for herself and her young son William, and a satisfactory status in Elmdon as well. One old lady remembers going up to the Hall to tea, as a little girl, when the family were away, and being allowed by Polly to ride on the Wilkes' children's rocking-horse in the nursery, but this would never have happened had the family been at home, for Polly, and no doubt the Wilkes too, would not have considered it proper. Very dignified, Polly always dressed in black. Her job was no sinecure, for in addition to her normal duties, she was responsible for feeding the guests when shoots were held at Lofts Hall. The beaters ate at the Wilkes Arms, but for days before the event Polly would be preparing the cold luncheon to be eaten at the Hall, at which game pie was the speciality. She would make the puff pastry, roll it out and then hang it in a bag in the cellar to chill. Then she would bring it up to the kitchen again, and repeat the whole process, before finally making the succulent pies. William, her son, made himself useful by cleaning horse brasses and tack, but he never had a proper job at the Hall, and when he grew up he joined the police force and went to work in London.

Polly was not the only connection the Greenhills had with Lofts Hall. In 1914, a girl called Annie Keen took the post of upper housemaid there. Her father had been coachman to a German prince, and she herself had worked at a mansion in Yorkshire and at Lambeth Palace before coming to the Hall. As she said years later, she always liked working in big houses because everyone had their own job to do, and there was plenty of company. Two weeks after her arrival, another housemaid took her out into the lane to learn to ride a bicycle. Enoch Greenhill happened to meet them, held the bicycle seat for her as she wobbled along, and arranged to see her again the following Wednesday. They courted for two years before they married, but as Enoch said later, once he saw Annie 'I knew I was hooked'.

Housemaids at Lofts Hall, *c*. 1914. (Annie Greenhill is third from the left)

Just as improved bus services after the Second World War opened up new chances of employment outside agriculture for Elmdon boys, so the girls were able to find work outside domestic service in the nearby towns. Several girls were employed in the laundries in Saffron Walden, and work in Spicers' factories in Sawston became as popular with the girls as with their brothers. Fewer and fewer young girls went into domestic work, and by 1964 there were no female living-in servants in Elmdon, and only four full-time dailies. Sixteen women, however, worked as part-time household helps, and there was one Italian *au pair* who was enlarging her experience of the world by travelling far from home in return for her board and pocket money.

Business heads

So far we have looked at the lower-status occupations, filled in the main by Elmdoners, and at service in private households which by its very nature demanded no capital outlay. But what of those who needed premises and stock, like the shopkeepers and publicans, or who required special equipment and suitable buildings, as the bakers, blacksmiths and wheelwrights did?

There were three possibilities open to such people in Elmdon in the last half of the nineteenth century, whether or not they were born in the parish. They could control their own business, either through purchase or inheritance; they could rent accommodation from the Lofts Hall estate, or they could find other owners willing to lease them the necessary premises, since about half the property in the village was out of the Wilkes family's hands, as we saw in chapter 1. If we look at the history of the two main shops in Elmdon from 1861 onwards, we shall find examples of each of these methods.

Mr Crisp's drapery shop, which also contained the Post Office and offered an upholstery service, stood in the High Street next door to John Brand's grocery and drapery store, although the rival establishments were separated by quite a considerable area of garden. The Crisps had arrived in Elmdon as a young married couple some time in the late 1830s, and had rented their shop and living quarters from Elizabeth and Rebecca Perry, of Poplars Farm, who had inherited a life interest in the property from their aunt. Although William Crisp was born in Little Eversden in Cambridgeshire and his wife Mary came from Wisbech, in the Isle of Ely,

118

they had lived in Saffron Walden for a time before coming to Elmdon and may have heard of the opportunity to rent the shop when they were there.

The Crisps continued to live over the shop, later adding groceries to the drapery business, until William died in 1874. His widow had been carrying on the business for three years, with the help of her unmarried daughter Eliza, when in 1877 she bought the property. By this time it had passed from Rebecca Perry to the next heir, a wheelwright living near Cambridge. He offered the shop, house and grounds to Mrs Crisp for £305, and after nearly forty years of renting the business premises, enough money had been saved to enable her to accept. She became the owner of the house and shop until she died in 1882. Mrs Crisp had several children among whom to share her possessions, and her executors therefore sold the Elmdon property to Eliza, the stay-at-home daughter, for £250, a sum which she raised on mortgage.

Shortly after her mother's death, Eliza, then aged 35, married George Wabon, a whitesmith or worker in tin, who was six years younger than herself and already her brother-in-law, through her younger sister's marriage to George's elder brother some four years earlier. They seem to have led a relatively uneventful life, continuing to run the shop under George's name, but giving up the Post Office in 1906. Although the shop continued as a grocery and drapery store, there was one brief period of glory, coinciding with the fashionable Sir James Bailey's tenancy of Lofts Hall, when George, probably hoping for patronage from this quarter, advertised himself in heavy type in Kelly's Directory as 'grocer, draper and metal worker; umbrellas, clocks and jewels neatly repaired'. Alas, Sir James died a year or two later, and the Wabon's entry in the Directory reverted to the more modest 'grocer and draper' in small print.

We do not know when George died, but by the end of the First World War Eliza Wabon had retired to Wells-next-the-sea in Norfolk, calling her house there 'Elmduna' in order to remind her of earlier days. She and George had no children to carry on the business, which was sold in 1920. With the sale, a family association with the shop covering over eighty years came to an end.

Elmdon's second shop was rather different, in that it belonged to the Lofts Hall estate. The occupant in 1861 was young John Brand, who at the same time held the tenancy of Hill Farm. John was born in Chrishall, one-and-a-half miles away, but for all

119

practical purposes he was an Elmdoner, since his ancestors had lived in the villages for generations, as the chart in figure 9 on pp.170-2 shows.

John Brand had taken over the tenancy of the shop from his widowed mother, who in turn had succeeded her late husband there. As we saw in chapter 4, John moved out of Hill Farm into Church Farm when it became vacant on the death of his uncle, and he then gave up the shop, presumably because he no longer needed a dual occupation to make ends meet, since Church Farm was twice the size of Hill Farm. The next shopkeeper was a Miss Mary Ann Clark from Cambridge, and she remained in possession at least until 1874. Around that time, however, John Brand's sister Harriet came back to Elmdon from Saffron Walden where she had gone to live when she married Jabez Chater, a florist and nurseryman. Jabez had almost certainly died, but Harriet was not left without a livelihood, for Miss Clark disappeared from the scene, and Harriet took over the shop which she continued to run for nearly forty years, until she was well into her 70s. She died in 1918, and it will come as no surprise to learn that the next tenant was her nephew, Ernest Brand, who was the younger son of her brother John. When the shop was put up for sale in 1927, it was bringing in an annual rent of £27 10s 0d, and Ernest was paying an additional £4 0s 9d for nearly two acres of land.[3] The shop was bought for £620, probably by Ernest himself, and he stayed on as shopkeeper for about ten years longer, before leaving for Bishops Stortford when he was nearly 60 years old.

It seems, then, that as Lofts Hall estate tenants the Brands had as much security of tenure in their shop as the Crisp family had done, even though the latter had bought their business. Once again, successive Squires appeared to favour Elmdoners rather than newcomers, and to allow tenancies to pass from one generation of a family to the next, just as they had done with their farming tenants.

However, in the case of both these shops, when the Crisp and Brand families were no longer concerned with them there was to be no more continuity of tenure from one generation to the next, and none of the future shopkeepers were to be Elmdoners, or even to have a known Elmdon connection.

In the case of the Brands' shop, part of the house was rented out as living accommodation to an Elmdon family unconnected with the business, and the remainder, including the shop itself, was occupied by a Saffron Walden man who is said to have been a butcher, although he is described elsewhere as a grocer and draper, just as Ernest Brand had been. His occupancy did not last long, for in 1940 he moved back to Saffron Walden. The shop was closed, and the property sold for use as a private house.

The Crisps' old shop continued rather longer, passing through the hands of a number of owner-occupiers, and the various sales give a striking picture of changing money values over a period of forty-one years. Eliza Wabon sold the shop in 1920 for £260, or only £10 more than she had paid for it thirty-eight years before. The buyer was Harry Easy, who took out a mortgage with the Victoria Oddfellows Lodge at Harston, a village near Cambridge from which he himself may have come, though there is no proof of this. Twenty-five years later, immediately after the Second World War, Mr Easy sold the business for £900, to a couple who re-sold it only a year later for £1,200. The next occupants, Mr and Mrs Robinson, came from Hertfordshire, and ran the shop very successfully for fourteen years. They are remembered as having everything in stock, and frequently travelling to London for supplies. In 1960, they sold the business for £4,980 to a man from a village some fifteen miles from Elmdon. He allowed the shop to run down for a year, and then sold the property for £5,250 to an owner who turned it into a private house, now known appropriately as 'The Old Stores'.[4]

Fortunately, the closure of what had been the Crisps' shop did not leave Elmdon without a grocery store at all. In 1943, Baker's Cottage, which had formerly been used as a pork-butcher's shop and an ale-house, was bought by a Wandsworth newsagent and tobacconist, and turned into a grocery and general stores. Either the proprietor did not enjoy living in Elmdon, or he had bought the business purely as a speculation, for a year later he sold it again to another Londoner. In the next four years the owners, all from London or its environs, changed four times, and between 1944 and 1948 the sale price more than doubled, rising from £1,150 to £3,000. In 1948, stability returned with the arrival of Mr and Mrs Woodward, who kept the shop for thirteen years before selling it to Mr and Mrs Macdonald. The latter were running the business at the time of the Elmdon survey in 1964, and are still doing so today, sixteen years after their first arrival in Elmdon from Cheshunt, in Hertfordshire.[5]

The sums of money which passed hands in the various sales of

Elmdon church from the Ickleton Road. Baker's stores is on the left, and the school on the right

Baker's Cottage were beyond the reach of what may be called the old Elmdon families. Those who had not taken advantage of the low prices for property obtaining at the time of the Lofts Hall estate sale in 1927 now found themselves priced out of the market by people from outside Elmdon. After the disappearance of the Lofts Hall estate, with its predisposition in favour of Elmdon families, and the opportunities it offered to rent business premises rather than buy them, Elmdoners' chances of turning shopkeeper in the village virtually disappeared, though one attempt was made in connection with the butcher's shop, as we shall see later.

To return to 1861, if we look at the two bakeries which were then operating in Elmdon and at what happened to them, we see once again that it was the Lofts Hall estate tenants who enjoyed continuity of tenure. One of the bakers was Charles Monk, who had come to Elmdon from Hertfordshire some time before 1841, and who ran a beer-shop as well as the bakery. In having a dual occupation, he was typical of many of the small tradesmen of Elmdon, who needed more than one line of business in such a small community if they were to make a reasonable living. It is probable that he rented his premises on Cross Hill, lying between the King's Head and the two village shops, but we do not know who the landlord was. Charles died late in 1861, and with his death the bakery closed. Neither of his teenaged sons who had been helping him in the business stayed on in Elmdon and the premises later became the public house known as the Carrier.

The second bakery was in Lofts Hall estate premises next door to Charles Monk's bake-house and beer-shop, and the picture there was very different. In 1841, the baker had been John Bowman, who years earlier had married Susannah, the young widow of one of the Elmdon Gamgees. It may well have been this marriage that turned John into a baker, for before that he had been a farm labourer. Susannah, however, 'one of thirteen children all healthy and strong'[6] was known to be an able woman of considerable character. With a low rent to pay — and in 1860 the annual charge for the 'cottage, lodges and small garden having a good bakery business' was only £14 0s 0d[7] — it would have been possible to take over an existing bakery without the expenditure of much capital.

When John Bowman died, Susannah carried on the bakery until her own death in 1865, at the age of 86. The tenancy of the business was then given to her daughter by her first marriage, Abigail Gamgee, who had married John Loveday. Abigail continued to run the bakery until she died in 1884, and the Lofts Hall estate then gave the tenancy to her son-in-law, Thomas Greenhill, one of the bricklayers of whom we read earlier in this chapter, who had married her daughter, Emily. It seems that although the tenancy was in Thomas's name, Emily did most of the baking, having worked both with her grandmother and her mother in the business. Men and women in Elmdon in 1964 remember the hot muffins she used to make, which she would split and cover with sugar. The Greenhills also sold coal and fish from the same premises. People used to have to fetch the coal themselves, but it cost less than 17 shillings a ton.

Emily died just before the sale of the Lofts Hall estate, and her son Walter bought the bakery. There his unmarried sister remained, turning out bread for the village and acting as relief organist at the church (but 'only when it suited her'), until the arrival of the bread delivery vans from outside killed the trade, and she retired to Saffron Walden.

There was only one butcher's shop in Elmdon in 1861. Like the other shops it was to be found on Cross Hill, and the buildings in which it was housed were almost certainly the property of John

Brand the blacksmith (not to be confused with the farmer and shopkeeper), whose father had been the owner at the time of the Enclosure Award. In 1861, the shop was being run by Robert Cowell, a young man from Audley End. The explanation of why he had come to Elmdon is not far to seek. His wife, Isabella, was John Brand's daughter, and no doubt his father-in-law was glad to let the premises to him.

However, in spite of the ownership of the business being in the family, it did not remain so for very long. Robert died in 1875, before he was forty, and though his widow carried on for a little while, she soon married again. Her new husband, like Eliza Crisp's, was her brother-in-law already, through her sister's marriage some years earlier to his brother. Like Robert Cowell, he was a butcher, but he lived in St James's, Westminster, and Isabella therefore left Elmdon.

The next occupant of the shop, George Hopwood, rented the premises for only two years, for the building was bought over his head by a rival butcher, Daniel Britton. For some twenty-five years Britton did a considerable business with Elmdon Bury Farm, being one of the chief buyers of its livestock. He finally sold up and went to Newport, and the shop was bought by Leonard Smith, a member of the Duddenhoe End farming family. Finally, in about 1920, the cottages containing the shop were sold to the Fisons of Elmdon Lodge farm, for use as tied cottages for their farm workers, and the shop was closed.

Almost immediately, a new butcher's shop opened in different premises, along the Ickleton Road. During the forty-four years it was in existence, this shop had three owners, none of them with any known Elmdon connection. The last owner, Frank Reeder, was still running the shop in 1964. He and his wife both came from the Isle of Ely, and even after nineteen years in Elmdon they did not think they had really been assimilated into the village. As Mr Reeder, a fenman, said with some feeling 'You'd have to have been here since Hereward the Wake to belong'. With his death in 1964, the shop and house were sold to a Saffron Walden building firm.

When this happened, the wife of an Elmdon farm worker tried to ensure that the village should continue to have a butcher's shop. She had worked for a butcher in a nearby village before her marriage, and Mr Reeder had been employing her as an assistant, instead of the usual butcher's boy. She persuaded the building

124

firm to rent the shop to her and for some months tried hard to make the business pay. She was handicapped by lack of capital, however, and as she could not afford to employ an assistant herself, the shop had to remain closed, losing custom, while she was out on the delivery round or buying supplies. After eighteen months, she received notice to quit, and the premises were pulled down. Elmdoners could no longer buy their meat in the village, but were dependent on travelling butchers from other places.

There was a time, from the early 1890s up to 1917, when Elmdon had two butchers' shops. As we saw earlier, in about 1893 George Hopwood arrived in the village and rented one of the cottages on Cross Hill formerly occupied by Robert Cowell the butcher, where he carried on the business. George came originally from the village of Hinxton, less than five miles from Elmdon, where his father was also a butcher, and he had gone off to work in the same trade in London. But his wife's health suffered from town life, and he was advised by the doctor that she should live in the country. A friend of his told him that the tenancy of the Green Man public house in Arkesden, in the next parish to Elmdon, was vacant, so he took it. He found the life uncongenial, however, and when the opportunity arose he moved with his family to the Cross Hill butcher's shop in Elmdon. After being turned out by Daniel Britton, George rented Baker's Cottage, where he not only continued the existing beer-selling business, but opened a pork-butcher's shop. In those days there was no compulsory slaughtering of animals in registered abbatoirs, and the butchery business was much more down to earth and open to the public eye. Individual butchers did their own killing, and George Hopwood would be seen driving a cart full of pigs, destined to become the Sunday dinners of his customers, and shouting to them to 'sit down, you devils', if they created any kind of commotion as they bowled along. The slaughterhouse at the back of the Cross Hill premises had a cesspool to collect the blood, and rats used to swarm there. George Hopwood's niece in Hinxton remembered that, as a small girl, one of her treats was to be allowed to go across the road to her uncle's shop to watch the animals being, slaughtered in the yard behind.

George Hopwood later added a carrier's business to his activities as a butcher and beer-seller, and it was through this that he met his death. He had taken a load down to the mill in Wenden Lofts and on the way back slipped, and was run over by his own cart. When

125

he died the butcher's shop closed, and though one of his sons came back to Elmdon from his job in London to help the widowed Mrs Hopwood, only the beer-selling part of the business survived for some years longer, before Baker's Cottage, as we have seen, became a grocery store.

There was one further shop in Elmdon, which was important to the children of the village but which was so small that it was simply contained in the downstairs room of an agricultural worker's cottage, and involved only a few shillings' worth of capital. This was the sweet shop run by Lydia Hoy, wife of a farm foreman, towards the end of the nineteenth century. Any children with a penny to spend would gather there, and if a number of them were in funds at the same time, perhaps as a result of carol singing or the performance of some holiday job, they would each put a half-penny into the common pool. They would then throw dice to find the winner, who acquired a handsome sum with which to buy sweets. Years later, Mrs Hoy's daughter carried on the same kind of small business from her own home, travelling to Saffron Walden for supplies of sweets as she needed them, just as her mother had done. Such 'businesses' as these, however, were only supplements to the family's main income, like the mole-catching or hurdle-making which, as we saw in chapter 4, some men took on after their day's work to make ends meet.

Two more businesses in Elmdon in 1861 demanded premises and equipment. Both of them were heavily dependent on the agricultural community for their work. These were John Brand's forge in the High Street, and the wheelwright's shop in the Ickleton Road which was occupied by Isaac Rollings. Although the Brands were primarily blacksmiths, they did wheelwrights' work as well, while the wheelwright's shop also had a smithy. These two businesses provide yet another example of the way in which shops and services were split between Elmdoners and outsiders.

John Brand was at least the sixth in a family line of blacksmiths in Elmdon, and although he rented from the Lofts Hall estate the ten acres of land which led him to be described as a farmer as well as a blacksmith in the 1851 census, the smithy was his own property, and could not be taken away from him as the land was in 1860. Two more generations of his family were to occupy the forge in their turn, as the family tree in figure 9 on page 170 shows, but in the end it passed out of the Brands' hands when it was bought by Mr Cross, the farmer. By this time, the two sons of Henry Brand, the last blacksmith of the family to work in Elmdon, had emigrated to London, no doubt as work fell off with the decline in the number of horses on the land. The Crosses used the forge largely for repairs to agricultural machinery, and it was still being worked for them in 1964 by a man whose grandfather was a blacksmith. Soon afterwards, however, he moved to a job in nearby Duxford where the wages were higher, and Elmdon was without a blacksmith for the first time in many hundreds of years.

Isaac Rollings at the wheelwright's shop, unlike John Brand, was not an Elmdon man. He had been born more than fourteen miles away, and had worked in Royston for a time before coming to Elmdon. His reason for leaving that town for the comparatively isolated village was almost certainly because his wife had inherited the wheelwright's shop where they were living and working in 1861. She was Elmdon-born, and had been a Miss Ann Cane before her marriage. The Canes had owned the wheelwright's business in Elmdon for at least two generations, and the previous owner had been a Miss Susannah Cane, so it is probable that Mrs Rollings came into the property through her.

Although one of Isaac Rollings' sons trained as a wheelwright, he did not take over the business when his father died in 1875. By then he may well have branched out for himself in another village. The next occupier, who is more likely to have rented than to have owned the premises, was an employee of Isaac's called Frederick Housden, who had come to Elmdon as a boy with his widowed mother when she married Robert Pilgrim, the Wilkes family's factotum. Although Frederick's son took over from his father, the end of the wheelwright's shop was near, and it finally closed in about 1912.

Public houses and beer-shops

As we have seen, in 1861 Elmdoners had the choice of two general shops, two bakeries, and two blacksmiths' and wheelwrights' establishments, but the greatest area of competition lay in the public houses and beer-shops. There were four of these at that time, and once again, two were run by Elmdoners and two by people born outside the parish.

The largest public house, with the highest standing, was the Wilkes Arms, owned by the Lofts Hall estate. It lay almost at the gates of the drive up to the hall, and as well as containing ten

127

rooms, it had ample outbuildings, including a barn, chaff house, granary bins, poultry house and stables for the guests' traps and horses. The inn sign was considered more distinguished than others in the village, for it bore the Wilkes's motto in Latin, which in translation read 'I trust not to my bow'.

It seems almost as if the Wilkes family considered the tenants of the Wilkes Arms as an extension of their own domestic staff for, as we shall see, its main business depended on patronage from the Hall. For this reason, in the nineteenth century at least, the tenants, like the Squire's upper servants, were not selected from the ranks of the villagers. In 1861 the tenant was Mrs Sarah Smoothy, widow of the previous tenant. When she died in 1865, she was replaced by another widow, a former housekeeper and cook at Lofts Hall whose husband had been Mr Wilkes's butler. Nothing is known of the next tenant, except that he was not an Elmdoner, but from 1889 to 1901 the inn was in the hands of John Britton, who came to the village some four years after Daniel Britton the butcher, and who must surely have been a relative of his, and possibly recommended by him.

There were to be four more holders of the licence before the Lofts hall estate was sold. The first was Henry Brand, son of the blacksmith, who took on the tenancy for a few years while waiting to step into his father's shoes at the forge. In doing this, incidentally, he was following the example of his own father, who also had to wait some years to inherit the forge and who had held the tenancy at the King's Head, as well as working for his father as a blacksmith. The second landlord came up from the Woodman public house in Duddenhoe End, and the third and fourth were Edward Jeffery and his widow after him.

The Jefferys, who had already been running the Carrier on Cross Hill for some years, were asked to take on the tenancy of the Wilkes Arms by Mr Wilkes himself. Even though Edward Jeffery was the licensee, his wife had a big part to play, for she was in charge of the catering. The horkey dinner mentioned in chapter 4 was held at the Wilkes Arms every Michaelmas day, when the rents fell due, and sixty estate tenants from Chrishall, Chishill and Duddenhoe End as well as Elmdon would have to be fed. The ovens were managed by Martha Greenhill, who lived next door, and to test their temperature she would put a pebble into each one. When the pebble turned white with the heat, she would know that the oven was ready for the Yorkshire puddings which accompanied the roast beef. Meanwhile, roast leg of lamb was also being prepared, and a huge piece of silverside would be boiling away in one copper, together with carrots and turnips, while plum puddings simmered in another. The meal was finished off with celery and cheese and washed down with beer. The rent dinner was followed a week before Christmas by a rather more select affair for the twelve men who paid tithes. Here the food was much the same, but instead of beer, punch was served, made from a blend of gin, brandy, stout, nutmeg and lemon juice. Other catering jobs included cricket teas in the summer, and meals for the fifty or so beaters when a shoot was being held from Lofts Hall in the autumn and winter. In addition, Mrs Jeffery often used to cook for parties at the Hall itself, and was noted for her apple pie with cream.

Edward Jeffery, the licensee, was well known in Elmdon for his wit. Like so many tradesmen in the village, he ran another business on the side and among other things he sold fish. One day he was on his round when he met the Squire of a neighbouring parish, who asked him what fish he had that day. 'Plaice, sir' said Jeffery. 'They say you should give place to the devil', remarked the Squire, attempting a pun. 'Oh no, sir, I can't afford to *give* it to you' replied Jeffery, and drove on, doubtless feeling very pleased with himself. By all accounts, he was an easy man to get along with, and he would allow his children and their friends to play soldiers with the old swords they had found in the attic, not even remonstrating with them when they slashed his cabbages to pieces with their weapons. But on one point he was adamant. No-one was allowed to talk at meal times, for then he 'wanted his peace'.

Once the Lofts Hall estate was sold, the demand for large-scale catering fell off, and the Wilkes Arms began to decline. A whole series of tenants came and went as business slackened, and finally in 1963 the inn was sold for conversion to a private house.

Although Elmdon boasted four inns and beer-houses in 1861, the peak time for this line of business came in the last years of the nineteenth century and the first decade of the twentieth, when the number of establishments had risen to six. It was not really surprising that beer-selling and pub-keeping proved such popular occupations. In the first place, in the days before the big breweries took over most of the beer was home-brewed, so that Elmdon families were in as good a position as anyone else to set up a beer-shop. In the second place, running an inn could be shared amongst members of the family, leaving the landlord free to take on other work as well. Then, the comparatively large number of establishments allowed some movement to take place from one to another. As we have already seen, Edward Jeffery was at the Carrier before he went to the Wilkes Arms, and there are at least five other examples of such movement between the Elmdon public houses and the Woodman down in Duddenhoe End. Finally, visiting the pub or the beer-shop was the major recreation for Elmdon men at this time. Those who worked on the steam ploughs and who lived rough during their week's work away from home would make up for it at weekends, and a good deal of drunkenness resulted. As old men in 1964 said, the beer was much stronger in those days, and with a shilling in your pocket you could not only buy your tobacco, but get drunk as well. Men would come out of the Carrier or King's Head at Cross Hill, and have to pull themselves along by the railings to get home. Many women were frightened by the drunkenness, but one formidable matriarch would roll up her sleeves and plunge into the mass of men at the bar when she felt it was time for her six sons to leave. As her grandson said years later, 'She wasn't afraid to go right into that crowd of men drinking. She knew if one of them set on her, her own sons would turn and bash him.'

Beer-selling, as opposed to running a public house, was a much favoured way of adding to a family's income. The Walters, at the Hoops beer-house, were a case in point. James Walters, the original owner, had been a master tailor, working by day in a small shop, which he owned, close to the Crisps' business, but living at the other end of the village in the Hoops, which was also his property and which he ran as a beer-house with the help of his wife. By 1861 James was dead, but two of his sons, John and James the younger, were still working as tailors, while his widow and his daughter Harriet ran the beer-shop.

The younger James married in his turn and had two sons who were also brought up to the tailoring trade. The three of them are remembered as sitting cross-legged in their shop, stitching away, and frequently singing, as they were a musical family. The jollity was muted as the years went by, for James became blind, and the tap, tap, tap of his stick would be heard as he walked up Cross Hill to the Carrier, where he would stand in the public bar, recite the Lord's Prayer, and make his way down the hill again. The tailoring business fell off, and James started a newsagency to make up his income. His son John continued this until 1926, when it closed. Meanwhile the beer-shop at the Hoops had been carried on by James's sister Harriet. It looks as if it was left to her personally by her mother, for she sold it to a brewer and two other men in 1900. At her death a few years later she was the owner of the four terraced cottages known as Manor Row, but she died intestate, and the property reverted to the Lord of the Manor.

From the early twentieth century, the beer-shops began to decline. The Hoops was the first to go, when it was sold to a retired police inspector in 1909 as a private house, and was followed in the 1930s by the beer-shop run by the wife of Henry Brand, the blacksmith, and a few years later by the beer-selling business in Baker's Cottage. By the end of the Second World War, Elmdon was left with three public houses, the Wilkes Arms, the King's Head and the Carrier. As we have seen, the Wilkes Arms had closed by 1964 and the other two public houses were struggling to continue, even though the old pattern of dual occupations was still in force. Just as Martha Nash, licensee of the King's Head in the 1880s, and her husband had sold coal and corn from the public house, and hired out a pony and trap for journeys to and from Audley End station, so their successors in the 1960s were running a small taxi and car-hire service, as well as keeping the public house going. The recently arrived licensee in 1964 had lived in the King's Head when her parents were the tenants in the 1930s, and had returned to Elmdon because she had enjoyed her childhood there so much, but she complained that the public house barely paid for itself. She was only able to continue because her husband had a remunerative job working in a Fleet Street newspaper office, to which he commuted nightly.

The Carrier at this time was enjoying a temporary advantage, for a juke box had recently been installed in the saloon bar and was attracting a good deal of custom, not only from people living in Elmdon but from other villages around. In time the novelty wore off, however, and in 1972 the public house finally closed, to be converted into a private house as so many other small businesses in Elmdon had been in recent years.

Conclusions

There were several major changes in the shops and services which Elmdon enjoyed between 1861 and 1964.

131

The first businesses to go were those run by the small, independent craftsman such as the bricklayer, the carpenter, the thatcher, the tailor and the shoemaker. Changing agricultural methods meant that ricks were no longer erected and thatched in the old way, but evolved into the ranges of stacked straw bales covered with black plastic sheets which are so often seen today. Hand-stitched corduroys and hand-made boots were replaced by cheaper manufactured goods, and larger firms from outside took over any major building work which was done in the village.

Domestic service changed out of recognition. In 1964, only two men were employed in private service, one as a gardener and general assistant and the other as a maintenance man at Lofts Hall; no women 'lived in' as domestic helps, and only four worked full-time in that capacity. On the other hand, as we saw earlier in the chapter, part-time domestic work remained a source of income for sixteen women in the village, and ten men worked as part-time gardeners. It was usually still possible in Elmdon in 1964 to find someone who would do small maintenance and repair jobs for private householders 'after hours'.

A major change over the period was the disappearance of what were essentially family businesses in which members of the family were absorbed until saturation point was reached. This applied not only to Elmdon-run businesses, but to those managed by people coming in from outside. Furthermore, if a vacancy existed and no suitable relative was available to fill it, then an Elmdon-born business owner would usually employ an Elmdoner, whereas a man from outside would tend to bring in someone from his own home village or elsewhere. For example, in 1861 the butcher's boy came from Audley End, just as the butcher himself did. Isaac Rollings, the wheelwright, who came into Elmdon in his late 50s, employed his own son. His other staff comprised a young man who, though brought up in Elmdon from the age of ten or so, had been born in Linton, and almost certainly two other workers from Finchingfield and Westleton in Suffolk respectively. The 1861 census does not tell us these men's employer, but both lived near Rollings' workshop and not down by the Brands' forge. Both had gone from Elmdon ten years later, by which time Isaac Rollings had died.

Elmdon businesses in the late nineteenth and early twentieth centuries were more dependent on local resources than they were in 1964. The village butcher bought his animals live from Elmdon farms, and might well fatten some of them up before slaughtering them himself. In 1964, the meat sold in Elmdon was brought in to the village, often from as far away as New Zealand, but even if home-killed, then from an abbatoir at some distance. Mrs Wabon and Mrs Chater would stock up their shops from a hawker's cart which came round the village once a month, while in the 1940s and 1950s, as we saw earlier, the owners of Baker's stores regularly visited London for their supplies.

Perhaps the biggest change came with the disappearance of easily-rented business premises. It seems that although an Elmdoner might inherit property which was already in the family, by the last half of the nineteenth century the situation had arisen whereby, once a business was put up for sale, it was likely to pass to outsiders. Elmdoners who were not already property owners had to depend on renting, and with the surge of owner-occupation of businesses as well as farms after the sale of the Lofts Hall estate, and the increasing value of buildings as potential private houses rather than as commercial undertakings, the leasing of premises was no longer in the owner's interest. Elmdoners were therefore squeezed out of the businesses remaining in the village.

By 1964, the commercial shops and services provided in Elmdon had been reduced to one grocery store, also housing the sub-Post Office, one butcher's shop, two public houses, an occasional taxi-service, and a petrol pump outside the village shop. Although the total population of the village had declined from 520 in 1861 to 321 in 1964, or by 38 per cent, thus reducing the demand for goods and services to some extent, it is the petrol pump which provides the real key to the decline, for as we saw in chapter 2, people living in Elmdon no longer had to shop in the village, since public transport or private cars had widened their range considerably. Even the public houses relied for part of their trade on people visiting Elmdon from nearby villages, and there was much coming and going between the different pubs. 'Come on, let's go down to look at the Lights of London' someone would say in the Carrier, referring to the string of electric light bulbs which hung outside the Woodman public house in Duddenhoe End, and a party of people would get into their cars and drive off, leaving the bar almost empty.

In 1964, too, only the part-time taxi service was run by an Elmdoner. All the other village businesses were in the hands of people who had come in from outside, and Elmdoners themselves were increasingly looking outside the village for their employment. What they did, and how the immigrants coming into Elmdon earned their livings, will be discussed further in chapter 11.

7
Marriage

Elmdon society in 1861 was described in the opening chapter as a
pyramid, with the Squire, himself a clergyman, at the apex; his
fellow clerics beneath him; the farmers beneath them, followed by
the workers in private service, and the shopkeepers, tradesmen and
craftsmen; and finally the agricultural labourers, who formed the
base of the structure. Up to now, we have looked at this society
largely in terms of the work done by each section, but several
other aspects also warrant consideration: the social backgrounds
of the members of each economic group; the degree to which they
married within their group, or within their own families, and the
ease with which they could move from one group to another.
These matters, and others, will be discussed with regard to the
majority of Elmdon men in 1861, that is to say, the labourers, in
Kinship at the core, the companion volume to this book. Here, it
is proposed to consider only the position of the other economic
groups.

The Squire and the clergy

'Robert went to school on Tuesday in good spirits; it was almost
perpetual motion with us while he was at home, the weather was
mild, and he kept moving from place to place, and now and then
some of his schoolfellows here, [so] that we miss him very
much . . .'.[1] Thus wrote Mary Ann Fiske, shown on line 4 of
figure 6 on pp. 136-7, in 1835 to her sister-in-law Hannah. The
'Robert' mentioned in the letter was Mary Ann's only son, and
twenty-three years later, as we saw in chapter 1, he was to change
his name from Fiske to Wilkes and become the Squire, as well as
the Vicar, of Elmdon. On the face of it, Robert's inheritance of
the Lofts Hall estate was an unlikely event, for John Wilkes (line
4), the last member of the Wilkes family to own the property,

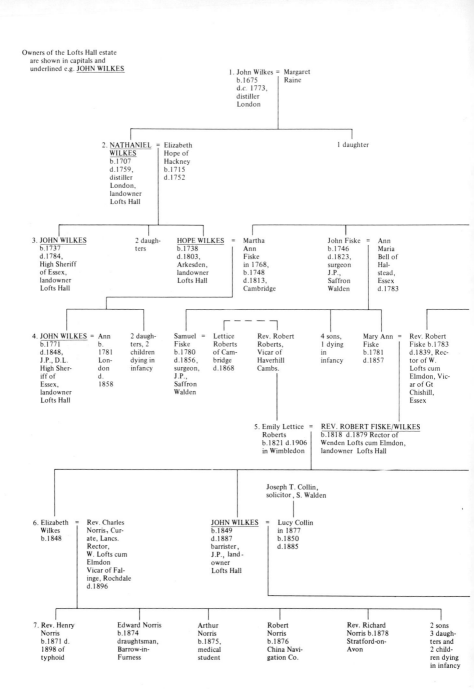

Owners of the Lofts Hall estate
are shown in capitals and
underlined e.g. JOHN WILKES

1. John Wilkes = Margaret
   b.1675   Raine
   d.c. 1773,
   distiller
   London

2. NATHANIEL = Elizabeth   1 daughter
   WILKES   Hope of
   b.1707   Hackney
   d.1759,   b.1715
   distiller   d.1752
   London,
   landowner
   Lofts Hall

3. JOHN WILKES   2 daugh-   HOPE WILKES = Martha   John Fiske = Ann
   b.1737   ters   b.1738   Ann   b.1746   Maria
   d.1784,   d.1803,   Fiske   d.1823,   Bell of
   High Sheriff   Arkesden,   in 1768,   surgeon   Hal-
   of Essex,   landowner   b.1748   J.P.,   stead,
   landowner   Lofts Hall   d.1813,   Saffron   Essex
   Lofts Hall   Cambridge   Walden   d.1783

4. JOHN WILKES = Ann   2 daugh-   Samuel = Lettice   Rev. Robert   4 sons,   Mary Ann = Rev. Robert
   b.1771   b.   ters, 2   Fiske   Roberts   Roberts,   1 dying   b.1781   Fiske b.1783
   d.1848,   1781   children b.1780   of Cam-   Vicar of   in   d.1857   d.1839, Rec-
   J.P., D.L.   Lon-   dying in d.1856, bridge   Haverhill   infancy   tor of W.
   High Sher-   don   infancy   surgeon, d.1868   Cambs.   Lofts cum
   iff of   d.   J.P.,   Elmdon, Vic-
   Essex,   1858   Saffron   ar of Gt
   landowner   Walden   Chishill,
   Lofts Hall   Essex

5. Emily Lettice = REV. ROBERT FISKE/WILKES
   Roberts   b.1818 d.1879 Rector of
   b.1821 d.1906   Wenden Lofts cum Elmdon,
   in Wimbledon   landowner Lofts Hall

Joseph T. Collin,
solicitor, S. Walden

6. Elizabeth = Rev. Charles   JOHN WILKES = Lucy Collin
   Wilkes   Norris, Cur-   b.1849   in 1877
   b.1848   ate, Lancs.   d.1887   b.1850
               Rector,   barrister,   d.1885
               W. Lofts cum   J.P., land-
               Elmdon   owner
               Vicar of Fal-   Lofts Hall
               inge, Rochdale
               d.1896

7. Rev. Henry   Edward Norris   Arthur   Robert   Rev. Richard   2 sons
   Norris   b.1874   Norris   Norris   Norris b.1878   3 daugh-
   b.1871 d.   draughtsman,   b.1875,   b.1876   Stratford-on-   ters and
   1898 of   Barrow-in-   medical   China Navi- Avon   2 child-
   typhoid   Furness   student   gation Co.   ren dying
                                                                         in infancy

Fig. 6 Wilkes genealogical table

136

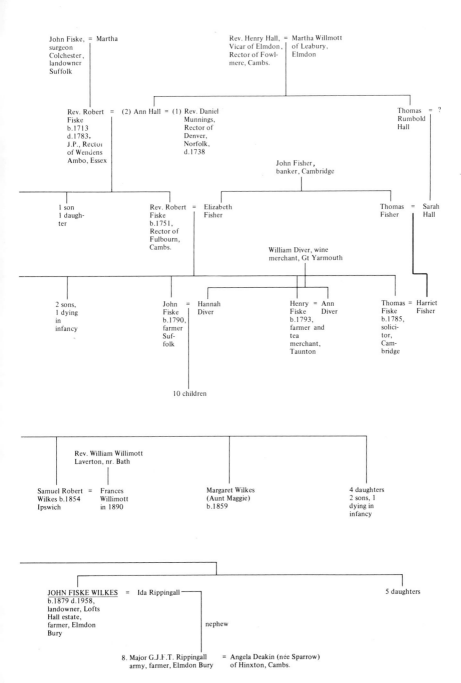

John Fiske, = Martha
surgeon
Colchester,
landowner
Suffolk

Rev. Henry Hall, = Martha Willmott
Vicar of Elmdon, | of Leabury,
Rector of Fowl- | Elmdon
mere, Cambs.

Rev. Robert = (2) Ann Hall = (1) Rev. Daniel
Fiske   Munnings,
b.1713   Rector of
d.1783,   Denver,
J.P., Rector   Norfolk,
of Wendens   d.1738
Ambo, Essex

Thomas = ?
Rumbold
Hall

John Fisher,
banker, Cambridge

1 son   Rev. Robert = Elizabeth
1 daugh-   Fiske   Fisher
ter   b.1751,
                Rector of
                Fulbourn,
                Cambs.

Thomas = Sarah
Fisher   Hall

William Diver, wine
merchant, Gt Yarmouth

2 sons,   John = Hannah   Henry = Ann   Thomas = Harriet
1 dying   Fiske   Diver   Fiske   Diver   Fiske   Fisher
in   b.1790,   b.1793,   b.1785,
infancy   farmer   farmer and   solici-
               Suf-   tea   tor,
               folk   merchant,   Cam-
                                      Taunton   bridge

10 children

Rev. William Willimott
Laverton, nr. Bath

Samuel Robert = Frances   Margaret Wilkes   4 daughters
Wilkes b.1854   Willimott   (Aunt Maggie)   2 sons, 1
Ipswich   in 1890   b.1859   dying in
                                                        infancy

JOHN FISKE WILKES = Ida Rippingall   5 daughters
b.1879 d.1958,
landowner, Lofts
Hall estate,
farmer, Elmdon   nephew
Bury

8. Major G.J.F.T. Rippingall   = Angela Deakin (née Sparrow)
   army, farmer, Elmdon Bury   of Hinxton, Cambs.

137

had nephews through the marriages of his two sisters to whom he could have left his land. But he passed these nephews over, and instead chose for his heir the son of a first cousin on his mother's side.

The full account of what happened will probably never be known, but old men in the district in the 1960s remembered as children hearing rumours of these long past events from their parents. It is likely that there was a family quarrel of some kind which caused John Wilkes to cut his nephews out of the succession. Once this had been done, it was after all not so strange that he should choose his first cousin once removed as his heir, for Robert Fiske, like his father before him, was Rector of Wenden Lofts and Vicar of Elmdon, and must have been better known to John Wilkes in his later years than any of his closer relatives.

As we saw in chapter 3, the Wilkes family came to Wenden Lofts in 1739, when John's grandfather, Nathaniel (line 2 of figure 6) bought the Lofts Hall estate. As the skeleton family tree in chapter 3 (figure 1) showed, Nathaniel was descended from a yeoman farmer of Shropshire, two of whose sons left that county to become malt distillers and citizens of London. The elder brother, Israel, founded the family fortune, and his only son, also called Israel and a malt distiller like his father, was well enough off to live in considerable style in Clerkenwell, in a handsome, brick-built house, approached by a paved court with iron gates, through which his coach would sweep, drawn by six horses. He and his wife were known for their hospitality and 'their house was resorted to by persons of rank, merchants, philosophers, and men of letters.'[2] It was in this atmosphere that Israel's three sons were brought up, and the middle boy, John, later became the famous radical, 'Liberty' Wilkes, the Member of Parliament.

The younger branch of the Wilkes family followed a very different pattern. Its founder, John Wilkes (line 1 of figure 6) was originally apprenticed to his brother Israel as a distiller. He also did well, and as we have already seen he left sufficient property to his son Nathaniel (line 2) not only to enable him to buy the Lofts Hall estate but to allow the family to add to it by purchase over the years. So while Nathaniel's cousin, Israel the younger, was running his business in Clerkenwell and entertaining a wide circle of men of the moment, Nathaniel was engaged in the pursuits of a country squire; and in the next generation, while 'Liberty' Wilkes was becoming a popular hero, his second cousins John and

138

Hope (line 3) remained in Essex. John held the office of High Sheriff of the county at one time, and Hope, the younger brother, who had been given his mother's maiden name, lived in Arkesden, on the south-east border of Elmdon parish. Contact between the London Wilkes and the Essex branch seems to have been slight, and even when 'Liberty' Wilkes was journeying through the county, there was no meeting between him and his relative at Lofts Hall.[3]

The Lofts Hall Wilkes, then, had moved in three generations from a background of yeoman farming in the West Midlands, through a successful business enterprise in London, to landowner-ship, the possession of a country seat, and the lordship of several manors, with all that that entailed in pre-enclosure days, when the office was by no means the empty title which it has now become. But when Hope Wilkes married in 1768, he took his wife from yet another kind of family. His bride, Martha Anne Fiske (line 3) was a clergyman's daughter, and the great majority of her male relatives were in the professions.[4] Her maternal grandfather, the Rev. Henry Hall (line 1) had at one time been Vicar of Elmdon, her grand-father on her father's side was a surgeon, as well as owning an estate in Suffolk, and her three brothers had entered the law, medicine and the church respectively. Indeed, the only male Fiskes shown in generations 1 to 4 who did not enter a profession were Martha's nephews, John and Henry (line 4), the two younger sons of the Rev. Robert Fiske of Fulbourn (line 3). Both were apprenticed to farmers. John finally became a tenant farmer in Suffolk, living in Metfield Hall, a large, agreeable house surrounded by a moat, but his brother Henry found farming uncongenial and with some spirit left his apprenticeship near Bury St Edmunds to set himself up as a tea merchant in Taunton. Even in a family as stable as the Fiskes appear to have been, there was room for some diversity.

When Hope and Martha Wilkes (line 3) were installed in Lofts Hall after the death of Hope's bachelor brother John, they and their children found themselves in touch with their Fiske relatives rather than with the London-based Wilkes. There were Fiske uncles, aunts and cousins in Saffron Walden, Cambridge and Fulbourn, all within easy visiting distance of Wenden Lofts, as well as in Suffolk. The closeness of the ties between these branches of the family is evident from the chart. In line 4, for example, we see that the Rev. Robert Fiske, brought up in Fulbourn, married his first cousin, Mary Ann Fiske, the daughter of the Saffron Walden surgeon, and was granted the livings of Wenden Lofts, Elmdon and Gt Chishill, which were all in the gift of his cousin, John Wilkes of Lofts Hall. Robert's brother Thomas, a Cambridge solicitor, also married a first cousin, this time on his mother's side. Then Robert and Thomas's two other brothers, the apprentice farmers, married sisters, Hannah and Ann Diver, who were the daughters of a prosperous wine merchant of Great Yarmouth.

If visits were not possible, the families kept in touch by correspondence. In the same letter that was quoted at the beginning of the chapter, Mary Ann Fiske (line 4) went on to enquire anxiously about the health of her sister-in-law's neighbours in Suffolk, adding 'Our neighbour Mrs Aldrich often enquires after you, she is very well but looks much older this last year, she is still our best neighbour'. The truth was that in a small, rural community like Elmdon there were very few neighbours whom the Fiskes would have considered suitable as friends. Mrs Aldrich, a clergyman's widow, was nearly 60 when the letter was written, and apart from her and the childless John Wilkes at Lofts Hall, there were no other members of the professional or landowning classes living in the immediate vicinity. No wonder, then, that Mary Ann and Robert's only son should be entertaining his school-fellows, or visiting them during his holidays, and that such pains were taken to keep in touch with relatives in the surrounding towns and villages.

When young Robert Fiske (line 5) grew up, he conformed to the family pattern. Like his father and grandfather, he entered St John's College, Cambridge, and he was the fourth in direct line in his family to take Orders. There was no difficulty in finding a parish, for his father had died when young Robert was only 21, and in 1843 he 'inherited' the livings of Elmdon and Wenden Lofts, in the gift of his father's cousin John Wilkes, just as we have seen that the Lofts Hall estate tenant farmers 'inherited' their farms from one generation to another. In 1842, he even seems to have married a family connection, as his father and so many of his uncles had done, for his wife was Emily Lettice Roberts (line 5), daughter of the Vicar of Haverhill, and it is difficult to believe that she was not in some way related to the Lettice Roberts (line 4) who had married his uncle Samuel. Figure 6 shows a possible relationship, but this has not been proved.

When Robert Fiske changed his name to Wilkes and came into his inheritance of the Lofts Hall estate in 1858, on the death of the previous owner's widow, he was already the father of six surviving children, and three more were born to him and his wife in the ensuing years. Two of these nine children died before coming of age, and we only know of three marriages in relation to the sons and daughters who grew up. Once again, the familiar pattern was followed, for Elizabeth (line 6) married a curate, who had been a student at Emmanuel College, Cambridge; Samuel's wife was a clergyman's daughter; and John, the heir, who had chosen the law rather than the Church for his profession, married the daughter of a Saffron Walden solicitor. Her name was Lucy Collin, and she may well have been related to the Rev. Joseph Collin, Rector of Strethall, who as we saw in chapter 1 was living in Elmdon in the 1860s and 70s.

In 1862, Robert Wilkes, by now installed in Lofts Hall with the cares of the estate on his shoulders, gave up the Elmdon living to his curate, and himself became curate of Wenden Lofts. In 1872, when the Elmdon and Wenden Lofts livings were again vacant, he kep them in the family by bestowing them on his son-in-law, Charles Norris (line 7), then working as curate-in-charge at Pendleton, Manchester. The Norrises came back to live in the familiar Elmdon vicarage where Elizabeth Norris had been brought up, and which had been built by her grandfather Fiske, with its splendid flower bed, 20 feet across, in the shape of a Maltese Cross cut out of the lawn in front of the drawing- and dining-room windows. They only stayed until a year after Elizabeth's father died, however, and then returned to a large industrial parish in Rochdale. From this time on, no members of the Fiske or Wilkes families held the Elmdon or Wenden Lofts livings, and a series of vicars with no known previous connection with the parish came and went.

It was in the next generation, which reached adulthood at the end of the nineteenth and beginning of the twentieth centuries, that the pattern set by six preceding generations began to break down. The Norrises produced a family almost on the scale of the Rev. and Mrs Quiverful in Trollope's *Barchester Towers*, for they had twelve children, ten of whom grew up. With a clergyman for a father, and a rector's daughter for a mother, it is not surprising that two of their seven sons entered the church. A third, also in the family tradition, read medicine, but two others broke new ground by becoming a draughtsman in Vickers' shipyard in Barrow-in-Furness, and an employee of the China Navigation Company

141

respectively. Close family links were maintained, however, and one of the Norris sons even retired to Elmdon, living in a bungalow which he had built for him on the edge of the village.

The young Norrises' cousin, John, better known as Jack, Wilkes (line 7) received a typical Fiske upbringing in that he was a student at Cambridge University, though at Trinity College and not St John's, and was later admitted to the bar at Lincoln's Inn, like his father before him. He never practised as a lawyer, however, and when he married, quite late in life, he chose for his wife the daughter of a Norfolk landowner who had no previous connection with Elmdon.

The Essex and Cambridgeshire Fiskes, then, were a family which kept up close links between the different branches. Intermarriage was common, particularly during the first half of the nineteenth century. The great majority of boys over several generations entered the professions. If a university training was required, Cambridge was the chosen seat of learning. Those who went in for medicine or the law usually gravitated to the towns of Saffron Walden and Cambridge, once they had qualified, while those who took Orders found themselves country livings, where they combined care for their parishioners with responsibility for the sometimes quite considerable acreages of glebe land which went with their office. With this background, born and brought up Elmdon, Robert Fiske Wilkes was a natural choice to succeed to the Lofts Hall estate, once John Wilkes (line 4) decided he must look outside his immediate family for his heir. By the turn of the century, however, signs of the changes which were to sweep away this apparently stable way of life had already made their appearance.

The farmers

We have already seen in chapter 4 that the majority of the farmers on the Lofts Hall estate in 1861 were interrelated. Figure 7 on page 143 sets out the marriages of members of Lofts Hall estate farming families in Chrishall and Wenden Lofts, as well as in Elmdon parish, during the whole of the nineteenth century. During this time, no marriages were recorded in the Elmdon parish registers for the farming families occupying the three Elmdon village farms which lay outside the estate, namely Poplars, The Lee and Bakers Farm which later became Elmdon Lodge. Indeed, for

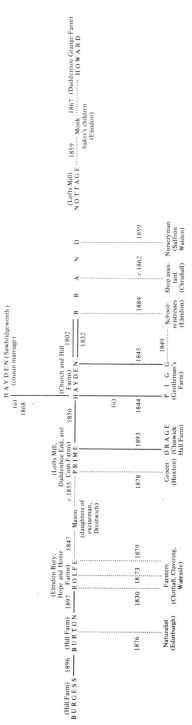

Key Each straight line (—— or |) represents one marriage between the two Lofts Hall estate families it connects. Lofts Hall estate family names are in capitals – e.g. PRIME.
Each dotted line (···· or ⋮) represents one marriage between a member of a Lofts Hall estate family and an individual outside such families.
The date of each marriage is given beside the marriage line. The marriages shown are those of Lofts Hall estate farmers, their sons and daughters.

(i) Tenants at Wenden Lofts Mill have been included, as some 40-50 acres of land went with the mill tenancy.
(ii) These marriages are of Lofts Hall estate farmers' sons who were not themselves farmers. One was a grocer and draper in Fulbourn, Cambs., the other a builder in Sawbridgeworth, Essex.

There were no recorded marriages in Elmdon for farming families on the three Elmdon village farms outside the Lofts Hall estate in the nineteenth century (Poplars, The Lee, Bakers'/Elmdon Lodge).

Sources: Elmdon parish marriage registers, 1800-99. Wenden Lofts and Chrishall parish marriage registers. 1841-71 Censuses.

Fig. 7   Diagram to show marriages of members of Lofts Hall estate farming families (i), 1800-99

many years both Poplars and Bakers Farm were occupied by unmarried tenants. The information available is biassed heavily towards the marriages of farmers' daughters, since it was then, as now, customary for a marriage to be celebrated in the bride's home church, and so the weddings of farmers and their sons to women living outside Elmdon parish are less frequently recorded in the registers. Nevertheless, figure 7 shows that of twenty-two marriages of Lofts Hall estate farmers, or their sons and daughters, nine, or 41 per cent, were to members born into other estate families, and that these marriages were distributed fairly evenly over the nineteenth century.

Did these 'inter-estate' marriages come about because certain farmers wished to cement relations with a working colleague; because marriages were sought with families which held a comparable social status; or simply because the offspring of the estate farmers were likely to have known each other from childhood and to have had plenty of opportunity to meet each other? It is impossible to answer these questions with any assurance after such a lapse of time, but it is noticeable that two-thirds of the recorded 'inter-estate' marriages took place between a group of small farmers, whose holdings were of 200 acres or less, namely the Haydens, the Piggs, the Brands, and Moses Prime while he was still tenant of Lofts Mill and its accompanying 45 or so acres. It would seem, therefore, that there was a marked tendency for the girls brought up on the smaller estate farms to marry either other small farmers who were also estate tenants, or their sons. On the other hand, one of the daughters of the Hill Farm tenant married John Rolfe's son up at Elmdon Bury, and Hill Farm was the smallest of the Elmdon farms while Elmdon Bury was the largest, so the practice was not invariable.

It is also noteworthy that by the time of his second marriage, Moses Prime had ceased to be a miller and small farmer and had become the tenant of over 300 acres, and his second wife came not from the ranks of the smaller farmers, to which he had formerly belonged, but was almost certainly the sister-in-law of John Rolfe at Elmdon Bury, which, as we have seen, was the largest farm in the parish. Furthermore, Moses Prime's daughter by his first wife married a grocer in Hoxton, an alliance which was similar in social standing to several other marriages of small farmers' daughters, while his daughter by his second wife, the sister-in-law of John Rolfe, married the tenant of the larger of the two Lofts Hall estate

144

farms in Chrishall, thus maintaining her position as a member of one of the larger farming families. For the Primes at least, social standing seems to have played an important part in the choice of a marriage partner.

Leaving aside the question of whether a farmer was a Lofts Hall estate tenant or not, how far did marriage take place between farmers and farmers' daughters? This was the case in ten out of the twenty-two marriages between 1800 and 1899 shown in figure 7, or 45 per cent, since seven of the men involved in the nine inter-estate marriages were themselves farmers. But more than half the marriages of farmers or their children were either to girls who were not farmers' daughters, or to men who worked in other occupations. Where did the farming families find their marriage partners outside farming?

A quick glance at figure 7 might well arouse surprise. For instance, how did the daughter of a small farmer in Elmdon meet a naturalist working in Edinburgh? What possible connection could there be between the tenants of Elmdon Bury and Duddenhoe End Farms and the family of an exciseman called Mason in Droitwich? We cannot give definite answers to these questions, but surmises may be made. For instance, John Rolfe's first wife died in 1844, leaving him with young children to look after. At the time of his second marriage, Miss Mason's place of residence was given as Elmdon Bury, and it seems very likely that she had come from Droitwich to work there as a housekeeper, or to take charge of the children, possibly in answer to an advertisement, and that the arrangement worked well enough to make it permanent. Once married, it would be only natural for her to invite her sister for a visit, and to introduce her to the young widower, Moses Prime. Miss Burton, from Hill Farm, might well have met her Edinburgh naturalist in much the same way, through taking a post in that city. Edinburgh might seem an unnecessarily long distance for her to travel, but she may possibly have been given an introduction to her prospective employers through the Elmdon-born Joseph Gamgee, who as we shall see in the next chapter had established himself and his family in Edinburgh and who, through his Veterinary School and his academic son-in-law, was likely to be in touch with scientists there. In both cases, the suggested answers depend on the mobility, not of the men, but the women. Daughters of small farmers, shopkeepers, or lower-paid officials, particularly if they were part of a large family, could not hope to remain at home until they married, as girls in the professional or landed classes did, but were expected to earn some kind of a living, even if only board and pocket money. As we saw in the last chapter, service in a private household, as a housekeeper, mother's help or governess, was an acceptable way of achieving this end. So, too, was taking employment as a schoolmistress, and as figure 7 shows, two girls who did this in Elmdon ended by marrying small farmers on the estate. In these cases, then, it was through the woman coming in to the man's environment, rather than the other way round, that acquaintance was first made, and in this respect, the marriage pattern of those concerned was very different from that of professional families such as the Fiskes.

Of course, there were several marriages in which both parties lived locally. In about 1862, for example, John Brand of Church Farm married the assistant in his uncle's grocery store in Chrishall, while both the Lofts Mill tenant who succeeded Moses Prime, and the Duddenhoe Grange tenant, married into the Monk family, who as we saw in the last chapter were Elmdon bakers. In Elmdon in the nineteenth century, marriage between the small farmers and shop-keeping families was by no means uncommon. This is not surprising, for if there was no room on the family farm or if no other tenancy were available, then a farmer's son was very likely to take up shop-keeping himself as an alternative way of earning a living. In addition, farming a small acreage and keeping a shop could run together, as they did for John Brand at Hill Farm.

The Lofts Hall estate lasted only twenty-seven years into the twentieth century, and no marriages of tenant farmers in Duddenhoe End were recorded in the Elmdon parish marriage register during that period. Figure 8 is therefore confined to showing the marriages of farming families in Elmdon village only, from 1900 to 1964, and to that extent it covers a smaller field than figure 7. Even so, the difference between the two diagrams is striking. First, and foremost, from 1900 onwards there was not a single marriage between one Elmdon farming family and another, whether estate tenants or owner-occupiers, while in the nineteenth century just over four out of every ten marriages fell into this category. Second, the percentage of marriages between farmers and farmers' daughters fell from 45 per cent between 1800 and 1899, to 29 per cent from 1900 to 1964. Finally, while both parties in nearly three-quarters of the nineteenth century marriages met each other while living in Elmdon, Chrishall or Wenden Lofts, only just under

Key   Each dotted line (⋮) represents one marriage between an Elmdon village farming family and an individual outside such families. There were no marriages between Elmdon village farming families, whether Lofts Hall estate tenants or not, during this period.

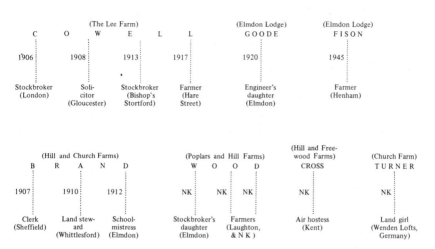

Sources: Elmdon parish marriage registers, 1900-64.
Elmdon survey, 1964.

Fig.   8   Diagram to show marriages of farming families, Elmdon village, 1900-64

three out of every ten did so in the twentieth century. There seems to be no clear reason why these sudden changes occurred, before transport facilities improved and while employment opportunities for women were still limited. One would expect the First World War to cause a social upheaval which would be felt in even the smallest village, but 43 per cent of the twentieth-century farming family marriages in Elmdon recorded in figure 8 took place before 1914. The depressed state of agriculture at the turn of the century might be thought to be a factor, making matches with other farming families less attractive, or it might be that the number of marriages being considered is too small to be representative of anything more than the special circumstances of a few individuals.

Non-farming occupations

We saw in the last chapter that there was a tendency for those born in Elmdon to be employed in the lesser jobs outside farming, while the majority of higher status occupations were filled by people coming in from outside. How far did these different occupational groups keep themselves to themselves, as the professional

147

class and, to a lesser extent, the farming families did during the nineteenth century, and how far did they overlap with other groups of a different status? Once again, did the turn of the century mark a break with long-established custom?

Details are known of fifty marriages in families living in Elmdon between 1800 and 1899 whose occupations lay outside the professions, farming, or labouring. In order to avoid breaking this total into a number of very small groups, table 39 (a) divides the marriages into two main categories, according to the type of family concerned. Group i covers those who may be assumed to have had a measure of independence in their own business or a degree of authority over others, namely shopkeepers and tradesmen, publicans and beer-sellers, heads of businesses, male head servants in private households, and schoolmistresses, and also includes their children. Group ii contains the employees of small businesses, lesser tradesmen and craftsmen, many of whom were employed directly by the farmers or the Lofts Hall estate, those with lower positions in private households, and their children.

A glance at table 39 (a) shows straight away that the two groups differed radically from each other. More than three-quarters of the Elmdon men and women in group i married spouses of equivalent standing, while only a quarter of those in group ii did so. Of the five exceptions in group i, two married into the small farmer

Table 39
(a) *Comparison of marriages of Elmdon village members of occupational groups i and ii and their children, by occupational grouping of spouse, 1800—99*

| | small-farmers | | Marriage to group i | | group ii | | labourers | | total |
	no.	%	no.	%	no.	%	no.	%	no.
Group i	2	9	17	77	2	9	1	5	22
Group ii	–	–	1	4	7	25	20	71	28

Group i contains shopkeepers, tradesmen, heads of businesses, male head servants in private households, and schoolmistresses, together with their children. In detail, the following occupations are covered: grocer, draper, baker, butcher, ironmonger, whitesmith, tailor, master plumber and glazier, master bricklayer, publican/beer-seller, owner or tenant of smithy and wheelwright's shop, butler, head gardener, schoolmistress. A marriage to the child of a farm bailiff is included in group i.

Group ii contains employees of small businesses, lesser tradesmen and craftsmen, those with lower positions in private households, and their children. It covers the occupations of employee blacksmith, employee bricklayer, carpenter, thatcher, painter, carrier, under-gardener, groom. Where a person holds more than one occupation, the highest status category has been used to classify him.

148

(b) *Marriages of Elmdon village members of occupational groups i and ii by place of residence of spouse, 1800–99*

| | Elmdon | | 0–5 | | 5–10 | | 10–20 | | over 20 | | not known | | total |
	no.	%	no.	%	no.	%	no.	%	no.	%	no.	%	no.
Group i	8	36	4	18	3	14	–	–	4	18	3	14	22
Group ii	21	75	5	18	1	4	–	–	1	4	–	–	28

place of residence of spouse at time of marriage within a radius in miles of

Source: Elmdon and Wenden Lofts marriage registers, 1800–99.

class, which could be considered a slight upward move socially, while the remaining three, who married down either into group ii or into the farm-worker class, were all the children of a publican who himself had risen to that position from being an agricultural labourer. The great majority of those in group ii, by contrast, married downwards into the labouring class, and only one upward marriage was made, by a carpenter who married a baker's daughter. The picture emerges of, on the one hand, a small group of shop-keepers, master craftsmen and head-servants who, together with their children, took considerable pains to marry others with a similar background, often having to go outside Elmdon in order to do so; and on the other, a larger group of lesser employees whose choice of partners was widened by a willingness to marry into the labouring class which formed the majority of Elmdon's population.

Table 39 (b) shows the extent to which each group found their marriage partners within Elmdon itself, and once again the contrast between the two groups is marked. In group i, both partners were living in Elmdon at the time of the wedding in 36 per cent of the marriages, but in group ii, the proportion rose to three-quarters. This is not surprising, as by restricting themselves to spouses of equal standing, group i members had only a small pool of suitable partners available within Elmdon itself, while group ii, by marry-ing into the labouring class, considerably widened its area of choice within the village.

As an illustration of the rather rigid marriage pattern of members of group i in the nineteenth century, let us look at the family of William Crisp, the grocer, draper and postmaster. Four of his five daughters grew up and were married in Elmdon church. Mary, the eldest, was 26 at the time of her wedding to William Curtis of Streatham. Her husband was not only a draper, like her own father, but was the son of a draper. We do not know how they met, but Mary may well have left Elmdon before marriage to work

149

as a draper's assistant in Streatham, having gained experience in this position in her father's shop. At all events, after marriage she and her husband disappeared from Elmdon, presumably to live near London.

The next daughter, Martha, married at 25. Her husband was a baker, as was her father-in-law, and came from Falkenden. She too left Elmdon after marriage. Eliza, next in age below Martha, in 1878 had to watch her younger sister, Juliana, marry while she herself was still single. Juliana's husband was an ironmonger called Robert Wabon. Like his brothers-in-law, he followed the same occupation as his father who was also an ironmonger. Although he may have come to live in Elmdon at some time after 1871, there is no evidence that he set up a business there, and it seems likely that he and his bride left Elmdon soon after they were married, although their destination is not known. Eliza, as the only unmarried daughter, was left with her widowed mother to keep the shop and post office going. As we saw in the last chapter, five years later her mother died, and within a few months she married George Wabon, a worker in soft metals and the brother of Juliana's husband, who joined her in running her Elmdon business. By then Eliza was 35 years old, and it is at least a possibility that this marriage resulted from her acquisition of the property, and that the two families concerned, already closely connected through the marriage of Juliana and Robert, viewed the arrangement as both suitable and convenient.

The patterns shown in the Crisp girls' marriages were common to almost all members of group i. In the majority of cases, the bridegroom was following the same occupation as his father had done; and just as only one of William Crisp's four married daughters remained in Elmdon, so most of the girls who married husbands of similar social standing had to go outside Elmdon to find a husband. Indeed, the only case of a marriage between two members of group i who were actually born in Elmdon, as opposed to those who had been living there for a period, occurred when James Walters, the tailor, married Ann Thurgood, daughter of the butler and cook-housekeeper at Lofts Hall. Even the brother-sister marriage of the Crisps and Wabons was paralleled in the Brand family, as we saw in the last chapter, when Isabella Cowell, née Brand, the widow of a butcher, married another butcher whose brother had married Isabella's sister Lucy some seventeen years earlier.

150

Table 40

(a) *Comparison of marriages of Elmdon village members of occupational groups i and ii and their children, by occupational grouping of spouse, 1900–64*

	group i		group ii		farm workers		total
	no.	%	no.	%	no.	%	no.
Group i	4	44	3	33	2	22	9
Group ii	–	–	6	40	9	60	15

To group i occupations listed in table 39 (a) above should be added chemist, chauffeur, and non-commissioned officer in the RAF.

To group ii occupations listed in table 39 (a) above should be added police constable, lorry driver, gamekeeper, seaman, and local organist.

(b) *Marriages of Elmdon village members of occupational groups i and ii by place of residence of spouse, 1900–64*

	Elmdon		0–5		5–10		10–20		over 20		not known		total
	no.	%	no.	%	no.	%	no.	%	no.	%	no.	%	no.
Group i	5	56	2	22	–	–	–	–	2	22	–	–	9
Group ii	8	53	5	33	–	–	–	–	1	7	1	7	15

Source: Elmdon marriage register, 1900–64

How far did these patterns continue into the twentieth century? A difficulty arises here in that only nine marriages for Elmdon residents in group i were recorded between 1900 and 1964, and this is really too small a number to be treated statistically. However, the very scarcity of marriages reinforces what we learnt from the preceding chapter, namely that a large proportion of the small family businesses disappeared during the period, and large domestic staffs with head servants became a thing of the past. Nevertheless, for the sake of comparison, table 40 (a) sets out the proportion of marriages in groups i and ii to members of various occupational groups. It shows that during the twentieth century, the majority of members of group i living in Elmdon no longer took their partners from their own category, but married downwards either into group ii or the farm-labouring class. In fact, the pattern of group i and group ii members was almost identical, with between 55 per cent and 60 per cent of marriages in each category being downwards to members of the group or groups below. As table 40 (b) shows, this similarity extended to the place of residence of the spouse as well, since around half the Elmdon members of both groups met their marriage partner in the parish.

151

But while group i members therefore showed a very definite change in marriage patterns, as the farmers had done, group ii continued much the same as in the nineteenth century.

As we saw at the beginning of this section, it was in group ii in the nineteenth century that most of the Elmdon-born workers and their families were to be found, while in group i, those born outside the parish predominated. It would therefore appear that the largely Elmdon-born group maintained its marriage patterns almost unchanged throughout the period of 164 years which we have been considering, with a considerable degree of intermarriage between itself and the families of farmworkers taking place, while the rigid pattern set in the nineteenth century by members of group i, in which those coming into Elmdon from outside predominated, broke down in the twentieth century. This might suggest that in the nineteenth century there was an 'insider - outsider' position similar to that described in so many present-day studies of villages, and that in marrying into their own category, group i members were able to keep themselves at arms' length from what might even then be termed 'the old Elmdon families'. First-hand evidence of such attitudes from the nineteenth century is lacking, but the words of an elderly widow talking to one of her young relatives in the 1930s may be of interest. She and her husband, neither of them Elmdoners, had come to the village towards the end of the previous century to run a small business, and she had stayed on after her husband's death. Noticing that the old lady seemed to have few friends and never stopped in the street for a conversation with passers-by, her young relative asked her why she did not talk to the other people in the village where she had lived so long. She replied 'Oh, I couldn't do that, they're villagers you see — just villagers.' And again, 'I might say "good morning" or whatever the time of day, but not talk, because they are only villagers, you know.' Elmdoners continued to touch their caps to her, but outside her own family, her only real contact was with the wife of the publican at the King's Head.

Even though the marriage pattern of group i changed abruptly in the twentieth century, the break in the way of life which the marriages indicate was neither as sudden nor as absolute as it might appear to be, since individuals established in Elmdon in the nineteenth century lived on into the twentieth and carried their attitudes with them, as did the elderly widow who has just been described. The Wabons, for example, are still remembered as 'an

152

old-fashioned couple - real old characters', while conversations with Elmdoners today often reveal evidence of mutual visiting and discussion of common affairs among small shopkeepers and businessmen from outside the village who have chosen to retire there. Some of these families still show a pattern of occupation and marriage very similar to that obtaining in the nineteenth century. A recent example, taken from the early 1970s, is of a man working in the drapery business who came to live in Elmdon with his parents when his father retired from running a credit drapery store. This man's grandfather, a butcher in Thaxted, had been apprenticed to Elmdon's butcher in the 1860s, and his recent marriage was to the widow of another butcher.

To sum up, then, during the nineteenth century there was a strong tendency for the landowning and professional classes on the one hand, and the higher status shopkeepers, tradesmen, business heads and head private servants of group i on the other, to marry within their own occupational group. This was only to be expected of the Squire, who through his wealth lived on a completely different scale to anyone else in the parish and who, by his distribution of church patronage, was able to select congenial clerical families to fill the benefices of Elmdon, Wenden Lofts, and Gt Chishill. In the case of group i, many members had come in from outside Elmdon and therefore had kin and contacts in other places. As we saw in the last chapter, it was not uncommon for this class to move from one locality to another. George Hopwood the butcher, for example, who was born in Hinxton, worked in London and Arkesden before arriving in Elmdon, while William Crisp, born in Cambridgeshire, had lived in Saffron Walden for a time before he settled into his shop in the High Street. It would not be surprising if these people felt themselves to be different from the long-established Elmdon families, and preserved their identity by marrying into similar families who more often than not lived outside the parish.

The farmers, on the other hand, had longer-standing links with Elmdon and the land, and once they acquired a tenancy it was likely to remain in their family for two or more generations, as we saw in chapter 3. Roughly two out of three of the Lofts Hall estate farmers in 1860 had been born in the estate parishes of Elmdon, Wenden Lofts or Chrishall, the others coming in from within a five-mile radius, and it would have been difficult for them to feel apart from the community, employing as they did such a large

153

percentage of its work force. Their family networks outside the three parishes were more limited than those of group i, and this is reflected in the fact that nearly three-quarters of their nineteenth-century marriages were to people living in either Elmdon, Wenden Lofts or Chrishall. Conversely, the tendency to marry into the same occupational group was less marked than in the case of the professional class and group i, for under half of the nineteenth-century marriages took place between families of Lofts Hall estate tenants, and slightly fewer between farmers and farmer's daughters. It looks as if the field of choice locally was too narrow to allow the farming families to marry entirely within their own group. They met this situation by marrying members of non-farming families who were living locally, whereas the shopkeeper class reacted to a similar situation by marrying into a family of comparable status living outside.

The farming families' tendency to choose marriage partners living locally was just as pronounced among the lesser craftsmen and tradesmen of group ii. Three-quarters of the marriage partners chosen by this group were living in Elmdon parish, and in only 8 per cent of the marriages did the partner come from more than five miles away. But marriage to members of families of comparable occupational standing was quite infrequent, covering only a quarter of the group's marriages. In the majority of cases, a partner was selected from the labouring class, and it looks as if remaining part of the Elmdon community was more important than maintaining occupational status. In any event, most of the lesser craftsmen worked for the farmers, or for the Lofts Hall estate, and would be in constant contact with the farm labourers, both at work and in the local public houses and beer-shops in the evenings. While the priority with the professional and landowning class and the members of group i was to marry a person from a comparable occupational group, in the case of the farmers and the members of group ii more importance was given to marrying someone who was already part of Elmdon or its immediate neighbourhood.

With the advent of the twentieth century, changes in these patterns occurred in the farming families and in group i, although group ii continued much as before. The farming families ceased to marry between themselves, and the percentage of farmers marrying farmer's daughters declined. The proportion of marriages to partners living locally dropped from over seven out of ten to under three out of ten. In short, the farmers' families became much less Elmdon-oriented in their choice of marriage partner. No doubt the dispersal of the Lofts Hall estate and the arrival of new families of owner-occupiers accelerated this trend, but it was already present in the marriages which took place before the sale of 1927.

While farming families were beginning to look outwards from Elmdon, group i families seem to have followed the opposite course. Over half their recorded marriages were to partners living in the parish, and 55 per cent were downwards to members of group ii or to farm labourers. The total number of marriages involved is so small, however, that it would not be justifiable to draw hard and fast conclusions from them.

8
Status and social mobility

Social roles in Elmdon

In earlier chapters we have seen how the different occupational groups in Elmdon contributed to the economic life of the village, and we have looked at all but the labourers in terms of their social backgrounds and their marriages. Nothing, however, has yet been said of the part each group played in the running of village affairs, whether by giving orders or by carrying them out. This question is covered in detail for the period following the sale of the Lofts Hall estate in the companion volume *Kinship at the core*. Here it is proposed to consider the matter only up until 1927, when the break-up of the estate began.

The Squire

'He lived and died among his people, being born and bred among them and only leaving his home for the purposes of education . . .' These words, from the obituary of the Rev. Robert Fiske Wilkes published in *The Guardian* on 26 November 1879, epitomise the almost princely role played by the Squires of Elmdon and Wenden Lofts in the nineteenth and early twentieth centuries. Even in 1964, old men and women, asked to name the important people in the village during their childhood, would simply say 'the Squire'.

Owners of Lofts Hall before Robert Fiske Wilkes inherited it in 1858, that is to say, members of the Wilkes family proper, had played a part in affairs well outside the boundaries of their estate, for two of them had served as High Sheriffs of Essex, and one as Deputy Lord Lieutenant of the county. Robert Fiske Wilkes, however, as his obituary suggests, confined his activities to running his estate and to fulfilling his duties to his parishioners, and neither his son nor his grandson, the last two in the line of squires, held any office other than that of Justice of the Peace.

156

Although Robert Fiske Wilkes was the only Lofts Hall estate owner to fulfil the dual role of squire and parson, his predecessors and successors were closely connected with the churches of Wenden Lofts, Elmdon and Gt Chishill in that, as we saw in the last chapter, they held the livings in their gift. This position continued, in fact, until 1928, when the last Squire sold the Advowson to Harrogate College. Later, in 1940, the Martyrs Memorial and Church of England Trust was appointed as Trustee of the Advowson, and thus became responsible for the appointment of Elmdon's Vicar.[1]

The Squire's interest in the churches, however, was not confined to choosing the clergy. The John Wilkes who died in 1848 was particularly concerned with the fabric of the church buildings, as tablets in St Dunstan's at Wenden Lofts and St Nicholas's in Elmdon confirm. In the former case, the inscription runs 'The old church was taken down and this one erected at the sole expense of John Wilkes, esquire, of Lofts Hall in the year of our Lord 1845 and 1846', while the message on the marble slab in the belfry tower of Elmdon church is even more specific, stating 'The Tower of this Church was effectually restored from its dilapidated state and improved by John Wilkes, Esq., of Lofts Hall, by an outlay of £662 1s 3d . . .' The next Squire, the Rev. Robert Fiske Wilkes, dismayed by the lack of a church in Duddenhoe End, converted one of the hamlet's barns into a place of worship, and also set in hand the rebuilding of the chancel of Elmdon church, although this was financed by subscriptions. These were officially voluntary, but if folk memory is correct, it seems that considerable, and much resented, pressure was brought to bear on local farmers, as the better-off members of the community, to give adequate donations.

As principal landowner in Elmdon, the Squire was in a position to affect not only the lives of his tenant farmers through his power to renew or terminate their leases, but to alter the physical appearance of the land surrounding the village. The survey of the estate carried out in 1860[2] makes it clear that the tenant farmers were not free to do just as they liked with the land they rented, but had to gain the Squire's permission first. 'The pieces of land nos. 263 - 268', wrote the surveyor, referring to a farm in the Duddenhoe End area 'are all small grass closes . . . The quality of the grass is very inferior . . . I therefore recommend that the Tenant be allowed to break up the whole of these fields and lay them into no. 262'. Furthermore the Squire felt quite free to make suggestions to his tenants which he expected to be adopted. 'Much improvement might be made on this Farm and George Nottage's land adjoining', states the surveyor, 'by stubbing up one or two small Groves and wide hedgerows situate between Grass Fields . . . In doing this, the ornamental Trees might be left standing in the Pastures. The Tenant should also be induced to reduce the size of the hedgerows and stub up the Bushes now allowed to grow in wide borders round the Pastures.' In this way, the pattern of fields and hedges around Elmdon was gradually modified.

As we saw in chapter 1, the Squire was responsible for the housing of nearly half Elmdon's population. Repairs to cottages could be expensive in relation to the rents received. In 1887, for example, one cottager paid an annual rent of £3 10s 0d, but against this was set the cost of repairs to a window, thatching the roof, insurance and a stamp on the lease which, together with the cost of the tenant's place at the annual rent dinner, came to £10 10s 3d[3]. New buildings were also needed from time to time. Soon after the last Squire, Jack Wilkes, removed to Elmdon Bury in 1906, he built a cottage for his farm foreman, costing £174 3s 8d, and a house for his bailiff for which he paid £388 9s 7d, a considerable sum in those days.[4]

The Squire incurred further responsibilities as an employer of labour, beyond paying wages and keeping rented cottages in repair. In 1895, for instance, the estate was paying pensions to three widows and to a retired coachman,[5] and in 1927, several of the cottages put up for sale were subject to life tenancies, rent free, for the occupants.[6]

Beyond his own tenants and employees, the Squire felt obligations towards the village as a whole. His subscription list for 1895[7] shows that he was contributing to clothing clubs in Chrishall and Elmdon, coal clubs in Elmdon and Duddenhoe End, the Wenden Lofts and Elmdon cricket club, the Foresters club, the Elmdon church choir, the Elmdon chimers, the handbell ringers, the bellringers, and the Elmdon harvest service; while outside these villages he supported Arkesden charities, Saffron Walden's hospital and horticultural society, the Agricultural Benevolent Society, and the Society for Promoting Christian Knowledge. The largest contribution, however, went to the Elmdon, Chrishall and Wenden Lofts schools.

As we saw in chapter 1, free education had been available from the foundation of Thomas Crawley's grammar school in 1559 until a new school was built in 1844. From then until 1891 a charge of a penny a week for each pupil was made, but children from all the different occupational groups attended, with the exception of the Squire's own children and those of the wealthiest farmers who employed governesses for their daughters and sent their sons to boarding school. However rigidly the parents might keep to their own occupational class, their children learned their lessons and repeated their tables together in the two-roomed schoolhouse, and farmers' children as well as their labourers' sons and daughters were reported as failing to make sufficient progress in their lessons or as breaking the school rules.[8] Robert Fiske Wilkes's own grand-children attended the school for a time, when their father was Vicar of Elmdon in the 1870s, and the various squires displayed considerable interest in it. This interest ranged from providing the land for the new building, to buying the used coal dust from the school's stove,[9] and the Squire frequently visited the classrooms, noting the progress of promising pupils. Jack Wilkes, for instance, tried to arrange for a particularly bright boy to enter a solicitor's office in Saffron Walden when he left school, although the boy in question had other ideas and managed to join the army.

Elmdon school group, c. 1907

159

The Squire was not only interested in the education of the children, he also provided entertainment for their parents. Old people in Elmdon in 1964 remembered attending concerts in the school to which Jack Wilkes would bring performers from Chesterford and even Cambridge, or going to dances held in the Squire's grounds, the proceeds being given to the church. On the occasion of the twenty-first birthday of the last Squire, Jack Wilkes, the whole village was invited to the birthday celebrations.

The Squire expected a certain return in exchange for his efforts on behalf of the village. First-hand accounts from those who remember the days before 1927, or who have had stories handed on to them by their parents, refer only to the last Squire, but it seems that his main requirements were respect and obedience. In the days before he had a motorcar, he expected to be saluted by the children as he passed through the village, and he reported any shortcomings in this regard to their parents. It could also be a dangerous matter to disagree with him, as his reaction to the attempt to form a branch of the National Union of Farm Workers, described in chapter 4, shows. It is only fair to say, however, that there are no accounts of anyone having finally lost their job as a result of an argument with him, although there is evidence that on one occasion he dismissed a man who later had to beg for his job back. He is said never to have forgiven the Squire for the humiliation which he felt he had suffered, going to the lengths of refusing to attend church during the Squire's lifetime, because the latter would be there, and continuing to absent himself after the Squire's death on the grounds that there was a memorial tablet to him erected in the building. Some people resented the degree of power which the Squire held — 'You couldn't go out of your back door without first asking the Squire' said one — but others felt differently. 'He was a good man, and would help if he could' was one comment, while a farm worker remembered him as 'a wonderful man', riding over the fields in his hunting pink. His aunt, who brought him up after his parents' death, was recollected as being 'very severe, but if she heard of anyone in want she would do something about it'. She, too, shared in the duties which fell to the Squire and his family, and used to hold annual tea-parties for the confirmation candidates, to each of whom she would present a little book. One Elmdon resident remembers that her book was called *Thoughts worth Thinking*, while the year before her sister had received *Leaves worth Turning*.

160

Tea at Elmdon Bury, c 1907. Jack Wilkes with two of his sisters and his Aunt Maggie (left)

The clergy

Elmdon was always predominantly a 'church' village. In 1829 Robert Fiske, the Vicar of Elmdon, recorded that, while no place had been built or set apart for Non-conformist worship, 'some of the dissenting ministers in the neighbourhood occasionally preach in a barn or private house'.[10] It was a different matter in Duddenhoe End, where in the same year congregations of eighty or so Dissenters were meeting in a licensed barn,[11] and it is possible that Elmdon villagers at that time who felt drawn to Non-conformism joined them there. Later on in the nineteenth century, it seems that a chapel existed for a time next to Baker's Cottage, now the village stores, but no one living in Elmdon in 1964 remembered it personally. In general, the vicar remained the undisputed representative of organised religion.

A few years after Robert Fiske Wilkes's son-in-law relinquished the Elmdon living to return to Rochdale in 1880, the Rev. Brabant-Smith arrived in the village. He was still there in 1927. Elmdon was fortunate in being served for more than forty years by a vicar who seems to have been universally liked and who also happened to be a first-class cricketer. Even so, he captained the village second team, while the Squire, a lesser player, led the first eleven. The vicar might visit his parishioners weekly, while his wife visited all the women who had babies, and villagers would go to him if they wanted to start clubs, or if they needed to go to hospital, but when it came to organising fêtes or entertainments in aid of the church, it was the Squire who took the lead.

Tenants of Lofts Hall

As we saw in chapter 3, Lofts Hall was let to tenants from 1905 until the sale of the estate. As befitted the occupants of such a large house, the tenants were wealthy, far wealthier indeed than the Squire, who was suffering at the time from a reduced rent roll and who had to provide for five sisters.

We do not know whether the Squire and his tenants were always on good terms, but clearly there were times when the latter saw their role in the village as very similar to his. For instance, within a year of their arrival Sir James Bailey and his daughter presented Elmdon with a Reading Room, a small brick building centrally situated across the village green from the church, where the girls could attend cookery, needlework and laundry classes, while the boys, for a fee of 2d a night, played billiards and held boxing contests 'with a proper ring, and gloves — we could do what we liked in there'. Some Elmdoners remembered that Sir James would have the children up to the Hall and give each of them a jug of broth, with plenty of meat in it. He also put on a fete one year, with an exhibition of garden produce, and later visited Ted Gamgee's plot, commenting on the neatness of the rows of lettuces, onions and beetroot. Lady Bailey, like the Squire, would visit Wenden Lofts school, and gave the children presents.[12] But not all the actions of the Baileys were well-received. Great opposition was aroused when Lady Bailey tried to close the footpath alongside the avenue leading up to the Hall, and the villagers refused to sign the petition for closure which was presented to them. There is, in fact, no reason to believe that the presence of the Baileys lessened the Squire's authority in the eyes of the village.

Sir James died in 1910 while having a Turkish bath in London, and his lease ran out two years later. The next tenants, who used the Hall largely for shooting parties, were Americans, and although they must have had a considerable effect on the prosperity of the tenants of the Wilkes Arms, whom they used as caterers, they did not participate in village affairs as the Baileys had done.

162

The farmers and shopkeepers

Like the Squire, his tenants at Lofts Hall, and the clergy, the farmers and shopkeepers felt themselves obliged to give to the village in money and in kind over and above what the law demanded of them, their contributions varying according to their income. Charles Rolfe, the tenant of Elmdon Bury, for instance, provided a tea for the schoolchildren each Christmas, highlighted by the distribution of sausage rolls, while Edwin Goode, the steam-plough contractor, made sure that every old person in the village received a present of coal or tea. Members of this group contributed 'voluntary' subscriptions to such charities as the church cleaning fund, ranging from Charles Rolfe's £2 2s 0d to 5 shillings each from the shopkeepers, blacksmith and wheelwright, and 2 shillings from the publican at the Carrier. In return, like the Squire, they expected a measure of respect and they saw themselves as being in a different category from the rest of the villagers. One way in which their higher status was recognised was by the allocation of reserved pews in church. 'Of course, they were privileged' said a farm worker's wife in the 1960s, but there must have been occasions·when the less well-off among them, faced with yet another subscription list, felt that the privilege had been paid for.

When it came to running village affairs, however, the major role of this group lay in the work they did for the Vestry, and its later replacement, the Parish Council. As we saw in chapter 1, in 1861 all the officers of the Vestry but one were farmers, the exception being a shopkeeper. The churchwardens were elected by the Vestry itself, but the constable, surveyors of highways, and overseers of the poor were appointed by the local Justices of the Peace, and the body as a whole was in no sense representative of all the inhabitants of the parish.[13] The most important duty of the Vestry was the assessment, collection and allocation of rates for parish relief, but the Elmdon Vestry minute book for the last half of the nineteenth century[14] shows that members dealt with a variety of other matters. For example, they examined the churchwardens' accounts, set up voluntary funds for church repairs (on the strict understanding that none of the money so raised should be used in payment of official fees) and, when faced with the need to elect members to serve on a local committee on school attendance under the provisions of the 1876 Education Act, chose the Vicar, the Squire and a leading farmer to fill the vacancies. When the Lofts Hall estate offered half-an-acre for the enlargement of the churchyard, they gratefully accepted and set up a sub-committee comprising two farmers and the blacksmith to oversee the work and raise the £16 0s 0d needed to pay for it.

In 1894 the Vestry was replaced by the Parish Council. A major difference between the two bodies was that Parish Council members stood for election, and this change was reflected in the composition of the first council, since it comprised three farm workers as well as three farmers and a blacksmith.[15] By 1897, two of the farm workers had dropped off the council, though whether this was through declining enthusiasm on the part of the electorate, or of the members themselves, or for some other reason, it is not possible to say. The third, George Greenhill, however, was still serving on the council in 1910, and although farm workers were never in the majority, their voice could at least be heard. Furthermore, there was presumably no reason why they should not have supplied a majority on the council if they had been prepared to stand and the electorate, of whom the lesser craftsmen and labourers made up the greater number, had so chosen. As it was, in the day-to-day matters of running the village the farmers played the major role, helped to a lesser extent by the shopkeepers and small business heads.

The lesser craftsmen and the farm workers

The groups we have looked at so far, though important in running Elmdon's affairs, were numerically small. The lesser craftsmen and the farm workers made up the great majority of the working population − more than eight out of every ten, in 1861. Their low wages precluded them giving money to the various fund-raising activities; none of them served on the vestry, and only a few were elected to the parish council.

At first sight, the social roles for which this group were cast would seem to be twofold − first, to be recipients of the benefits bestowed upon them by the more prosperous members of the community, and second, to be an audience before whose eyes the more powerful members of village society played their parts. Nevertheless, the lesser craftsmen and farm workers had another overwhelmingly important function in village affairs: they did the work. When one of the Elmdon Bury barns caught on fire, it would have been completely destroyed if the villagers had not turned out to keep the flames in check until the fire brigade could be summoned, and the Squire recognised the value of their action by giving them a special dinner in thanks. Miss Wilkes's hostel, which she set up in one of the Lofts Hall lodges in order to train females for posts in domestic service, required *de facto* a supply of girls willing to attend. The names of farm workers and their wives might not appear on subscription lists, but they figured largely when necessary tasks, such as cleaning the church, cutting its hedges, clearing out its gutters, and laundering its surplices were allocated. These were the people who rang the church bells, blew the organ, wound the clock and lit the boilers, and though some of the work was paid for, other activities were undertaken voluntarily.

A good illustration of the roles played by these different groups in dealing with an unusual event may be found in the minutes of the Vestry meetings held in 1887 to determine the best way of celebrating Queen Victoria's golden jubilee.

The first meeting opened with the chairman reading two letters from the Squire setting out his proposals for the occasion. These included the gift of 2s 6d to all people of the Queen's age and upwards; the provision of a tea for the women and children; and a dinner to be given to the labourers if funds allowed. He himself would subscribe £10 0s 0d, his mother £5 0s 0d and Miss Wilkes '10 shillings with the offer of personal assistance'.

Various alternative suggestions were then put forward, including one that the men, women and children should all have a tea, and another that employers of labour should give their workmen a dinner on the employer's premises, the unemployed joining them with financial support from the general fund. In the end, generosity prevailed and it was decided that a communal dinner would be held, preceded by a special service in Elmdon parish church with bell-ringing, and followed by a cricket match between Elmdon and Duddenhoe End. There would be other sports such as foot-racing, leaping and tug-of-war, and prizes would be provided from the general fund. Tea would be served at five o'clock, and the celebrations would close with a display of fireworks.

Principles decided, the second meeting of the Vestry proceeded to work out the detailed organisation. The Squire provided the venue for the dinner, which was to be held in the Hunting Park. The farmers, shopkeepers and heads of businesses arranged for the food supply, with the publicans producing two pints of beer for each man, and the Elmdon bakers and shopkeepers providing bread. Responsibility for the cooking of 500 pounds of meat was divided between a publican and a baker who looked after the roasting beef; a farmer who would arrange for the boiled beef, and the village blacksmith who would be responsible for the mutton. Potatoes would be boiled in a copper in the high pasture and Mrs Wilkes would supply pepper, mustard and salt. Only one outstanding question remained, minuted despairingly as 'Puddings: who will cook?'

Mr Housden, the wheelwright, was appointed secretary and Mr Negus, the carpenter, and Mr Greenhill, the baker, were made foremen of the work committee. Twenty-four labourers, together with an indeterminate number of 'lads in regular work', were to be asked to help in putting up a stage for the entertainment, in return for a pint of beer each, paid for from the general fund. Thus the Squire proposed action and contributed money and accommodation; the farmer and shopkeeper members of the Vestry made decisions and took executive responsibility, as well as subscribing; and the farm workers fulfilled their normal role as recipients, audience and providers of labour.

Very little change in the way things were run had occurred when peace celebrations were being planned after the First World War, over thirty years later. The special committee set up to deal with this event was larger than the Vestry meeting, and it included the Squire, but its male membership still consisted of the farmers, shopkeepers, heads of businesses and head servants, and excluded the labouring class. It did, however, have a number of women members, of similar social standing to the men, and to that extent signs of progress were present.

Peace celebrations at Lofts Hall after the First World War

Social mobility in the nineteenth century

It is not difficult to imagine a service in Elmdon church in the 1860s at which the Squire, in his role of vicar, and a cross-section of village society joined without a second thought in singing the verse from the hymn 'All things bright and beautiful' which goes

> The rich man in his castle,
> The poor man at his gate,
> God made them, high or lowly,
> And order'd their estate.

Nevertheless, it was by no means impossible to rise or fall, even if only a short distance, in the social scale. As we saw in chapter 7, the Fiskes were remarkably stable throughout the century, but in the large family of the Rev. Robert Fiske of Fulbourn the two younger sons did not follow professional careers, but were apprenticed to farmers. Once he had learned the business, the elder of the two became, not an owner-occupier, but a tenant farmer of only 230 acres[16], which by Elmdon standards only just brought him out of the small farmer category, while the younger, disliking farming, became a tea merchant. Both these young men married the daughters, not of professional men as their brothers and cousins did, but of a wine merchant — well-to-do no doubt, but certainly associated with trade.

Tenant farmers, on the other hand, would make efforts to buy land of their own, and in Wenden Lofts in 1871 James Rolfe, who rented Hope and Home Farms from the Lofts Hall estate, was described in the census not only as a farmer, but as a land-owner as well. As we have seen, however, there was often no room for younger sons of the smaller farmers on the land, and they therefore had to leave the farming class and become shopkeepers or tradesmen. Sometimes a determined young man could reverse the position. As we shall see in the Brand family history which follows, by the early nineteenth century William Brand had left Elmdon for Chrishall, where he became in turn schoolmaster, shopkeeper, and tenant farmer, managing to acquire quite an amount of house property on the way.

As chapter 7 showed, throughout the nineteenth century the shopkeepers and small business heads managed to maintain their social position to a very marked degree, while the children of lesser craftsmen and tradesmen were not only much more likely to ally themselves with the families of farm workers, but in the case of the sons, frequently became agricultural labourers them-

167

selves. Occasionally an individual would rise from the labouring class, like James Baker who became tenant publican of the King's Arms, and was later able to buy Baker's Cottage and set up his own beer-shop there. The most dramatic example of all, however, was that of Joseph Gamgee. He started work in 1809, when he was 8, at Elmdon Bury, but he had such an aptitude for working with horses that at 15 years old he left the farm for a job with the Hertfordshire Hunt, and from there moved on to Sicily to look after the hunters and race horses of Prince Petrullo, a large land-owner. He saved enough money in Sicily to return, on foot, to England and enter himself as a student of the London Veterinary College of St Pancras, and he gained his diploma in 1823, with the assurance of the authorities that 'no Student had come up under more disadvantages of early education and none had passed with Greater distinction'. He returned to Italy and set up a veterinary practice in Florence, but by 1861, he was settled in Edinburgh, a renowned expert on the causes of lameness in horses, helping his son John to run the New Edinburgh Veterinary College. Another son, named Joseph like his father, became Professor of Surgery at Birmingham University, and the author of standard works on fractures and wounds. A third son was appointed Professor of Physiology at Manchester University and was made an FRS at the age of 31, and a grandson, D'Arcy Wentworth Thompson, became an internationally famous biologist, holding the position of Professor of Natural History in St Andrews University for a record sixty-four years.[17]

Such cases were rare. In general, Elmdon society in the nine-teenth century was remarkably stable, and usually such movement as there was disturbed only the fringes of the different occupational categories.

The Brand family

The Brands of Elmdon first appear in the records in 1556, when Richard Brand made his will,[18] and they may well have been established in the village for many years before that; Elmdon's parish registers do not go back farther than 1618, and it is only after that date that it is possible to trace the history of the family in any detail. Although the Brands were exceptional in that no other family of farmers and craftsmen maintained themselves in Elmdon for such a long period, their case history may be used to show some of the ways in which different branches of the same family could rise and fall in the social scale.

The blacksmith Brands

The family tree, figure 9, begins with the John Brand whose will[19] was proved in 1683. He was a blacksmith and shopkeeper, and as he signed his will with a mark instead of a signature, it would seem that he was a man who had acquired a respectable amount of property without the benefit of much formal education. He left to his wife Hannah 'two houses in Elmdon, with two shops and all other outhouses'. After her death, his own house was to go to his elder son John and his heirs, while the younger son, Robert, was to receive the second house, together with the neighbouring shop and smithy and adjoining copyhold land, provided that both sons paid their sister, Susannah Godfrey, the sum of £20 0s 0d within a year of the death of their mother. Susannah herself was left her parents' feather bed and bedding. So here is the first appearance of the Brands as blacksmiths, shopkeepers and small farmers, roles which, as we have seen in earlier chapters, some of them were to continue to fill right into the twentieth century.

It is likely that the elder son, John (see line 2 of the tree), had already established himself in Chrishall, a mile-and-a-half from Elmdon, by the time of his father's death, which may account for the younger son, Robert, being left the Elmdon smithy. At all events, John and his wife Mary had at least four children, three of whom were baptised in Chrishall and one of whom was buried there, although Ellen, who died when she was only 24, was buried in Elmdon. John himself died in Chrishall in 1721 and is described in the burial register of that parish as 'Old John Brand'. Unfortunately there is no record either in the Elmdon or Chrishall baptismal registers of the John Brand (line 3) who is shown in the tree as probably being John and Mary's son. Nevertheless, we know that he lived for part of his adult life in Elmdon, filling the office of churchwarden, and as there is no record of his likely uncle Robert either marrying or having children, it could be that he ended by inheriting property both from Old John Brand in Chrishall and from Robert in Elmdon.

The probability that the Brands owned property and land both in Chrishall and Elmdon during the seventeenth century becomes a certainty by the time generation 4 on the tree is reached, for John,

169

Fig. 9 Brand family

THE BRAND FAMILY

Key Names in capitals are of Brands who spent much of
their lives in Elmdon

The underlining of a date – e.g. b.<u>1767</u> – indicates that the event was recorded in the Elmdon
parish registers

The underlining of an individual indicates an Elmdon
connection through birth, occupation or landholding.

A broken horizontal line indicates that the relationship
is only a possibility and has not been proved.

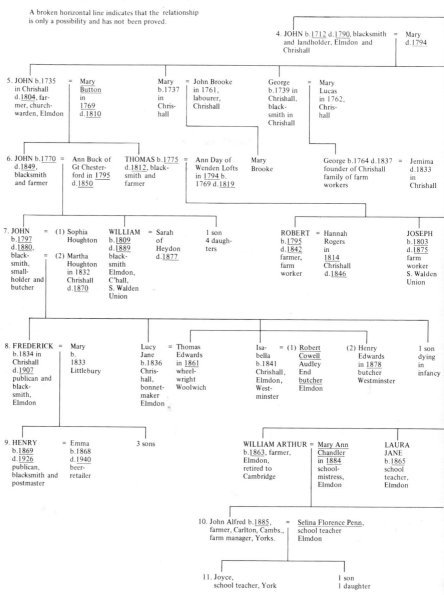

4. JOHN b.<u>1712</u> d.<u>1790</u>, blacksmith = Mary
and landholder, Elmdon and   d.<u>1794</u>
Chrishall

5. JOHN b.1735 = Mary   Mary = John Brooke   George = Mary
in Chrishall   <u>Button</u>   b.1737 in 1761,   b.1739 in Lucas
d.<u>1804</u>, far- in   in   labourer,   Chrishall, in 1762,
mer, church-   <u>1769</u>   Chris- Chrishall   black-   Chris-
warden, Elmdon d.<u>1810</u> hall   smith in   hall
                                                      Chrishall

6. JOHN b.<u>1770</u> = Ann Buck of   THOMAS b.<u>1775</u> = Ann Day of   Mary   George b.1764 d.1837 = Jemima
d.<u>1849</u>,   Gt Chester-   d.<u>1812</u>, black-   Wenden Lofts   Brooke   founder of Chrishall   d.1833
blacksmith   ford in <u>1795</u>   smith and   in <u>1794</u> b.   family of farm   in
and farmer   d.<u>1850</u>   farmer   <u>1769</u> d.<u>1819</u>   workers   Chrishall

7. JOHN   = (1) Sophia   WILLIAM = Sarah   1 son   ROBERT = Hannah   JOSEPH
b.<u>1797</u>   Houghton   b.<u>1809</u>   of   4 daugh-   b.<u>1795</u>   Rogers   b.<u>1803</u>
d.<u>1880</u>,   d.<u>1889</u>   Heydon   ters   d.<u>1842</u>   in   d.<u>1875</u>
black-   = (2) Martha   black-   d.<u>1877</u>   farm,   <u>1814</u>   farm
smith,   Houghton smith   farm   Chrishall   worker
small-   in 1832   Elmdon,   worker   d.<u>1846</u>   S. Walden
holder and   Chrishall C'hall,   Union
butcher   d.<u>1870</u>   S. Walden
                           Union

8. FREDERICK = Mary   Lucy = Thomas   Isa-   = (1) Robert   (2) Henry   1 son
b.<u>1834</u> in   b.   Jane   Edwards   bella   <u>Cowell</u>   Edwards   dying
Chrishall   1833   b.1836 in <u>1861</u>   b.1841   Audley   in <u>1878</u>   in
d.<u>1907</u>   Littlebury Chris- wheel-   Chrishall,   End   butcher   infancy
publican and   hall,   wright   Elmdon,   <u>butcher</u>   Westminster
black-   bonnet- Woolwich   West-   Elmdon
smith,   maker   minster
Elmdon   Elmdon

9. HENRY   = Emma   3 sons   WILLIAM ARTHUR = Mary Ann   LAURA
b.<u>1869</u>   b.1868   b.1863, farmer, <u>Chandler</u>   JANE
d.<u>1926</u>   d.1940   Elmdon,   in <u>1884</u>   b.1865
publican,   beer-   retired to   school-   school
blacksmith and retailer   Cambridge   mistress,   teacher,
postmaster   Elmdon   Elmdon

10. John Alfred b.<u>1885</u>,   = Selina Florence Penn,
farmer, Carlton, Cambs.,   school teacher
farm manager, Yorks.   Elmdon

11. Joyce,   1 son
school teacher, York   1 daughter

170

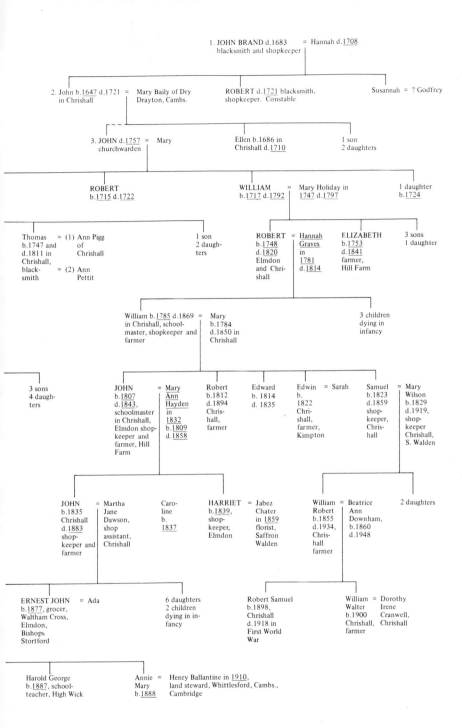

1. JOHN BRAND d.1683   = Hannah d.1708
blacksmith and shopkeeper

2. John b.1647 d.1721 = Mary Baily of Dry   ROBERT d.1721 blacksmith,   Susannah = ? Godfrey
in Chrishall   Drayton, Cambs.   shopkeeper. Constable

3. JOHN d.1757 = Mary   Ellen b.1686 in   1 son
churchwarden   Chrishall d.1710   2 daughters

ROBERT   WILLIAM   = Mary Holiday in   1 daughter
b.1715 d.1722   b.1717 d.1792   1747 d.1797   b.1724

Thomas   = (1) Ann Pigg   1 son   ROBERT   = Hannah   ELIZABETH   3 sons
b.1747 and   of   2 daugh-   b.1748   Graves   b.1753   1 daughter
d.1811 in   Chrishall   ters   d.1820   in   d.1841
Chrishall,   Elmdon   1781   farmer,
black-   = (2) Ann   and Chri-   d.1814   Hill Farm
smith   Pettit   shall

William b.1785 d.1869 = Mary   3 children
in Chrishall, school-   b.1784   dying in
master, shopkeeper and   d.1850 in   infancy
farmer   Chrishall

3 sons   JOHN   = Mary   Robert   Edward   Edwin   = Sarah   Samuel   = Mary
4 daugh-   b.1807   Ann   b.1812   b. 1814   b.   b.1823   Wilson
ters   d.1843,   Hayden   Chris-   d. 1835   1822   d.1859   b.1829
              schoolmaster in   hall,   Chri-   shop-   d.1919,
              in Chrishall, 1832   farmer   shall,   keeper,   shop-
              Elmdon shop- b.1809   farmer,   Chris-   keeper
              keeper and   d.1858   Kimpton   hall   Chrishall,
              farmer, Hill   S. Walden
              Farm

JOHN   = Martha   Caro-   HARRIET   = Jabez   William   = Beatrice   2 daughters
b.1835   Jane   line   b.1839,   Chater   Robert   Ann
Chrishall   Dawson,   b.   shop-   in 1859   b.1855   Downham,
d.1883   shop   1837   keeper,   florist,   d.1934,   b.1860
shop-   assistant,   Elmdon   Saffron   Chris-   d.1948
keeper and Chrishall   Walden   hall
farmer   farmer

ERNEST JOHN   = Ada   6 daughters   Robert Samuel   William   = Dorothy
b.1877, grocer,   2 children   b.1898,   Walter   Irene
Waltham Cross,   dying in in-   Chrishall   b.1900   Cranwell,
Elmdon,   fancy   d.1918 in   Chrishall, Chrishall
Bishops   First World   farmer
Stortford   War

Harold George   Annie = Henry Ballantine in 1910,
b.1887, school-   Mary   land steward, Whittlesford, Cambs.,
teacher, High Wick b.1888   Cambridge

171

born in Elmdon in 1712, left a will[20] which shows that he held land in both parishes, and in Little Chesterford, five miles east of Elmdon, as well. This will provides evidence that the Brands looked on Elmdon as their home village and Chrishall as their second string, because the Elmdon land was left to the eldest son, John (b.1735 – see line 5) for his life, and had then to pass to his son, while the Chrishall land was left outright to John's youngest brother Thomas who, incidentally, had married as his first wife Ann Pigg, of the Chrishall farming family. The middle son, George, like Thomas, was a blacksmith living in Chrishall, but he did not inherit any land, possibly because he was already set up in business. He did, however, receive a legacy of £50 0s 0d, and an equal share in the proceeds of the sale of the Little Chesterford copyhold land, along with his brothers and sisters.

Having disposed of his land in his will, John Brand (line 4) turned his attention to his grand-daughter, Mary Brooke (line 6) who seems to have been living with him and his wife. He not only left her £20 0s 0d, but also 'the bed whereon she commonly sleeps in my now dwelling, with bedding and furniture from the same room'. On the face of it, the testator's wife Mary did not do as well as one might expect, for all she got was an income of £2 0s 0d a year from the Elmdon property, a further £2 0s 0d a year from the Chrishall lands, a lump sum of £60 0s 0d, and her choice of household goods other than those earmarked for her grand-daughter.

It might be thought that with John Brand (line 5) settled in the Elmdon property, and his brother Thomas in Chrishall, this side of the family would now split into two branches, each in future keeping to its own parish. This, however, was not the case. Two generations later, the Elmdon Brands were still using Chrishall as a place for the eldest son to go while waiting to inherit the Elmdon forge. John Brand (line 7) for instance, and his second wife Martha had four children in Chrishall, before returning to Elmdon after the death of John's father in 1849. It was this John Brand (line 7), incidentally, who was the Lofts Hall estate tenant of ten acres in 1860, and who lost his tenancy the following year because he had let the land go back so badly.

As we saw in chapter 6, the Elmdon forge passed from John Brand (line 7) to his eldest son Frederick (line 8), and then to Frederick's second son Henry (line 9). Both Henry's sons, however, left Elmdon in the early twentieth century to work in London, and the forge was finally sold to the owner of Hill farm in the 1940s, after having been in the same family for at least nine generations. It remains to be seen what happened to the younger sons of the blacksmith Brands who did not inherit the business.

The labouring Brands

In general, the younger sons of the forge-owning Brands became blacksmiths like their elder brothers, probably working at first as apprentices in the smithy. This was true of the first example we have of a son of a Brand blacksmith who did not inherit land, namely George (line 5) who, as we have just seen, inherited a sum of money from his father but no property. There is no reason to suppose that he did not continue as a blacksmith for his working life, but the same was not true of his own son, also called George (line 6). Young George had to compete with his two cousins, John and Thomas (line 6) who were the sons of the senior line, for any work going in the Elmdon forge, and his father had no property in Chrishall for him to take over. Instead, he became a farm labourer and the founder of a family of agricultural workers who lived in Chrishall throughout the nineteenth century.

The same story is repeated in the next generation. Thomas (line 6), like George, was a younger-son blacksmith, though he may have inherited land, but not the smithy, from his father. He died in early middle age, and his will[21] shows him to have been comparatively prosperous, or at least to have thought himself to be so, for he directed that his farming business be carried on jointly by his wife Ann and his eldest son Robert, who was only 17 when his father died, under the direction of his executors, William Truslove Rolfe and James Hayden, both Elmdon farmers. His remaining four sons and two daughters were each to receive £100 0s 0d on attaining their majorities. It seems likely, however, that the area farmed was insufficient to support this large family without the help of a second occupation, for by his death in 1842, Robert (line 7) had declined from farmer to farm labourer; and Joseph, the youngest brother, was also a farm labourer. True, these boys were particularly unlucky in that their father died before the younger ones were old enough to be apprenticed to a trade, and they were also of the generation which suffered the upheavals and reorganisation resulting from the Elmdon enclosure of 1824

173

described in chapter 3. Even so, Joseph, who at the time of the enclosure owned a cottage and garden in Duddenhoe End, ended his days in the Saffron Walden workhouse, where he died in 1875. Surprisingly, this was a fate shared by his cousin William (line 7) who, as third son of the owner of the Elmdon forge, trained as a blacksmith and was employed in that capacity while his brother John was the head of the business, but who, nevertheless, clearly had been unable to put by enough money to save him from the Union in his old age. Furthermore, both William's sons were farm labourers, and one of his daughters married a farm worker from Langley.

So far, we have looked at the Brands who, as eldest sons, inherited the Elmdon smithy and a ready-made position in life, and at their younger brothers, who usually worked as blacksmiths even if in a subordinate capacity, and their descendants, most of whom joined the farm-labouring class. There remained another branch of the family descended from William and Mary (line 4) who, as far as we know, had nothing to do with the work of the forge.

The farming and shopkeeping Brands

William Brand (line 4) was the youngest of three sons, although the middle boy died when he was seven. As we have seen, John Brand, William's eldest brother, inherited the forge, and owned land in Elmdon and Chrishall, but there is no indication that he was a shopkeeper. It is quite possible, therefore, that William as the younger son took over the Elmdon shop that had once been the property of his greatuncle Robert (line 2), although this is only a supposition, and if he did so, then he may have supplemented his income by farming land in Elmdon's open fields, in the same way that his great-great-grandson John (line 8) tenanted Hill Farm in 1861, as well as keeping the shop across the road in Elmdon High Street. Certainly, William's daughter Elizabeth owned two strips of open field land at the time of the Enclosure Act of 1824.[22]

With each succeeding generation, the problem had to be faced of what to do with the eldest son before he inherited whatever business his father was running in Elmdon, and how to find occupations for younger sons. The junior branch of the Brands, descended from William and Mary (line 4) met this in much the same way that the senior branch of blacksmiths did, that is, they left Elmdon for Chrishall, until such time as an opportunity came to return. The case of William Brand (line 6) and his children will serve as an illustration of this.

William Brand seems to have gone to Chrishall in the first place as a shopkeeper, an occupation he held in 1814 when his son Edward (line 7) was baptised in that village. Two years later, he had taken advantage of the temporary closure of Elmdon's free grammar school,[23] which was normally open to boys from Chrishall

The first term, ratio, and number of terms given,
to find the sum of all the terms.
Rule. Find the last term as before, then subtract the
first from it, and divide the remainder by the ratio less
1; to the quotient of which add the greater; gives the sum
required.

A Man bought a horse and by agreement was to give a
farthing for the first nail three for the second &c there
were four shoes and in each shoe nails what was the
worth of the horse

Robert Brand's arithmetic book, *c.* 1824

as well as Elmdon, to open his own small school in a room in his house. The arithmetic exercise book of his young son Robert (line 7) survives,[24] and shows that the pupils were expected to cope with a variety of esoteric subjects such as alligation without time, double position, conjoined proportion, arithmetical progression and geometrical progression. It was under this last heading that Robert learned how to deal with the problem of the cost of shoeing a horse, referred to by Mr Weller Senior in *Pickwick Papers*, when he said of the sanctimonious Mr Stiggins 'Borrows eighteenpence on Monday, and comes on Tuesday for a shillin' to make it up half-a-crown; calls again on Vensday for another half-crown to make it five shillin's, and goes on, doubling, till he gets it up to a five pund note in no time, like them sums in the 'rithmetic book 'bout the nails in the horse's shoes, Sammy.' The illustration on p.175 shows the working out of this problem in Robert Brand's beautiful copperplate handwriting.

William's Chrishall enterprises clearly prospered, and as time went on he was able to add farming to his other activities. The Chrishall rate book for 1855[25] shows that, some forty years after his arrival in the village, he was renting Building Hall farmhouse, another farmhouse and 412 acres of land from Lord Dacre; 22 acres from the Lofts Hall estate; a house and 5 acres from Martyns Charity; and 2 acres of land, known as 'Cuckoos', from the Rev. Everit. He also owned a house and 17 acres of land, and nine cottages in the village which he let. In the same year, his second and third surviving sons, Robert and Edwin (line 7), were together renting 319 acres and the farmhouse of Chiswick Hall Farm in Chrishall from the Lofts Hall estate, and his youngest son Samuel had taken over the family shop, renting a further 4 acres of land, and three cottages for sub-letting. The only son not to have remained in Chrishall was the eldest, John, who, as we shall see later, returned to Elmdon.

When William died in 1869 at the great age of 84, he had outlived this son, John (line 7) by more than twenty years. In his will he left his real estate to his oldest surviving son, Robert, for life, and afterwards to his younger grandson, William Robert (line 8) and his heirs.[26] His personal estate, stock, crops and effects were to be shared equally between his sons Robert and Edwin. The stock-in-trade of the Chrishall shop, then being run by Samuel's widow, was left to her for life or until remarriage, and then to Samuel's children. Once again, the same pattern emerges — farming was for

176

the older sons in the family, shopkeeping for the youngest, for whom no land was available. As for William's three grandchildren in Elmdon, John, Caroline and Harriet (line 8), he does not seem to have had the same interest in them as he had in the members of the family who stayed with him in Chrishall, for he only left John £80 0s 0d, and the girls £10 0s 0d apiece.

Robert Brand (line 7) never married, and his brother Edwin, as we saw in chapter 4, moved to Kimpton in Hertfordshire, but Samuel's son William Robert (line 8) stayed on in Chrishall, taking over the tenancy of Building End Farm in his turn. On William Robert's death, his son Walter (line 9) continued as tenant on the same farm and he finally bought the property towards the end of the 1950s. Walter retired in the early 1970s, and he and his wife now live in the house in which Walter's great-grandfather taught the village children so many years ago.

William's eldest son, John (line 7), as a young man had worked in Chrishall as a schoolmaster, like his father before him. However, when the opportunity came he returned to Elmdon to take over the grocer's and draper's shop there. A few years later his position in Elmdon was consolidated when he became the beneficiary of his great-aunt Elizabeth (line 5) who had been the tenant farmer of 64 acres of land in Elmdon open field belonging to the Lofts Hall estate in 1790, and who lived in the homestead which later became known as Hill Farm. As we saw in chapter 4, he took over the tenancy of Hill Farm, as well as continuing to run the shop, and he and his descendants almost uninterruptedly remained tenants of the Lofts Hall estate at Hill or Church Farms, and village shopkeepers, right up until 1927. By this time school-teaching had been added to the occupations traditionally followed by Elmdon Brands. As we saw earlier, John Brand (line 7) had been a schoolmaster in his Chrishall days, and two generations later his grandson, William Arthur (line 9), married the village school-mistress, while William Arthur's sister Laura herself taught in the Elmdon school for a few years. William Arthur's son John (line 10) also married an Elmdon school-teacher, while John's brother Harold won a scholarship to university, going on to be a grammar-school teacher. In the next generation, John's daughter Joyce (line 11) became a teacher in York.

As we saw in chapter 4, John Brand (line 10) was a member of the last generation of the family to live in Elmdon, but in fact he had left the village before the Lofts Hall estate was finally sold in

177

1927. While his father was still tenanting Hill and Church Farms, John looked after a small farm at Carlton, some fifteen miles away, which his father owned. However, the enterprise failed, John found work as a farm manager in Yorkshire, and when William Arthur retired to Cambridge in 1927 the Brands' connection with Elmdon farming ceased.

Each individual in each family has his or her own story, but it is fair to ask how typical in broad outline the Elmdon Brands were of other farmers in the district. They were exceptional in the length of time they survived in the village; but a comparison with the Piggs of Chrishall over the last hundred years is of interest. By the second half of the nineteenth century, both families farmed roughly the same acreage and were tenants of the Lofts Hall estate. William Arthur Brand (line 9) and Thomas Pigg were both elder sons who inherited the farm tenancies held by their fathers. Both married Elmdon school-teachers. Their younger brothers, Ernest Brand (line 10) and Jason Pigg, both became grocers outside their home villages. In the next generation, both John Brand and Charlie Pigg failed at farming in the 1920s and left the district.

Conclusions

We may draw the following conclusions from this family history covering nearly 300 years. First, for many years the Brands moved between Elmdon and Chrishall, with Elmdon being regarded as the home village to which several family members dying in Chrishall were brought home for burial.

Second, while it is clear from the Brand wills which have been preserved that the testators in general tried to be fair to all their children, in fact the eldest sons who inherited indivisible property, such as a blacksmith's shop, were able to maintain their position, and to some extent that of their children, while the descendants of the younger brothers were likely to lose ground and become farm labourers. On the other hand, lack of inherited property could act as a spur to a man wishing to strike out for himself. William Brand, descendant of a younger son, took what opportunities he could find in Chrishall and ended by farming the largest acreage of all the Brands in the two parishes.

Finally, the limited opportunities of employment in Elmdon and Chrishall for most of the period we have been considering

178

resulted in a pattern of occupation which recurred constantly over the years. Brands were blacksmiths, small landholders and shop-keepers for at least six generations before the changes brought about by the enclosures of the early nineteenth century gave some fortunate ones the chance to farm on a larger scale, as tenants of local landowners, while reducing the less fortunate to the ranks of the farm labourers. Even by the mid-twentieth century, only one additional occupation, that of school teaching, had been added to the list.

By the early twentieth century, too, knowledge of family connections between the farming and shopkeeping, blacksmith and labouring Brands had been lost, although this is not surprising in view of the fact that the ancestor common to all three had lived seven generations earlier.

9

Migration in the mid-nineteenth century

We have already looked at the opportunities available to those who were Elmdon-born for earning their livings in the village between 1861 and 1964; at how their isolation was lessened as transport facilities improved; and at how the marriage patterns of various groups altered with the twentieth century. These changing conditions naturally had an effect on the numbers of people coming to live in Elmdon, and on those leaving it to settle elsewhere.

The population in 1861

Elmdon parish, containing both Elmdon village and Duddenhoe End hamlet, had a population of 731 persons in 1861, more than two-thirds of whom lived in the thriving community of Elmdon village. There were many families with young children, and indeed, in the village itself four out of every ten people were under 15, as table 4, p.19, shows. The population of the parish as a whole[1] however, had already passed its peak, and had entered on a period of decline which was to continue for seventy years, up to 1931 (see table 41).

Although the parish had absorbed just over 200 additional people between 1801 and 1851, the year when the population was at its greatest, it was unable to contain all the natural increase of its inhabitants during this period, and some families and individuals had to leave. As table 42 shows, the percentage of population increase in Elmdon parish in the fifty years from 1801 to 1851 was less than half that experienced in Great Britain as a whole, and lower than the rate either for Essex, the county in which Elmdon lay, or even for Suffolk, its predominantly rural neighbour. As an instance of the scale of this emigration, 318 more births than deaths of Elmdoners were recorded in the parish registers between 1821 and 1851, so that if no immigration or emigration had taken

180

place, and assuming that all births and deaths were recorded in the registers, the population would have risen from 601 in 1821 to 919 in 1851, instead of the 743 recorded by the census.[2] As immigration into the parish certainly did take place during the period, the figures indicate that emigration took place on a considerable scale.

Table 41
Population of Elmdon parish, 1801—1961

year	males	females	total population	% increase or decrease
1801	268	266	534	
1811	260	287	547	+ 2.4
1821	293	308	601	+ 9.9
1831	358	339	697	+ 16.0
1841	343	337	680	− 2.4
1851	384	359	743	+ 9.3
1861	362	369	731	− 1.6
1871	371	346	717	− 1.9
1881	316	298	614	− 14.4
1891	296	299	595	− 3.1
1901	262	282	544	− 8.5
1911	266	267	533	− 2.0
1921	259	244	503	− 5.6
1931	239	235	474	− 5.8
1941	−	−	−	−
1951	236	250	486	+ 2.5
1961	238	252	490	+ 0.8

Source: Censuses, 1801—1961

Table 42
Population increase in Elmdon parish, Essex, Suffolk and Great Britain, 1801—51

	Elmdon parish (i) %	Essex (i) %	Suffolk (i) %	Gr. Britain (ii) %
Population increase 1801—1851	39.1	63.5	56.1	98.2

(i) Source: 1851 Census, Vol. I, Division IV, Eastern Counties
(ii) Source: *Long term population distribution in Great Britain - A Study*. Department of the Environment, 1971, table 1.5

It is not surprising that some emigration should occur, for, as we have already seen, the parish was heavily dependent on agriculture. Virtually all the land, except for small areas of woods and copses, had already been brought into production, and there was a limit to the number of men who could be absorbed into full-time employment. When a farm labourer died, he might be replaced by one of his sons, but there would still be no room for the others, and many families had more than two boys. There were cases, of course, where several brothers succeeded in spending their adult lives in Elmdon as farm workers, thus strengthening their families' positions in the village, but they could do so only at the expense of other families who were forced by economic necessity to look for work elsewhere, and who, as a consequence, disappeared from Elmdon altogether. With the size of the labouring population being governed by the number of jobs available on the farms, the need for servicing industries was also limited. Craftsmen's and tradesmen's families, too, found it necessary to emigrate.

Local emigrants

The emigrants did not all go very far however. Figure 10 shows that in 1861, 242 people who had been born in Elmdon parish were living outside its borders, but within a radius of eight miles from its centre. Eleven more were to be found in Cambridge, the nearest town to Elmdon with a population of over 25,000, and some thirteen miles away as the crow flies. There is no means of knowing exactly what proportion of all emigrants these individuals represented, although, as we shall see later, a detailed study of those who left Elmdon between 1851 and 1861 shows that just one quarter of the emigrants during that decade settled locally.

Even a cursory inspection of figure 10 will show that the majority of the local emigrants had moved to parishes in which the principal village lay no more than four miles away from the centre of Elmdon parish. Thus, as table 43 shows, roughly six out of every ten local emigrants were living within an hour or two's walk of their birthplace and so could keep in touch with their kin either in Elmdon village or Duddenhoe End hamlet. As we can see from table 43 there were more female local emigrants than males, and a higher proportion of these females settled further away from Elmdon parish. As we look more closely at the people who left, we shall see the causes for these differences.

The detailed schedules of the 1861 census taken in the parishes to which they had moved tell us a good deal about these local emigrants. They ranged in age from a week-old baby to the 87-year old widow of a farm labourer. Within these limits, however, their age structure differed noticeably from that of the settled

182

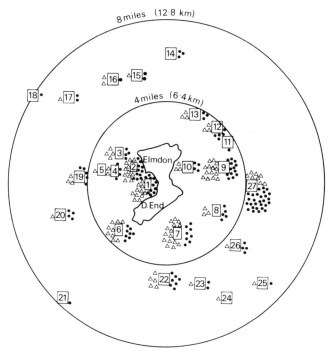

Fig. 10 Distribution of local emigrants from Elmdon parish, 1861

Towns and principal villages in parishes where local emigrants
from Elmdon parish were living in 1861

No.	Town or parish	Population in 1861	No.	Town or parish	Population in 1861
1	Wenden Lofts	61	15	Thriplow	502
2	Chrishall	643	16	Fowlmere	560
3	Heydon	270	17	Melbourn	1,637
4	Great Chishill	473	18	Kneesworth	280
5	Little Chishill	110	19	Barley	809
6	Langley	410	20	Barkway	1,221
7	Arkesden	506	21	Great Hormead	660
8	Wendens Ambo	419	22	Clavering	1,047
9	Littlebury	974	23	Rickling	502
10	Strethall	41	24	Quendon	165
11	Little Chesterford	276	25	Widdington	409
12	Great Chesterford	1,027	26	Newport	886
13	Ickleton	721	27	Saffron Walden	5,474
14	Whittlesford	395	28	Cambridge	26,361

183

Table 43
Settlement of local emigrants by distance from Elmdon, 1861

	males		females		total	
	no.	%	no.	%	no.	%
Within 4 mile radius	79	72	78	55	157	62
4–8 mile radius	25	23	60	42	85	34
Cambridge	6	5	5	3	11	4
Total	110	100	143	100	253	100

Source: 1861 census

community which had been left behind in Elmdon village. There were also marked differences between the age structures of the male and female emigrants themselves.

Age structure

Naturally enough, there were considerably fewer children among the local emigrants than in the Elmdon village population for, as we saw in chapter 1, Elmdon parents tended not to send their daughters away to work until they were at least 14, and at that age their sons were still living at home, learning their jobs on the land. Nearly all the emigrants of 14 and under had been brought away from Elmdon by their parents, and were still living with them. In the 15–29-year-old age group, however, the percentage of girl emigrants rose sharply (see table 44(a)) strengthening the view that parents considered their daughters old enough to manage a job away from home by the time they entered this group. To these young girls leaving Elmdon to work must be added those in the upper part of the 15–29 age bracket who had married outside the parish, often going to live in their husbands' village. The greatest rise in the proportion of male emigrants, on the other hand, as

Table 44
(a) *Age structure, female local emigrants from Elmdon parish, compared with Elmdon village, 1861*

Age	female emigrants		females, Elmdon village
	no.	%	%
0–14	15	10	43
15–29	38	27	22
30–44	34	24	12
45–59	35	24	11
60+	21	15	11
Total	143	100	99

184

(b) *Age structure, male local emigrants from Elmdon parish, compared with Elmdon village, 1861*

age	male emigrants		males, Elmdon village
	no.	%	%
0–14	24	22	39
15–29	23	21	25
30–44	34	31	14
45–59	10	9	14
60+	19	17	8
Total	110	100	100

Source: 1861 census

table 44 (b) shows, came in the 30–44 age group — the very group which in Elmdon village experienced a marked decline in numbers — indicating that sons left home later than daughters.

Marriage

Although the proportions of married and single local emigrants varied little between the sexes, it is apparent from table 45 that the proportion of Elmdon girls going to live in the birthplace of their husband was just over double that of men going to live in their wives' home villages. Even so, over a quarter of the married men had in fact moved to their wives' town or village, indicating that kin links were important when looking for a job and a house outside the husband's own territory. A fifth of all the male emigrants' marriages were to another Elmdoner, but here it is worth noting that none of the dozen couples involved had moved further than three miles from the centre of Elmdon parish. Squeezed out by increasing population pressure, they went no further than they had to in order to make a living.

Table 45
Birthplaces of spouses of local Elmdon emigrants, 1861

married Elmdon emigrants	spouse born:								total
	in Elmdon		in the place where the couple were living in 1861		elsewhere		not known		
	no.	%	no.	%	no.	%	no.	%	no.
Males	12	20	16	27	29	49	2	3	59
Females	12	14	49	58	19	22	5	6	85

Source: 1861 census

185

If we look at the unmarried emigrants, we find from table 46 that roughly nine out of every ten unmarried males were living either with at least one parent, or with other kinsfolk. Only three bachelors were lodging independently of their relatives, but nearly half the girls were in this position. The explanation lies in the differing occupations of the two sexes.

Table 46
Unmarried local emigrants from Elmdon parish, 1861 by residence

| | males | | females | |
	no.	%	no.	%
Still living with at least one parent or step-parent	29	74	16	42
Visiting or living with other relatives	7	18	3	8
Visiting families not known to be kin	—	—	1	3
Living independently of family	3	8	18	47
Total	39 [i]	100	38 [ii]	100

(i) One single man in Saffron Walden workhouse and one in Addenbrooke's hospital have been omitted from the total
(ii) Two single women in Saffron Walden workhouse have been omitted.

Source: 1861 census

Occupations of local emigrants

As table 47 (a) shows, the pattern of occupations among the male emigrants was remarkably similar to that prevailing in Elmdon village. In other words, emigration was taking place throughout the whole male working community and was not confined to a single occupation, such as farm labourer. For women emigrants, however, one occupation dominated all others in a way that it had not done in Elmdon village itself. If a girl did not emigrate to marry, in nearly nine out of ten cases she entered living-in domestic service (see table 47 (b)). At an age when her wage-earning brother would be living with parents or other relatives, she would be away from home, receiving her board and lodging as part of her wages. The 'living-in' aspect of domestic service provided girls with the equivalent of the tied cottage which often went with the married farm labourer's job. For both married farm workers and domestic servants, the problem was to find work. Once that had been achieved, the question of accommodation was automatically solved. It was not so easy for the unmarried farm labourer, on the other hand, who was unable to live with parents or relatives. By the

186

mid-century it was no longer the custom, in Elmdon at least, for farmers to take in unmarried farm workers who were not related to them and provide them with board and lodging in the same way that they did their female workers. In 1861, there was only one such young farm worker living in his employer's farmhouse, a rather isolated settlement some two miles from the village. In general, young men in those days did not housekeep for themselves, and a tied cottage was of little use without a wife to look after it and to cook the meals. The difficulty and expense of finding suitable lodgings may help to account for the small number of single working men living independently of their families.

Table 47
(a) *Occupations of local male emigrants compared with males employed in Elmdon village, 1861*

| | emigrants | | Elmdon villagers |
	no.	%	%
Professional	1	1	1
Farmers (including working sons)	7	8	5
Domestic service	4	4	3
Craftsmen, tradesmen and their workers	19	22	25
Farm employees	57	65	66
Total:	88	100	100

(b) *Occupations of local female emigrants compared with females employed in Elmdon village, 1861*

| | emigrants | | Elmdon villagers |
	no.	%	%
Farmers	–	–	2
Domestic service	26	87	44
Craftsmen, tradesmen and their workers	2	6.5	29
Farm employees[i]	2	6.5	25
Totals:	30	100	100

(i) The individuals concerned were both in Saffron Walden workhouse at the time of the census.

Source: 1861 census

Finding employment

When an Elmdoner left the parish to work elsewhere locally, what decided where he or she should go? Many factors of which we must remain ignorant may have come into play, but there is evidence to show that links of kinship or acquaintance were important to both sexes. We have already seen that more than one out of every four married men emigrating locally had ended up in their wife's village, and that some young single men had been despatched from Elmdon to live with relatives while working outside the parish. Links such as these must have been very valuable in enabling the men concerned to obtain employment for, as we saw in chapter 1, in Elmdon village itself it was rare in 1861 for a non-Elmdoner to hold a job on the land, and the same position may well have held in other villages. Girls, too, were not often sent to situations about which nothing was known. Familiar names are to be found among the girls' employers. For example, Ruth Jeffery was working for William Pigg, who farmed in Barkway, and it is hard to believe that he was not related to the Piggs on the Lofts Hall estate. In Saffron Walden, Mary Ann Hammond was servant to William Chater, a nurseryman and florist, of just the right age to be father of Jabez Chater who had married Harriet Brand from Elmdon and who was living nearby. Also, one member of a family would find a job in the same locality for another. In Barley, the two unmarried domestic servants from Elmdon who were working in separate households were sisters; the elder must surely have had some hand in finding the younger's job for her. These were by no means isolated cases.

The questions as to why more females emigrated locally than males and why more women than men were to be found further away from the parish, can now be answered. More girls left Elmdon parish than boys partly because a greater proportion left home on marriage, and partly because they went outside to work at an earlier age, being provided with board and lodging at their place of employment. Girls went rather further afield than men within the locality because jobs in domestic service at a distance from Elmdon were open to them just as much as in places closer at hand. Saffron Walden, too, which lay just outside the four-mile radius, was a draw to Elmdon girls, because its large middle-class population provided a number of places for them. The majority of the male emigrants, on the other hand, were farm workers, and since the population pressures which had caused them to leave Elmdon were presumably also operating in nearby villages, it was easier for them to break into a tight employment situation close to home where they had relatives, or might be personally known to their new employer, than it would have been in a strange village a few miles further off.

There seems, in any case, to have been a desire among these

local migrants to stay as close to home as possible. It is remarkable how Cambridge, only fifteen miles off by road, attracted so small a proportion of Elmdoners in relation to its size and job opportunities. Although clearly it would not draw men who wanted to continue working on the land, it did offer a chance to break away from farm labouring, for example by working on the railway, or as a jobbing gardener, or as a porter in one of the colleges, all jobs held there by Elmdoners in 1861. Only a tiny number, however, took these opportunities.

So far we have looked at the people who left Elmdon parish before 1861 and settled near enough to it to keep in some kind of contact with their relatives and friends if they wished to do so. But many problems remain unsolved. A detailed study of the population changes which took place in Elmdon village between 1851 and 1861[3] may throw some light, not only on what proportion of emigrants settled locally, but also on who the emigrants were, and on how far they were replaced by people coming in from outside the parish.

The migration pattern of Elmdon village, 1851—61

Elmdon in the mid-nineteenth century has so far been described as a stable community with an ordered way of life. It may come as a surprise, therefore, to realise that of the 528 inhabitants of the village in 1851, very nearly half had vanished from the scene ten years later, while 47 per cent of the population in 1861 consisted of individuals who had not been present a decade before, (see table 48 (a) and (b)). In fact. this scale of movement was not new to English villages, as Peter Laslett and John Harrison showed in their study of population turnover in Clayworth and Cogenhoe in the seventeenth century.[4] A closer look at who came and who went, however, may show us something of the mechanics of this constant change in the population, as families expanded and contracted, and as new faces appeared in the village streets.

Those disappearing between 1851 and 1861

The loss of nearly half the population between 1851 and 1861 was not of course due entirely to long-term inhabitants of Elmdon leaving to live elsewhere. Twelve out of every 100 individuals present at the time of the 1851 census had died before ten years

189

Table 48
(a) *Population loss, Elmdon village, 1851−61*

		males		females		total	
		no.	%	no.	%	no.	%
Disappearing	through death	30	11.0	32	12.5	62	12.0
between	temporary visitors	2	1.0	1	0.5	3	0.5
1851 and 1861	emigrants	90	34.0	97	37.0	187	35.5
In Elmdon, 1851 and 1861		145	54.0	131	50.0	276	52.0
Total population, 1851		267	100	261	100	528	100

(b) *Population gain, Elmdon village, 1851−61*

		males		females		total	
		no.	%	no.	%	no.	%
In Elmdon, 1851 and 1861		145	58.0	131	48.5	276	53.0
Entering	through birth	64	25.5	74	27.5	138	27.0
between	temporary visitors	4	1.5	2	0.5	6	1.0
1851 and 1861	immigrants	37	15.0	63	23.5	100	19.0
Total population, 1861		250	100	270	100	520	100

Source: 1851 and 1861 censuses

elapsed, the young and the old suffering the heaviest losses. Then a handful of people who happened to be paying visits to families or friends on the day the census was taken had returned home, and cannot be considered true emigrants. But once deaths and temporary visits have been taken into account, 187 people, or 35.5 per cent of all those who were present in 1851, left their homes in Elmdon to live outside the village before 1861 (see table 48 (a)).

The question 'where did these emigrants go?' is quickly answered. Roughly a quarter of those leaving during the decade found themselves within eight miles of Elmdon, and it is these people who followed the patterns described in the first section of this chapter. But the fate of almost all the remaining three-quarters of the emigrants is unknown. A shepherd and his wife had moved on to Barrington, ten miles away from Elmdon village, while a girl had found herself a place as a house servant in Buntingford, some twelve miles off. Thanks to notes made by the vicar against the names of those he confirmed during the decade, we know that three boys emigrated to Australia. These teenagers, incidentally, were all sons of small tradesmen. For the remaining 136 emigrants, all that can be said is that they moved beyond the range of easy contact with Elmdon. London may well have been a magnet

190

drawing many of them into urban life, but this is supposition. Certainly none of them went to the much closer town of Cambridge.

Considerably more is known about who these emigrants were, than about their destinations. Like all the working male emigrants described in table 47 (a), the working men and boys who left between 1851 and 1861 represented a cross-section of the whole male community. But were they young men in search of a new life, leaving their parents behind in Elmdon, or were they household heads, taking their families with them?

Table 49 shows that a man heading a household in Elmdon in 1851 had twice as good a chance of staying on in the village as did a male who had not yet set himself up in a separate establishment. Only one out of every five household heads emigrated during the decade, while two out of five of the other males of all ages did so. A man who had not only a job, but also a cottage, a wife and children in Elmdon, was not automatically precluded from emigrating, but he was more likely to be able to maintain his position in the village than a young, unmarried man.

Emigrants from Elmdon between 1851 and 1861, therefore, fell into two groups — those who emigrated with their families, and those who left independently. Let us look first at the family groups.

Table 49
Emigration of male household heads[i] from Elmdon village, 1851–1861

	male household heads 1851		male non-household heads 1851		all males	
	no.	%	no.	%	no.	%
Dying	17	19	13	7	30	11
Returning visitors	—	—	2	1	2	1
In Elmdon, 1851 and 1861	56	61	89	51	145	54
Emigrating	18	20	72	41	90	34
Totals	91	100	176	100	267	100

(i) These were men who at the time of the 1851 census were shown as head of the household in which they lived. A married man living with his parents is therefore not included as a household head.

Source: 1851 and 1861 censuses

Families emigrating from Elmdon, 1851–61. As we have already seen from table 49, emigration was not an issue for the majority of male household heads in Elmdon in 1851. Some of them died before 1861, but just over six out of every ten of them stayed on in the village. However, the eighteen male household heads in 1851 who did move before 1861 were not the only people with dependants to leave Elmdon during the decade. They were joined by young married couples who had been living with parents, or in lodgings, in 1851, and by other young men who married after the census was taken. In addition, a carpenter's wife became widowed, and went away with her son and daughter. In all, twenty-seven family heads and fifty-one dependents left, accounting for 42 per cent of all the emigrants.

The carpenter's widow was exceptional in leaving Elmdon with her children, for the death of a male household head did not usually result in the family's disappearance from the village. Ten of the male household heads who died between 1851 and 1861 left dependent children as well as widows, and the carpenter's family was the only one to go away. But neither he nor his widow were Elmdoners, and no kin link has been traced between them and anyone else in the village. The widow found work as a char-woman in Saffron Walden. She was living there in 1861, still managing to keep her son and daughter, then aged 10 and 12, at school. The other widows with children were all able to stay on in Elmdon. Most of them in 1861 were still living in the same cottage that they had been occupying with their husbands ten years earlier. Only one of them was having to be helped by parish relief, and all but one of the others had found a job of some kind, varying from working in the fields or taking in washing, to running the former husband's small business. One can only guess at how hard times must have been for them, but at least Elmdon society in the mid-nineteenth century was flexible enough to contain a number of families in difficult circumstances, so that they were not forced into the workhouse in Saffron Walden.

All but one of the families leaving Elmdon village between 1851 and 1861, then, was headed by a male breadwinner. Once again, these household heads represented a cross-section of the male community. One of them was the Squire himself, since it was in 1858 that he came into his inheritance of the Lofts Hall estate and left the vicarage in Elmdon for the Hall in Wenden Lofts parish. Another was a tenant farmer who went off to better himself on a

considerably larger holding eight miles away. Others were tradesmen, like the village policeman turned straw-bonnet manufacturer,
who in 1851 was running a cottage industry employing eight
young women, or Charles Walters, the rag-and-bone dealer; this
group included a number of men who, in any case, were not
Elmdoners and who were not held to the village by kinship ties
when a better opportunity presented itself elsewhere. When they
left Elmdon, they moved right away, for none of them was living
within eight miles of the village in 1861.

Individuals who emigrated singly, 1851—61. Family heads,
their wives and children made up just over four out of every ten
people leaving Elmdon. The other emigrants were primarily young
people. Table 50 shows that only four of them were over 30 years
of age. Of the rest, some were non-Elmdoners who came in to
work and then left again, like the housemaid at the vicarage, or
the two teenaged carpenter's apprentices from Hertfordshire,
living in 1851 with the master carpenter Joseph Smith; a few were
Elmdon girls leaving to marry outside; two were women in special
circumstances; but the great majority were young people emigrating
to work, and leaving parents behind them in the village. The boys
in general went further away than other emigrants from Elmdon,
for only 15 per cent of them settled within eight miles of the
parish centre, compared with the average of 25 per cent for all
emigrants. The girls, though, were much closer to this average, 27

Table 50
Individual emigration from Elmdon village, 1851—61

Category	male		female		all	
	no.	%	no.	%	no.	%
Over 30 years of age	1	2	3	5	4	3.5
Previous immigrants leaving	6	11	7	13	13	12
Elmdon girls marrying outside	—	—	6	11	6	5.5
Miscellaneous(i)	—	—	2	4	2	2
Young people leaving to work	47	87	37	67	84	77
Totals	54	100	55	100	109	100

(i) One woman was a young widow who lost first her baby and then her
husband, and presumably returned to her own people in Ickleton. The other
was looking after an invalid brother, who was suffering from water on the
brain, in 1851 and was at an age when, if she had had no domestic commitments,
she would probably already have left Elmdon.

Source: 1851 and 1861 censuses

193

per cent of them settling locally. Two of the boys had returned to Elmdon to live by 1871; a handful of the girls came home to be married in the parish church; but the great majority slipped away from Elmdon altogether. Indeed, of the thirty-seven girls leaving to work between 1851 and 1861, only seven came back to be married from home, whether to an Elmdoner or an outsider, giving some idea of the extent to which links were broken. Many of the other girls must have married, but the ceremony was not performed in Elmdon.

Those coming to live in Elmdon between 1851 and 1861

Although, as we have seen, nearly half Elmdon's population in 1851 had disappeared ten years later, either through death or emigration, there were only eight fewer people living in the village by the time the 1861 census was taken than there had been in 1851. Clearly, a large number of people had come into Elmdon to take the place of those who departed. Indeed, table 48 (b) shows that 47 per cent of the village population in 1861 were new to the scene. Who were these newcomers, and how did they fit into the established social order?

By far the largest group numerically were the children born to families living in the village. Over a quarter of the whole village population in 1861 had been born within the last ten years to parents living in Elmdon. This high birth rate naturally had its effect on emigration. Some families had as many as ten children over a period of twenty years and although when conditions became too cramped at home, an older child would perhaps stay with a grandparent or other relative as a temporary measure, there was increasing pressure on the older children, and particularly on the girls, to find work away from home. With births outnumbering deaths by more than two to one, it was no wonder that emigration from Elmdon should run at 35.5 per cent, compared with an immigration rate of only 19 per cent.

Movement into Elmdon from outside was therefore considerably less than emigration from the village. Even so, it may seem strange that there should be immigration at all, with so many Elmdon people free to fill the jobs and cottages available. The explanation is first, that certain jobs were considered either to be outside the reach of Elmdoners, or at least to be of a kind that were usually shared between them and outsiders, as we saw in chapter 6, and

194

second, that just as kinship ties were important in establishing Elmdon parish emigrants in villages nearby, so immigrants to Elmdon were helped by their links with families already established there. In these cases it seems reasonable to assume that relatives used their influence to help their kin to acquire work and housing in the village. If we look more closely at those coming in, either as family groups or as individuals, we shall see that only three of the working immigrants between 1851 and 1861 appear to have had neither a job which was traditionally open to an outsider, nor a kin connection in the village.

Immigrant families. When the twenty-seven families we have already discussed emigrated from Elmdon between 1851 and 1861, some of the housing and jobs they left behind were taken up by Elmdon men, who were thus able to marry and start a family without leaving the village. But by no means all the vacancies were filled in this way. In fact, seventeen family heads and forty-two dependants came into Elmdon during the decade, representing 59 per cent of all the immigrants. In this, immigrants and emigrants differed considerably. While only about four out of every ten emigrants left as part of a family group, compared with six out of ten leaving as individuals, the position with the immigrants was the other way round.

All these incoming family heads either had jobs which it was quite usual for non-Elmdoners to hold, or had kinship connections in the village. In the first category, we find the two clergymen living next door to each other on Cross Hill who were described in chapter 1. One of them had come in to help the Rev. Robert Fiske Wilkes with his parish duties when he became Squire and moved to Lofts Hall. No Elmdoner, other than the Squire himself, was in any way trained to fill the position of curate of Elmdon, and the post had necessarily to go to an outsider. The other clergyman, the Rector of Strethall, was almost certainly a friend of the Squire, and as Steward of the Manor of Elmdon Bury helped him with the Manor Court and its business. Also, a farmer had emigrated during the decade, so it is not surprising that another should come in to replace him. This 'incomer' was in fact John Brand, born in Chrishall, whose family connections with Elmdon dating back to the seventeenth century were described in chapter 8. There was a new farm bailiff at Poplars Farm who had no known Elmdon connections, but Miss Perry, the farmer, seems always to have employed non-Elmdoners as a matter of principle. A new butcher from Audley End had set up shop on Cross Hill, but his wife was Elmdon-born, and his father-in-law owned the premises. The head gardener at Lofts Hall was from Norfolk, but the Hall nearly always employed outsiders in its top jobs. The blacksmith and tailor who appeared between 1851 and 1861 had both been born in Elmdon, even though they had been away from it for some time; the wheelwright almost certainly came because his wife was connected with the family who had owned the forge in 1851. Two carpenters replaced one who left and another who died, and no Elmdon connection has been traced in their case, but it was quite usual for non-Elmdoners to come into the village to work at this particular trade. The only woman family-head was a widow who had been living in Elmdon nearly thirty years before, when her daughter was born, and now had a widowed sister living in the village. Finally, of the five agricultural labourers who came in as family-heads, all had been born within Elmdon parish. Two had come up from Duddenhoe End, and the others had returned after a spell of work elsewhere.

For a married man to find a job in Elmdon, therefore, it seems to have been necessary either to offer a skill which was in short supply in the village at the time, or to have a strong connection by birth, previous residence, or marriage. It is interesting to note, incidentally, that returning agricultural labourers were able to find work on the land for the sons they brought back with them, as well as for themselves. Once the family was re-established, the boys were embraced by the prevailing system in Elmdon whereby virtually all the male children in the labouring class served their apprenticeship on the land.

Individual immigrants. Table 51 shows that women coming in to Elmdon singly between 1851 and 1861 outnumbered single men by three to one. The cause lies in the fact that two-thirds of the girls entered to marry men living in the village. Some of these girls were Elmdon-born, having left home to work before 1851, but returning later to marry a boy they had known since childhood. An even greater number came from a single outside parish, that of Littlebury. Between them, the Elmdon and Littlebury girls represented just over half the incoming brides. When it came to working immigrants, however, the numbers of men and women were equal. Because most young Elmdoners who had left the

196

Table 51
Individual immigration into Elmdon village, 1851–61

Category	male		female		all	
	no.	%	no.	%	no.	%
Over 30 years of age	3	30	1	3	4	10
Miscellaneous[i]	–	–	1	3	1	2
Girls marrying into Elmdon	–	–	20	65	20	49
Young people coming to work	7	70	9	29	16	39
Totals:	10	100	31	100	41	100

(i) This individual had returned to look after her grandfather, a widower in his 80s. She also contributed to the household by doing field work.

Source: 1851 and 1861 censuses

village did so through lack of work there, it was natural enough that they should outnumber single immigrant workers by more than four to one. Only twenty people came in as individuals to work, compared with eighty-four leaving Elmdon for that purpose during the decade.

Considering the men first, we can see on a small scale how the same factors which influenced Elmdon males when they emigrated locally had their effect on boys and men coming into the village. Three of the ten male immigrants had kinship links in Elmdon, like young Robert Pigg who was working on his uncle's farm. Another four were doing jobs outside agriculture. Joseph Brooks, for instance, was butcher's boy in the Cross Hill shop and, incidentally, came from the same village as his employer. Only three farm workers entered who had no known kinship link in Elmdon. These ten male immigrants met the housing problem in different ways. Two of them were living with relatives, as we saw earlier that some of the Elmdon emigrants did; three more were living-in with their employers; and two bricklayers, who may well have been in Elmdon on a temporary job, were staying at the King's Head. Only three had had to find themselves lodgings with village families.

All but two of the females coming in to work formed part of the steady flow of domestic servants from outside Elmdon who cleaned and cooked at the vicarage and the larger farms, and who then either married or moved on to other places. The exceptions were Miss Perry's companion at Poplars Farm, who was a young relative of a former companion there, and Harriet Toysbee, the village schoolmistress from Islington of whom we read in chapter 6.

Conclusions

As we have seen in earlier chapters, Elmdon's economy was based firmly on agriculture, and for the majority of men and boys in the village, the prime essential for remaining there was to acquire and keep a job on the land. Improvements in agricultural methods, however, were steadily cutting down the number of farm workers needed. As table 52 shows, in the twenty years between 1851 and 1871, the number of acres worked by one farm labourer, averaged over five Elmdon farms, rose from 26½ to 30, so that when elderly workers died or retired, it was not always necessary to replace them by younger men. About nine jobs were lost in this way over a twenty-year period, at a time when the birth-rate was high and a large number of young people were reaching the age when they wanted to marry and settle down. However, the economic system, described in chapter 1, which gave Elmdon its stability, precluded changes which might absorb these young people by creating new work for them, and so emigration was forced on them. On the other hand, a farm worker who had retained his job on the land into adulthood and who then married and rented a cottage, stood a good chance of being able to stay on in the village.

In the service industries, conditions were rather different. Some of these workers were native to Elmdon, and for them much the same pressures applied as in the case of the farm workers, for the demand for their services was limited by the size of the total population. But others were outsiders who came in as part of a constant stream of skilled or semi-skilled workers. They stayed for a while and then, unless they happened to marry into the village, they left again to be replaced by others.

Table 52
Changes in the agricultural labour force, Elmdon village, 1851–71

Farm(i)	no. of acres worked per farm labourer	
	1851	*1871*
Elmdon Bury	23.5	28
Lee Bury	24	28
Elmdon Lodge	29	33
Church	26	31
Poplars	30	30
Average	26.5	30

(i) Figures are not available for Hill Farm

Source: 1851 and 1871 censuses

In order to migrate into Elmdon, it was generally necessary either to have kin-links in the village, or to be doing a job which Elmdoners did not normally expect to fill. If an outsider set up a business in Elmdon, even if he did so through a link with his wife's family as Robert Cowell the butcher did, then he might well employ outsiders himself; or an individual employer, like Miss Perry, might make a point of employing non-Elmdoners. But few of these outside employees stayed long. On Poplars Farm, for example, Miss Perry's bailiff and her entire house staff, male and female, had changed each time the census was taken. For a farm worker to come into Elmdon and become part of the base supporting the occupational pyramid above it, he needed in all but exceptional cases to have had previous residence in the village or to have relatives there.

The result of this migratory pattern was to reinforce the innate conservatism of Elmdon. The young, and possibly the more enterprising married men, left. Those who came in from outside were usually either transients, or else fitted into the prevailing system rather than acting as agents of change.

10

The changing population

In the last chapter, we looked in some detail at the movements of the whole population of Elmdon village between 1851 and 1861, a period when the total number of inhabitants was near its peak. In order to trace migration patterns up to the mid-twentieth century, however, a different way of assessing how far people moved in and out of the village will have to be found because the full national censuses naming everyone in Elmdon are only available up to 1871.

Fortunately a workable substitute for the censuses can be found in the registers of electors, which list all eligible voters for parochial, county and parliamentary elections from 1885 onwards. These rolls have been published at least once a year since they first came out, except in certain years during the two world wars, so it is possible to extract detailed information from them about voters coming into and leaving Elmdon[1]. Admittedly, from 1885 to 1918 the suffrage was limited, and not all males of 21 years and over were listed, since bachelor sons living at home, domestic servants living-in and those of no fixed abode were debarred from voting, along with the great majority of women. For the first eighteen years of the twentieth century, therefore, we can only consider a proportion of adult males living in Elmdon, consisting largely of family heads. Universal adult male suffrage was introduced in 1918, however, and from then on all males of 21 years and over are listed, to be joined ten years later, in 1928, by all adult females.[2]

The electoral registers tell us no more than the voter's name and partial address, but a considerable amount of additional information about many of those listed is available from the 1964 survey. This makes it possible to some extent to match the detail provided by the mid-nineteenth century censuses, and to make a direct comparison of population turnover and migration trends for all those aged 21 and over living in Elmdon village for the decades

1851–61 and 1949–59. Later, we shall look in a more limited way, through the adult male population only, at the period from 1899 to 1949.[3]

Adult population turnover, 1851–61 and 1949–59

The years between 1851 and 1959 saw great social and economic changes. Elmdon people lived through the agricultural depressions of 1875–84 and 1891–9 which drove so many country families off the land. In the First World War a generation of young men from the village made contact with the outside world through service in the armed forces. A further period of depression in the 1920s was intensified from 1929 to 1933, and only six years later the Second World War broke out. These were events which affected the whole nation, but Elmdon also experienced changes which were hardly felt outside the parish, although they were of great importance to the people in the village. The sale of the Lofts Hall estate in 1927 meant that from that time on the Squire no longer owned half Elmdon, and strangers were able to buy cottages which had previously been rented to villagers, while the introduction of daily bus services after the Second World War freed those living in Elmdon from the necessity of finding work there, either on the land or in those small service-industries which had survived, since it became possible to travel instead to nearby factories and towns. Indeed, it was perfectly practicable to commute to work in London, via Audley End station, and to appreciate country living during the evenings and at weekends. In addition, the total population of the parish had declined by no less than a third between 1851 and 1951 (see table 41, p. 181).

How far had these events changed Elmdon's migration pattern by the middle of the twentieth century? Table 53 (a) and (b), setting out the population movements of all Elmdon village residents of 21 years and over between 1851–61 and 1949–59 provides the somewhat surprising answer that in terms of the overall figures for disappearances, appearances, and those remaining in Elmdon, there was slightly less movement of adults between 1949–59 than there had been over a hundred years ago. Even the overall population decline of a third which the whole parish experienced between 1851 and 1951 was not fully reflected in the adult village population, which had been reduced over the same period by only 12 per cent. If we look simply at the pro-

Table 53
(a) *Turnover of population aged 21 years and over, Elmdon village, 1851–61*

	males		females				all	
	no.	%	no.	%	no.	%	no.	%
Total population, 21+, 1851	129	51.8	120	48.2	–	–	249	100
through death	21	16.3	21	17.5	42	16.9	104	41.8
Disappearances								
through emigration	35	27.1	27	22.5	62	24.9		
Still in Elmdon, 1861	73	56.6	72	60.0	–	–	145	58.2
Still in Elmdon, 1861	73	59.4	72	53.7	–	–	145	53.7
through reaching majority	32	26.0	23	17.2	55	21.4	112	43.6
Appearances								
through immigration	18	14.6	39	29.1	57	22.2		
Total population 21+, 1861[i]	123	47.9	134	52.1	–	–	257	100

(i) Excludes 1 male and 2 female visitors

Sources: 1851 and 1861 censuses. Parish registers

(b) *Turnover of population aged 21 years and over, Elmdon village, 1949–59*

	males		females				all	
	no.	%	no.	%	no.	%	no.	%
Total population, 21+, 1949	107	48.9	112	51.1	–	–	219	100
through death	15	14.0	7	6.3	22	10.1	88	40.2
Disappearances								
through emigration	29	27.1	37	33.0	66	30.1		
Still in Elmdon, 1959	63	58.9	68	60.7	–	–	131	59.8
Still in Elmdon, 1959	63	63.6	68	62.4	–	–	131	63.0
through reaching majority	10	10.1	5	4.6	15	7.2	77	37.0
Appearances								
through immigration	26	26.3	36	33.0	62	29.8		
Total population, 21+, 1959	99	47.6	109	52.4	–	–	208	100

Sources: Registers of Electors for Elmdon (village district), qualifying dates 10 June 1949 and 10 October 1959. Parish registers. Elmdon survey, 1964.

portion of men who emigrated, rather than died, in each decade, we see that the correspondence is exact, since 27.1 per cent of the 1851 and 1949 male populations had left by the end of each ten year period.

Does this mean that the population of Elmdon village was more stable in the mid-twentieth century than it had been a hundred years earlier? Closer examination of the tables shows that in some respects the overall figures are misleading. More people died between 1851 and 1861 than between 1949 and 1959 and even though the proportion of men emigrating was identical, the

202

Table 54

(a) *Entrants into Elmdon village, 21+ age group, 1851—61*

	males		females				all	
	no.	%	no.	%	no.	%	no.	%
A. *With Elmdon connection*								
Reaching age of majority[i]	32	64	23	37.1	55	49.1		
Former residents returning[ii]	4	8	5	8.1	9	8		
Non-Elmdoners married to an Elmdon resident, or returning former resident	2	4	17	27.4	19	17	86	76.8
Other kin links	2	4	1	1.6	3	2.7		
B. *No known Elmdon connection*								
Coming to work in Elmdon	9	18	5	8.1	14	12.5		
Coming to live, but working outside	1	2	–	–	1	.9	26	23.2
Wife or relative of male working immigrant	–	–	11	17.7	11	9.8		
Total entrants[iii]	50	44.6	62	55.4	–	–	112	100

(i)   Includes all those born and brought up in Elmdon, or living there in 1851, who reached the age of 21 between 1851—61. Some of these individuals were away in 1851, either working or at school.
(ii) Covers former residents, who were already over the age of majority in 1851, returning to Elmdon
(iii) Excludes 1 male and 2 female visitors

Sources: 1851 and 1861 censuses. Parish registers.

(b) *Entrants into Elmdon village, 21+ age group, 1949—59*

	males		females				all	
	no.	%	no.	%	no.	%	no.	%
A. *With Elmdon connection*								
Reaching age of majority	10	27.8	5	12.2	15	19.5		
Former residents returning	4	11.1	2	4.9	6	7.8		
Non-Elmdoners married to an Elmdon resident, or to returning former resident	4	11.1	6	14.6	10	13	41	53.2
Other kin links	2	5.6	5	12.2	7	9.1		
'Weekender' pre-1949 turned permanent resident	1	2.8	2	4.9	3	3.9		
B. *No known Elmdon connection*								
Coming to work in Elmdon	6	16.7	2	4.9	8	10.3		
Coming to live, working outisde	4	11.1	1	2.4	5	6.5		
Retired people and widows	–	–	2	4.9	2	2.6	36	46.8
Wife or relative of male working immigrant	–	–	8	19.5	8	10.4		
Not known	5	13.9	8	19.5	13	16.9		
Totals	36	100.1	41	100	–	–	77	100

Sources: Registers of Electors for Elmdon (village district). Qualifying dates 10 June 1949 and 10 October 1959. Elmdon Survey 1964. Parish registers.

women's emigration rate was higher in the later period. If deaths are ignored, therefore, it appears that a slightly greater proportion of people left the village in the mid-twentieth than in the mid-nineteenth century. The main changes, however, occurred in the immigration pattern, and these are analysed in greater detail in table 54 (a) and (b).

The major difference between people joining Elmdon's adult community from 1851–61 and from 1949–59 is immediately apparent from the tables. In the mid-nineteenth century, just over three-quarters of the entrants into the adult group of villagers had a definite connection with Elmdon, while a hundred years later this proportion had dropped to only a little more than half. If we look more closely at the different kinds of link which entrants had with the village, we see that the greater part of this change in balance was due to the differing proportions of young people born or brought up in Elmdon who reached the age of 21 during the decade. Almost half the people entering the adult group between 1851 and 1861 fell into this category, compared with roughly two out of every ten between 1949–59. The overall population loss of a third which the parish experienced between 1851 and 1951 was due more to a decline in the size of the average Elmdon family than to rural depopulation in the sense that large numbers of houses were left empty.

Leaving aside these young people, the proportions of men and women with Elmdon links who actually immigrated are not dissimilar. In each decade, people who had lived in the village at some previous stage in their lives came back to it. Between 1851 and 1861, for example, the widowed Mrs Elcock returned. A Chrishall woman, she had lived in Elmdon some thirty years before and was probably drawn back to the village by the presence of her sister, who had married an Elmdon man. A hundred years later, it was happy memories of her childhood in Elmdon which brought the tenant of the King's Head back to the village. Fewer women came in through marriage to Elmdon men between 1949 and 1959 than between 1851 and 1861, reflecting in part the declining numbers of Elmdon-born men living in the village, though this was offset to a limited extent by a rise in the number of non-Elmdon men entering as a result of marriage to Elmdon women. Both in the mid-nineteenth and mid-twentieth centuries, people came either to live with relatives or to be near them, like William Harris, a middle-aged bachelor farm worker who came to

204

live with his brother and sister-in-law in the 1850s, or the woman in the 1950s who returned to look after her widowed brother. But as table 54 (b) shows, the twentieth century produced one new type of immigrant who had a previous connection with Elmdon. This was the 'weekender', who owned a house which he or she visited intermittently, before finally turning it into a permanent home. Statistically, the numbers entered under this heading in the table are almost insignificant, but nevertheless, they do indicate a new factor in Elmdon's migration pattern.

Former 'weekenders' were not the only different kind of immigrant coming into Elmdon between 1949 and 1959. A hundred years earlier, only one adult entrant was living in Elmdon but working outside, and as he was the Rector of Strethall, a neighbouring parish which in 1861 contained only forty-one souls, he may well have spent more time in Elmdon than outside it. But by the mid-twentieth century, five adults who came in during the decade were spending their working days outside the parish, and three of them were daily commuters to London. Another new category was composed of widows or retired single women who had come to live in Elmdon not for the support that relatives already there could give, but simply because it was a pretty village and one in which leisure could be enjoyed.

Although by 1949 some adults were coming into Elmdon for rather different reasons than the immigrants of a hundred years ago, there was one category whose relative importance changed remarkably little. The proportion of those immigrants without village connections who came to work in Elmdon as well as to live there was only marginally less in 1949—59 than in 1851—61. There were, however, considerable changes in the way these immigrants were employed. The most noticeable of these was first, that while in the mid-nineteenth century a third were craftsmen, none fell into this category in 1949—59; and second, that all but one of the 1949—59 male immigrants were working in agriculture, indicating that Elmdoners themselves were taking advantage of the recent improvement in transport to leave the land and work in nearby factories, or on the buses instead. On the women's side, there was a marked decline in the importance of full-time domestic service as an occupation.

To sum up, the two main changes in migration patterns between 1851—61 and 1949—59 lay first in the declining numbers of children born into Elmdon families and reaching the age of 21 while still living in the village, and secondly, to a less marked though still significant extent, in the increasing proportion of adults coming in who had no previous links with Elmdon. If the overall figures alone are considered, however, there was almost no change in the pattern of adult population movement at the beginning and end of the periods we have been discussing. Both 1851—61 and 1949—59 were decades in which economic conditions favoured farming, and were therefore likely to reinforce stability in Elmdon which contained no industry except agriculture. But this stability had not been maintained throughout the whole period; the national and local crises described earlier had caused fluctuations in turnover at different times in the intervening years. In order to understand this more fully, let us look at the movements of men who had the vote from 1899 to 1949, bearing in mind that for the first two decades, as we saw earlier in this chapter, those concerned were mainly household heads, whereas for the rest of the period they included all men of 21 years and over.

Migration, 1899—1949

Table 55 sets out the proportions of male voters who departed, arrived or stayed in Elmdon throughout each decade from 1899 to 1949. At the beginning of this period, the depression of the 1890s was ending. In any case, as chapter 4 showed, Elmdon had been cushioned from its worst effects by the introduction of Edwin Goode's steam-plough contracting business at Elmdon Lodge farm, which created jobs for a number of village men. The ensuing decade was one of slow recovery, and it is perhaps not surprising to find that the emigration rate for male voters was very similar to that of all adult males in 1851—61, as was the proportion of men coming in who were either Elmdoners reaching the age of 21, or who had a close link with the village. An increase did occur in the percentage of those coming in without any known connection with Elmdon, though as the numbers involved were so small it did not mark a dramatic change. These incomers included two publicans, a farm bailiff, a policeman, a farmer and a carpenter, who were just the kind of 'stranger' immigrant familiar to Elmdoners in the mid-nineteenth century, as well as a farm worker and six men whose occupation is not known. One individual who was in Elmdon in 1899, but had left before 1909, was a new type of resident, however. He was Tregonwell Monro, who hired rooms in

206

Table 55
Turnover of male voters, Elmdon village, 1899–1949

	1899–1909		1909–19(i)		1919(i)–29		1929–39		1939–49	
	no.	%	no.	%	no.	%	no.	%	no.	%
Total male voters at beginning of decade	62	100	68	100	107	100	96	100	96	100
Disappearance through death	14	22.6	14	20.5	13	12.1	13	13.5	15	15.6
through emigration	16	25.8	16	23.5	37	34.6	23	24	24	25.0
(Disappearance subtotal, braced)	30	48.4	30	44	50	46.7	36	37.5	39	40.6
Still in Elmdon village at end of decade	32	51.6	38	56	57	53.3	60	62.5	57	59.4
Still in Elmdon village at end of decade	32	47.1	38	52.1	57	59.4	60	62.5	57	53.3
with Elmdon connection(ii)	24	35.3	24	32.9	20	20.8	14	14.6	22	20.6
Appearances without Elmdon connection	12	17.6	11	15	19	19.8	22	22.9	28	26.1
(Appearances subtotal, braced)	36	52.9	35	47.9	39	40.6	36	37.5	50	46.7
Total male voters at end of decade	68	100	73	100	96	100	96	100	107	100

(i) From 1899 to 1918, unmarried sons living at home, living-in domestic servants, and men of no fixed abode were excluded from the lists of voters, which otherwise included men of 21 years and over. In 1918, universal male suffrage for men of 21 years and over was introduced. The spring 1919 Register of Electors living in the parish of Elmdon fortunately listed separately those who joined the Register under the new regulation. It has therefore been possible to compare like with like for the decades 1899–1909 and 1909–1919, that is to say, men aged 21 and over excluding bachelor sons at home, living-in domestic servants and those of no fixed abode up to 1919; and all men aged 21 and over from 1919 onwards.

(ii) This covers those Elmdoners who reached the age of 21 during the decade; non-Elmdoners who married into established Elmdon families; and those who had other kin links with established Elmdon families.

Sources: Registers of Electors, 1899, 1909, 1919 (spring), 1929, 1939 and 1949. Parish registers.

Church Farm from the widowed Mrs Brand, and he figured in the subscription lists to village charities which were so familiar to the better-off families in Elmdon at that time. What exactly he was doing in the village we do not know, and indeed he did not stay long, but he may well have been an early representative of those who came, not to earn a living, but simply because they thought Elmdon a pleasant place to live.

Although 1899–1909 was a decade in which no great change in population movement might be expected, and none was experienced, the next ten years were a different matter, for they included the period of the First World War. This major national event did not apparently affect the migration figures of Elmdon at all. In fact, marginally smaller proportions emigrated and immigrated, and a correspondingly higher proportion remained in the village, compared with the previous decade. The voters concerned, however, were household heads and therefore older, rather than younger, men. One might expect their sons who, before the war, were excluded from voting because they were unmarried and living at home, to show a different pattern. However, they do not seem to have done so. In 1918, thirty-six Elmdon men were serving in the armed forces.[4] Before 1921, three of them had died on war service, and one after the war; ten had decided to live elsewhere; but twenty-two, or 61 per cent, were back in the village, compared to the 51 per cent of the old-style voters who stayed in Elmdon from 1909–19. The war brought its tragedies to Elmdon, for twelve young men from the parish were killed between 1914 and 1919, but it did not immediately alter the old pattern of village life.

With the decade 1919–29, the period of greatest change in Elmdon's migration pattern was reached. As table 55 shows, over a third of the adult males left, compared with under a quarter both in the preceding decade, which covered the First World War, and the following ten years which included a period of intense depression. This increased movement away from the village may in part have been a delayed reaction to the new experiences brought to younger men through war service, making it difficult for them to settle down again. Certainly, in the reverse direction, at least one ex-serviceman came into Elmdon as a stranger at this time. He was an ex-army Captain who became a poultry farmer, specialising in Rhode Island Reds, and he entered into village affairs by becoming honorary secretary of the Elmdon Conservative Club.[5]   His commercial venture, however, was probably unsuccessful, for he soon left. As we have already seen, agriculture was far from healthy in the 1920s, and it was difficult to prosper in any branch of farming at that time. Even so, the major cause of the increased emigration rate during this decade was almost certainly the breakdown of the old system of land-holding, when the Lofts Hall estate was sold. As we saw in chapter 6, the Squire preferred tenants from Elmdon families, and from the time in 1922 when he tried unsuccessfully to dispose of his property, villagers must have felt uncertain of what the future would hold. When the sale was actually made in 1927, the old farmers like William Arthur Brand and Oswald Prime retired, making room for newcomers from outside, and forty-three houses and cottages in Elmdon village were put on the market. They were not in the main bought by Elmdon people, and certainly not by farm workers (see p. 116, chapter 6). The resultant changes in house ownership must have given the final impetus to those Elmdoners who were thinking of moving elsewhere.

It was during the 1920s that Elmdon's first London commuter arrived (see chapter 2, p. 35). He used to drive by pony trap each day to Audley End station, and take the train to the City where he worked in a stockbroker's office. Nor was this the only thing for which he was remembered. He lived in The Hoops, and as a Four Square Gospeller, he used his house for meetings of the Glad Tidings group. Neighbours from their windows would watch with amazement the total immersion of converts being baptised in the garden, to the accompaniment of hymns played on the harmonium - a very different scene from the days when Harriet Walters, the tailor's daughter, and her mother ran The Hoops as a beer-shop.

Incomers of this kind, who lived in Elmdon but worked outside, became more numerous as time went on. While a greater proportion of the adult male population emigrated in the 1920s than at any other time in this century up to 1959, the percentage of immigrants with Elmdon connections dropped, so that those in this category coming in between 1919 and 1929 formed only just over a fifth of the adult male population in 1929, compared with a third, ten years earlier. During the next decade, 1929–39, this trend became even more pronounced, as table 55 shows, and for the first time the proportion of strangers coming in exceeded that of young Elmdoners reaching the age of 21, together with immigrants who had links with the village. Emigration, on the other hand, was back to where it was for the bulk of the period from 1899 to 1949. Regardless of national events such as depression or war, about a quarter of all men aged 21 and over left Elmdon during each decade, except during the 1920s.

It is understandable that the Second World War should have little effect on population movement in Elmdon, for the need to make the country as self-sufficient in food as possible meant that agriculture was declared a reserved occupation. Many Elmdon men were therefore bound to stay where they were, and were not free to join the forces. Nevertheless, six men from the parish died on active service, their names being inscribed on the memorial tablet in Elmdon church. After the War, the introduction of the daily bus service was a stabilising influence, for job opportunities in Elmdon itself were no longer a major factor in determining whether a man could stay there.

To sum up, changes in the proportions of overall population turnover were remarkably small throughout the period we have been considering, and the greatest changes occurred as a result of local rather than national events. From 1919 onwards, however, an increasing number of those immigrating had no previous connection with the village. The question remains as to how far these strangers supplanted the older Elmdon families. After all, the incomers in this category in each decade from 1899 onwards made up anything from a seventh to just over a quarter of the whole adult male population, as table 55 shows, and with this proportion of outsiders arriving every ten years, one might expect a considerable displacement of the families already established in Elmdon.

To answer this question, let us look not at emigrants or immigrants, but at the settled portion of the population, both male and female, who were present at the beginning and the end of the decades 1851–61 and 1949–59. Table 56 (a) and (b) shows that while there was indeed a drop in the proportion of adults who were related to established Elmdon families, either by birth or marriage, this amounted to only about 20 per cent over a hundred years, for both sexes. Even as late as 1959, roughly two out of every three adults in Elmdon had kin links with established families, and the claim made by an incomer in the 1960s that everyone in Elmdon was related had a modicum of truth in it. The reason for this lay in the fact that most of the immigrants with no kin connection did not settle permanently in the village. Indeed of the 92

Table 56
(a) *Men aged 21 plus, in Elmdon village in 1851 and 1861*[i] *and 1949 and 1959*[ii] *by kin connection*

| | 1851–61 | | | | 1949–59 | | | |
	no.	%	no.	%	no.	%	no.	%
Those with Elmdon kin links								
Born in Elmdon or brought up in an established Elmdon family	63	86.3	63	86.3	33	52.4	42	66.7
Non-Elmdoners married into an established Elmdon family	–	–			9	14.3		
Those with no known Elmdon kin links								
Working in Elmdon	10	13.7	10	13.7	14	22.2	21	33.3
Working outside, retired or occupation not known	–	–			7	11.1		
Totals			73	100			63	100

(i) The men present both in 1851 and 1861 formed 56.6% of all adult males present in 1851
(ii) The men present both in 1949 and 1959 formed 58.9% of all adult males present in 1949

(b) *Women, aged 21 plus, in Elmdon village in 1851 and 1861*[i] *and 1949 and 1959*[ii] *by kin connection*

| | 1851–61 | | | | 1949–59 | | | |
	no.	%	no.	%	no.	%	no.	%
Those with Elmdon kin links								
Born in Elmdon or brought up in an established Elmdon family	29	40.3	62	86.1	26	38.2	46	67.5
Non-Elmdoners married into an established Elmdon family	32	44.4			17	25.0		
Other kin connections	1	1.4			3	4.4		
Those with no known Elmdon kin links								
Working in Elmdon	1	1.4	10	13.9	4	5.9	22	32.5
Dependents of men immigrants with no kin connection	9	12.5			16	23.5		
Retired	–	–			2	2.9		
Totals			72	100			68	100

(i) The women present in 1851 and 1861 formed 60% of all adult females present in 1851
(ii) The women present in 1949 and 1959 formed 60.7% of all adult females present in 1949

Sources: 1851 and 1861 census. Registers of electors for Elmdon (village district), qualifying dates 10 June 1949 and 10 October 1959. Elmdon survey 1964. Parish Registers.

211

adult males in this category from 1899 to 1949, over six out of every ten left again after a single decade. Only five of them died in Elmdon, though three more lived there up to their retirement, and in only six cases did a son or daughter of one of these immigrants remain in the village, either to marry into an Elmdon family or to become in their turn an established Elmdoner through birth or upbringing. After a hundred years, Elmdon's population was still made up partly of transients who stayed only a comparatively short time, and who formed a minority, even if a growing one, and a majority who belonged to a core of well-established families.

So far, we have looked broadly at Elmdon's pattern of migration, and in greater detail at those entering the village, between the mid-nineteenth and mid-twentieth centuries. But what of the members of established Elmdon families who emigrated during this time? They were, after all, individuals driven by their own ambitions or needs. What caused some families to stay while other went and why, within each family group, did some members spend their lives in Elmdon while others emigrated? The histories of the six old Elmdon families still present in the village at the time of the 1964 survey,[6] which were drawn on in chapter 4 to assess the degree of change in the farm workers' group between 1861 and 1930, provide evidence on which to base at least partial answers to these questions.

Migration in the six families

The six families differed considerably in the length of time they had been living in Elmdon. Two of them, the Hayes and the Hoys, were certainly established by the mid-seventeenth century and possibly earlier. For most of the eighteenth century, family members held small acreages in the open fields, and at the same time worked as craftsmen and tradesmen. Some of them were thatchers, others were plumbers and glaziers, publicans or carpenters - trades which later on were often held by non-Elmdoners, as chapter 6 showed. At this time, they were property owners in a small way, and were able to hand down cottages and land in Elmdon to their children.[7] Changing conditions, however, worked against them. Both families had sold their open field land before the Enclosure Award of 1829, and the Hayes and Hoys who stayed in Elmdon in the nineteenth century became farm labourers.

The Greenhills and the Gamgees came to Elmdon later in the

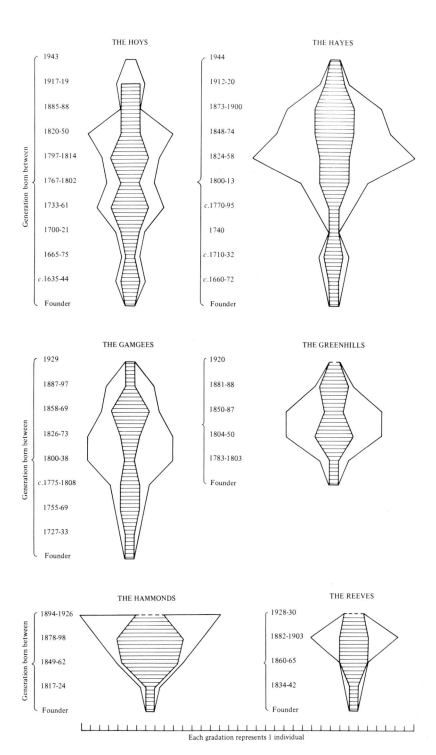

Fig. 11 Six Elmdon families

213

eighteenth century, and established themselves through marriages to Elmdon girls. Richard Greenhill, who came from Heydon only three miles away, was a bricklayer. It was his grandson, James, who became the master bricklayer described in chapter 6, and whose early death in 1859 signalled the end of the family business, and the entry of some of the family into farm work in the second half of the nineteenth century. The Gamgees, in contrast, were said to be of foreign origin, either French or Italian,[8] and the earliest members of the family to live in Elmdon probably started out as farm labourers. By the late eighteenth and early nineteenth centuries, however, a Gamgee was holding the responsible job of farm bailiff, and this man's son became both a wheelwright, and the father of the Gamgee who was to leave Elmdon for a veterinary career first in Italy and then in Edinburgh (see chapter 8). The Gamgees who stayed in Elmdon continued to work on the land, except for one who took over his maternal grandfather's job as a carrier.

The last two families, the Hammonds and the Reeves, arrived in Elmdon early in the nineteenth century. The founders of the Elmdon branches were both agricultural labourers, with wives from outside the village, and from the start they lived the lives common to farm workers which by this time the Hayes, Hoys and Gamgees were also sharing. Only some of the Greenhills remained in the small craftsmen's and tradesmen's group.

Family size

The varying backgrounds of these families before the mid-nineteenth century did not make any marked difference to the numbers of their men who were able to remain in Elmdon. Figure 11 illustrates the expansion and contraction of males born into each family, from its founding father (or in the case of the Hoys and Hayes, from its first recorded ancestor) up to the latest generation becoming adult before 1964. The whole shape of each family's diagram represents the total number of males surviving infancy who were born in Elmdon in successive generations, while the shaded central core shows the proportion who spent their lives in the village. Looking at the diagrams for all the families except the Hammonds, it quickly becomes apparent that from 1635 right up to 1964, regardless of family background or occupation, the numbers of men staying on in Elmdon in each generation varied from one to four, and never exceeded the latter figure. This applied regardless of the number of males born into a family in a particular generation. For example, only one of the nine male Gamgees born between 1800 and 1838 avoided emigration, but two generations later, four out of only six males were able to do so. It seems as if Elmdon at all times was able to absorb a limited number from each family group, but beyond this point the rest of the men had to go, whether they were few or many.

A look at the Hammond family diagram, however, does not support this supposition. Robert Hammond had settled in Elmdon by 1816, and nearly thirty years later the first of his seven Hammond grandsons was born. No fewer than six of the seven boys stayed in Elmdon for the greater part of their lives. How did such a new family manage to upset the established pattern?

The six Hammonds who stayed were all brothers, and it was their cousin who emigrated. The boys were part of a family with so many children that their names were remembered by the next generation through a sort of jingle. 'That's how they taught us to know 'em, see' said one of their descendants. 'We used to say Jim, Tim, Tom, Bob, Harry, John, Liddie, Jinnie, Liza.' These were the young men mentioned in chapter 6 who used to drink in the Carrier in the evenings and whose mother would march into the bar and order them home when she thought they had been there long enough. Five of the boys were farm workers all their lives, but Harry left the land for a spell in the army during the Boer War, before returning to Elmdon and a job as a butcher's assistant. It seems likely that the remaining brothers all worked on Elmdon Bury Farm at one time or another. Unfortunately no wages books for the period are available to prove whether this was the case, but tradition in the village has it that 'they were all up at the Bury'. In those days a good deal of farm work, and particularly the harvesting, depended on men working together as a unit (see chapter 4, p. 84) and it could be that as each Hammond boy grew up, his father or older brother already on the team at Elmdon Bury would exert influence to get him in as well. None of the other families we have been considering produced so many brothers, as opposed to cousins, in one generation as the Hammonds did, and possibly existing farm labourers worked less hard to get jobs for nephews or cousins than they did for sons or brothers.

The Hammonds managed to maintain an exceptionally large number of their males in Elmdon in the next generation too,

215

although instead of being one group of brothers, as their fathers had been, the seven men concerned were drawn from four groups of cousins. But after this, the core of Hammonds staying on in Elmdon reverted to the same pattern which the other families showed. It is interesting to note that the six families in the male line taken together were split up into 19 different households in 1964, just as they had been over a hundred years earlier in 1861.

Jobs and housing

If family size in general had little influence on the numbers of related men spending their lives in Elmdon, what was it that made some stay and others go? Individual choices and preferences, which are seldom recorded, should never be discounted. Nevertheless, the basic necessities of any worker, in the present as in the past, are a job and a house. In Elmdon in the nineteenth and early twentieth centuries, up to the sale of the Lofts Hall estate, these two needs went hand in hand, for as we saw in the last chapter, the village was dependent on agriculture, and once a farm worker's job had been won, a tied cottage, or one rented from the Lofts Hall estate, followed as a matter of course. If we consider the fifty-nine men staying in Elmdon who were born into the six families from 1800 to 1899, the youngest of whom would have reached 21 just as the Squire was deciding to dispose of his estate, we find that forty-five of them, or three out of every four, worked on the land. To these men, so long as they retained their job, housing was a problem only in so far as they wished to live in one rather than another of the various tied or low-rental cottages which were attached to the estate and to the other Elmdon farms. It seems too as if estate employees who reached retirement during this period retained their cottages. As chapter 8 showed, the Squire protected his elderly tenants in 1927 by selling their cottages subject to rent-free life tenancies.

This close association between housing and jobs is confirmed if we look at those members of the six families born in the nineteenth century who left Elmdon. Of the twenty-two men whose occupation after emigration is known, eighteen moved to work which carried accommodation with it. Eight went as farm labourers, and presumably were allocated tied cottages by their employers. Private service took another four, one becoming a butler, another a chauffeur, a third a gardener — all jobs which carried housing of a sort with them. The fourth was Joseph Gamgee who, as we saw in chapter 8 left home first to work as a hunt servant at Puckeridge, and then as stud-manager to Prince Petrullo in Sicily, but presumably even he did not have to worry about where he would live, since lodgings would go with each of these positions. Two further emigrants became publicans, two joined the army, and two the police — all jobs where accommodation was provided. There remain only four men who would have had to find housing for themselves after leaving Elmdon — a coal porter, two post office workers, and a horse-bus driver.

When we come to look at the men of the six families who were born in the twentieth century, most of whom would have been looking for jobs and houses at the time of, or later than, the break up of the Lofts Hall estate, rather a different picture emerges. Although agriculture remained of great importance as a source of employment right up to the end of the Second World War, and all but two of the thirteen men from the six families who remained in Elmdon began their working lives on the land, four of the older generation took advantage of the increased job opportunities offered as a result of the new daily bus service in 1947 and changed from farm work to other occupations. It might have been thought that housing problems would prevent them from taking this course of action, but one man was able to stay on in his tied cottage, even though he no longer worked for the farmer who owned it, while the other three all obtained council houses.

The first six council houses in Elmdon were erected in 1921. Curiously Tudor in appearance, they were built on land formerly part of the Church living, and were appropriately known as The Glebe. It was fortunate for the old Elmdon families that this extra housing provision came before the sale of the Lofts Hall estate, for it helped to compensate for the loss of some of the cottages bought by outsiders at the 1927 and 1930 sales. It must always be remembered, however, that roughly half the houses in Elmdon village never belonged to the estate. Ownership has not been established in all cases, but certainly a number had been bought as investments by local people, and were rented out, just as were some of the old Lofts Hall estate cottages after the sales. Elmdoners therefore were not dependent solely on the new council houses and the farmers' tied cottages with their traditional insecurity of tenure, at least until after the Second World War when rising house prices made selling more attractive to the owners than letting. By the time this happened, though, more council houses were being put up in Elmdon, and by 1964 there were twenty-five of them, all but three being occupied by families in which the head of the household or his wife had been born in Elmdon. If we look at the six family members in the male line heading nineteen households in Elmdon in 1964, we find that ten of them, or more than half, were in council houses, five were in tied cottages, three rented their houses, and only one owned his property. He was Edward Gamgee, who had been given the cottage by his sister, as we saw in chapter 6.

It looks, then, as if the six families had solved their housing problems as easily in the twentieth century as in the nineteenth, but this was not entirely the case. Whereas in the last half of the nineteenth century, jobs had been hard to get but housing was not difficult to find,[9] the situation had been reversed by the 1960s. The older men in the six families indeed benefited greatly both from council housing and from the various rent acts which gave them security of tenure in all but the tied cottages. Their sons, however, who had no difficulty in finding work outside Elmdon in local factories, and who thanks to modern transport could live at home, just as their counterparts had done in the 1860s, met with considerable difficulties when they wished to marry. Picturesque but unmodernised cottages no longer came on the market for the £30–£120 which they fetched at the Lofts hall estate sales, but were sold at prices well beyond the reach of most Elmdoners. In addition, new building in the village was limited by the planning authorities to 'in-filling'. If a young Elmdoner in the 1960s wished to stay in the village after marriage and work outside agriculture, he needed to acquire a council house, but these rarely fell vacant. The safe housing which the older generation of the six families acquired enabled them to retain their position in the village, but their sons were often forced to look for accommodation in a nearby development village such as Sawston or Duxford, where housing estates were allowed, or even further afield. While in the nineteenth century it was lack of work which caused members of Elmdon families to emigrate, in the mid-twentieth century the majority of those going left because of lack of housing.

I I

Elmdon in 1964. The continuity
and the change

If, like the mythical observer at the beginning of chapter 1, the
Rev. Robert Wilkes had been able to revisit the village in 1964, he
would almost certainly have made straight for the parish church
on Cross Hill, for it had been the centre of his working life for
nearly twenty years, and the restoration of its chancel, a project
dear to his heart, had not been completed until 1879,[1] the year
of his death. But once he had seen that the interior of the church
had changed little since then, and that his likeness, carved on a
corbel over the vicar's stall, was still in place, he would have felt
free to look at the rest of Elmdon. As he descended the steep
path from the church to the old vicarage where he had been born,
he would have been surprised by the absence of movement in the
scene. There would be no horses striking sparks from the flints in
the rough road as they went down the hill to be shod at the
Brands' forge or pulled carts and wagons into the yards at Hill or
Church Farms; no village women visiting the two grocers' and
drapers' shops below Charles Monk's beer-house; no smell of freshly
baked bread from Susannah Bowman's premises; and no children
playing up and down the road. Instead, he would see that the
bakery and shops had been turned into private houses, and it
might be many minutes before he was startled by a passing car.
Clearly, the structure and organisation of village life were very
different from his day. If he had been able to pursue his investigations further, in which areas would he have found the greatest
changes?

Population

A longer stay in Elmdon would confirm Robert Wilkes in his first
impression that the village was a quieter place than it used to be,
for as table 57 shows, the total population had dropped from 520

219

Table 57
Age structure, Elmdon village, 1964(i)

	0–14 yrs		15–29 yrs		30–44 yrs		45–59 yrs		60+ yrs		not known(ii)		all	
	no.	%	no.	%	no.	%	no.	%	no.	%	no.	%	no.	%
Males	37	23	26	16	22	14	32	20	37	23	4	3	158	49
Females	21	13	31	19	28	17	31	19	44	28	5	3	160	50
Sex not known	3	100	–		–		–		–		–		3	1
All	61	19	57	18	50	16	63	20	81	25	9	3	321	100
All, 1861	214	41	123	24	68	13	65	12	50	10	–		520	100

(i) The Elmdon Survey grew out of a series of unstructured interviews carried out as a form of training in field-work techniques by students of the Anthropology Department of Cambridge University. Although practically all residents of 21 years and over appearing on the Register of Electors for 1964 were seen, the interviews were spread out over a period, and did not refer to one specific day as did the 1861 census figures. Nor was a direct question asked on age, since at the time a statistical study was not envisaged. Entries in the parish registers for those born or dying in Elmdon, and material in the students' notebooks both in 1964 and at later periods in the case of those born outside Elmdon, have enabled a division of the 1964 population into 15-year age groups to be made. It must be pointed out, however, that the figures in table 57 should be looked on as an informed estimate rather than as completely accurate.

(ii) All over 21 years of age

Sex ratio: 98.75

Sources: Register of Electors, Elmdon village, 1964. Parish registers, Elmdon. Elmdon survey notebooks. Table 4, chapter 1.

220

people in 1861 to 321, a decrease of 38 per cent. Nor could he fail to be struck by the decline in the numbers of children about the streets. The proportion of under 15s had been halved since he had relinquished the Elmdon living a hundred years ago, and if the whole 0—14 age group had been mustered at Cross Hill for a village occasion, it would only have contained sixty-one boys and girls, compared with 214 in 1861. If his visit had been in term-time, children would have been even more conspicuous by their absence, for all those aged 5—14 would have been at school, while in 1861 roughly a third of this group were neither pupils nor at work, but were simply living at home without any formal occupation. Conversely, he would surely have been surprised at the number of elderly people he met, since in 1964 those aged 60 and over made up a quarter of the total population, while in 1861 they had only represented one out of every ten inhabitants. In his time, 60 per cent of the people he met in the village were likely to be under 30 years of age. By 1964, the balance had tipped the other way, and six out of ten were 30 or over. Elmdon had become a village with a predominantly middle-aged or elderly population.

Household structure

Although there were almost 200 fewer people in Elmdon in 1964 than in 1861, Robert Wilkes would have noticed very little change in the number of houses it contained. He would see that some cottages had been pulled down and others amalgamated or sub-divided, and he could not fail to remark the new council housing which lay in the eastern half of the village, along the Ickleton road. But while in 1861 there were 115 separate households, in 1964 this number had dropped by only one. Indeed, the correspondence would be exact if not for the fact that one particularly large family had been allocated two adjoining council houses in order to make room for the six unmarried children and their cousin who, with the household head and his wife, made up the establishment. As table 58 shows, the difference between 1861 and 1964 lay not in the amount of housing stock available, but in the smaller groups which the dwellings accommodated. While only 29 per cent of Elmdoners in 1861 were living either alone or with one other person, excluding servants, by 1964 this proportion had almost doubled, standing at 54 per cent. In 1861, Elmdon Bury farm-house housed John Rolfe, his second wife, four children and two

221

Table 58
Size of households, Elmdon 1964, excluding servants[i], visitors and lodgers not known to be kin

no. of house- hold members	no. of households	no. of individuals	% of all households	% of all house- holds, 1861
1	20	20	18	(6)
2	41	82	36	(23)
3	17	51	15	(17)
4	21	84	18	(19)
5	8	40	7	(8)
6	3	18	3	(9)
7	1	7	1	(7)
8	1	8	1	(6)
9	1 [ii]	9	1	(3)
10	–	–	–	(1)
11	–	–	–	(1)
not known	1 [iii]	1	1	–
	114	320	101	(100)

(i)   Only one household in 1964 contained a 'servant'.
(ii) In this instance, the family had been allocated two council houses
(iii) The household head refused to be interviewed

Sources: Register of Electors, 1964. Parish registers, Elmdon. Elmdon survey notebooks. Table 6, chapter 1.

living-in servants, while a hundred years later, its only occupant was the last Squire's widow. Down at the King's Head, the publican and his wife in 1964 were installed in accommodation which in 1861 had contained a family of seven, quite apart from occasional strangers who put up at the inn.

The declining size of Elmdon households in general was naturally reflected in changes in household structure, set out in table 59. The proportion of people living entirely alone had trebled by 1964, while at the same time the proportion of extended family households containing relatives over and above the household head, his wife and their children had halved. Another marked change lay in the reduction of households with living-in domestic servants. There were nine such establishments in 1861 and only one in 1964. Even in this solitary case, the help was only part-time, since the 'servant' was not a regular employee, but an Italian *au pair* girl.

Incomers

If Robert Wilkes had wanted to find out how many Elmdoners in 1964 were descended from the men and women who had been his own parishioners, and had asked who the people he met in the street were, he would certainly have heard some familiar names,

Table 59
Household Structure, Elmdon, 1964

		without servants no.	with servant no.	total no.	total %	total, 1861 %
1. Solitaries	(a) widowed/divorced	9	1	20	18	(6)
	(b) single	10	–			
2. No family	(a) co-resident siblings	5	–	6	5	(7)
	(b) non-related residents	1	–			
3. Simple family households						
	(a) married couples, alone	33	–			
	(b) married couples with child(ren)	38	–	78	68	(74)
	(c) widowers with child(ren)	2	–			
	(d) widows/separated/divorced with child(ren)	5	–			
4. Extended family households						
	(a) extended upwards	1	–			
	(b) extended downwards	1	–	6	5	(11)
	(c) extended laterally	4	–			
5. Multiple family households						
	(a) secondary unit down	1	–			
	(b) secondary unit down, with upward extension	1	–	2	2	(2)
6. Indeterminate		1	–	1	1	–
7. Not known		1	–	1	1	–
Totals		113	1	114	100	(100)

Sources: Register of electors, Elmdon village, 1964. Parish registers, Elmdon. Elmdon survey notbooks, table 11, chapter 1.

for there were still Gamgees, Greenhills, Hammonds, Hayes, Hoys and Reeves in the village. Indeed, as an Elmdon farmer said in the early 1960s, if you passed a man whose name you did not know and said 'Good morning, Mr Hammond', you had a 50 per cent chance of being right. This was of course an exaggeration, but in fact, direct descendants of these six families in the male line, and their wives, accounted for 17 per cent of Elmdon's total population in 1964, and others were related to them through the female side. The extent of these relationships is discussed fully by Marilyn Strathern in *Kinship at the core*. But as Robert Wilkes went on his way he would meet more and more people who had no roots in Elmdon. Old Mrs Bowman's cottage and bakery, for instance, was occupied by a widow from Chile, who had moved there to be near her recently arrived daughter and son-in-law, the latter commuting daily to his work as a chartered accountant and solicitor in London. Even the Wilkes Arms was now a private house, occupied in the school holidays by the wife of a business-man in Baghdad, and her two children. Robert Wilkes was familiar with Elmdon in the days when nearly three-quarters of its inhabitants had been born in the parish, and probably christened by him or his father. How far had the position changed in 1964?

Birth and marriage

Table 60 shows that in 1964 the proportion of Elmdon inhabitants born outside the parish had more than doubled since 1861, and now included nearly six out of every ten individuals. At first sight, this might imply that outsiders were in the majority and that established Elmdon families had been swamped by incomers but,

Table 60
Population by place of birth, Elmdon village, 1964

| | born in Elmdon parish[i] | | | born elsewhere[ii] | | | total | |
	no.	%	(1861) (%)	no.	%	(1861) (%)	no.	%
Males	69	44	(81)	89	56	(19)	158	49
Females	60	37.5	(65)	100	62.5	(35)	160	50
Sex not known	3	100	–	–	–	–	3	1
All	132	41	(73)	189	59	(27)	321	100

(i) Elmdon parish has been used rather than Elmdon village because the 1861 census did not distinguish between those born in Elmdon village and Duddenhoe End hamlet, both in Elmdon parish. In 1964, 2 males and 5 females had been born in Duddenhoe End.

(ii) This category includes 8 males and 9 females who were either members of established Elmdon families or who were raised in Elmdon from early infancy.

Sources: Elmdon parish registers. Elmdon survey notebooks, table 7, chapter 1.

as we shall see later, this was not the case, although some degree of dilution had indeed occurred. One of the reasons for the sharp increase in the proportion of people born outside the parish lay in the changing pattern of marriage. As table 61 shows, the partners in 38 per cent of all marriages in 1861 had both been born in the parish. In 1964, the proportion had dropped to 5 per cent, and instead, Elmdon men and women were finding their spouses from a wider area. The incoming marriage partners, although increasing the proportion of those in the village who had been born outside Elmdon, did not remain 'outsiders' in the usual sense of that word,

224

Table 61
Elmdon village, marriages, 1964

Elmdon-Elmdon marriages[i]			husband b. Elmdon wife b. elsewhere[ii]			wife b. Elmdon husband b. elsewhere			both born elsewhere[iii]			all	
no.	*%*	*(1861) (%)*	*no.*	*%*	*(1861) (%)*	*no.*	*%*	*(1861) (%)*	*no.*	*%*	*(1861) (%)*	*no.*	*%*
4	5	(38)	21	27	(44)	12	15	(3)	42	53	(14)	79	100

(i)   This category includes 1 case where the wife was born in Duddenhoe End.
(ii) This category includes 4 cases where the wife was raised in Elmdon.
(iii) This category includes 1 case where both husband and wife were raised in Elmdon, 1 case in which the wife was raised in Elmdon and 3 cases where the husband was raised in Elmdon.

Sources: Elmdon parish registers. Elmdon survey notebooks, table 10, chapter 1.

but became part of the Elmdon family into which they married. Their own relatives from outside Elmdon therefore had a link with Elmdon too, and might enter the village as a result, as the nephew of Jack Wilkes' widow did when he took over Elmdon Bury Farm.

Another change which table 61 reveals is that there had been a considerable increase since 1861 in the proportion of marriages in which the husband came to live in the wife's birthplace, thus reversing the usual pattern. In 1861, this had occurred in only 3 per cent of the marriages, compared to 15 per cent in 1964.

Whether the incomers entered as marriage partners or as outsiders with no previous connection with Elmdon, Robert Wilkes would have been astonished by the distances from which some of them had come. As table 62 shows, in 1964 only just over a quarter of the incomers had been born within a ten-mile radius of Elmdon, compared with three-quarters in 1861, while the proportion of those born over twenty miles away rose to 60 per cent. Not only had people arrived from all parts of the United Kingdom, but individuals had been born in Germany, Gibraltar, Italy, Switzerland, the USA and Chile. Elmdon had never been isolated from other small settlements. By 1964 it was clear that improved means of transport in general, and the widespread use of private cars in particular, had opened up the village to people drawn from areas far beyond the neighbouring parishes. No longer could family ties be kept up only within walking distance. One couple had recently come to live in Elmdon especially to give support to elderly relatives who, however, lived not in the village but in Saffron Walden, five miles distant as the crow flies, but only a matter of minutes away by car.

Table 62
Population by distance of birthplace from Elmdon, 1964

	no.	%	(% in 1861)
up to 5 miles	43	23	60
5 - 10 miles	8	4	15
10 - 20 miles	10	5	8
over 20 miles	114	60	11
not known	14	7	6
total	189	100	

Sources: Elmdon parish registers. Elmdon survey notebooks, table 9, chapter 1.

Reasons for immigration

As we saw in the last two chapters, being born outside Elmdon did not necessarily mean that an incomer had no kinship ties bringing him or her to the village. How far had the nature of these ties changed since 1861? Table 63 shows that while nearly half the incomers in 1861 were connected with established Elmdoners through birth or marriage, the proportion by 1964 had dropped to three out of ten. Conversely, women and children coming into Elmdon because they were dependants of newly immigrant males rose to 34 per cent in 1964, compared with only 17 per cent in 1861. Incomers previously unconnected with the village outnumbered those who were linked to families already established there, and to that extent, Elmdon families had indeed lost ground to the newcomers.

Table 63 also shows that there was a new category of incomer in 1964. Even in 1861, Robert Wilkes was used to seeing immigrant parishioners settle into the village for a few years and then leave again, but these, as we saw in chapter 6, were largely shopkeepers, craftsmen or domestic servants, all of whom came to work as well as to live in Elmdon. By 1964, 15 per cent of all incomers were household heads who were living in Elmdon simply because they had found housing and living conditions to their liking. Some of them were retired, but others left the village each day to go to work, whether locally or in London, and even if their wives used the village shop and their children attended the village school, they themselves were part of Elmdon only in the evenings and at weekends.

226

Table 63
Those living in Elmdon village, 1964, who were not born in the parish

	no.	%	(1861) (%)	no.	%	(1861) (%)
With kinship connections						
Women who had married men already established in Elmdon village	30	16	(31)			
Men who had married women already established in Elmdon village	16	8	(2)			
Children with 1 or both parents born in Elmdon	11	6	(14)	137	72	(79)
Miscellaneous family connections in Elmdon	10	5	(14)			
Miscellaneous family connections, immigrant family	4	2				
Wives accompanying immigrant husbands	33	17	(11)			
Those entering as children of immigrant parents	33	17	(6)			
Without kinship connections						
Coming to Elmdon to work:						
males	17	9	(14)			
females	7	4	(7)	52	28	(21)
Coming to Elmdon for housing						
males	20	11	(−)			
females	8	4	(−)			
Total				189	100	

Sources: Elmdon parish registers. Elmdon survey notebooks, table 8, chapter 1.

The position in 1964

How far, then, had Elmdon's total population in 1964 been diluted
by immigrants who had no connection with other families in the
village? As we have seen, table 60, showing that 41 per cent of
people in Elmdon had been born within the parish, is a poor guide
to the true position, because the great majority of spouses marrying
into Elmdon families had come from outside. There are further
reasons. First, individuals who, though actually born outside
Elmdon, were either members of old-established Elmdon families,
or who had been brought up in the village from early infancy and
so were in practical terms part and parcel of village life, appear as
outsiders; and second, children recently born in Elmdon to immigrant parents who might well stay for only a year or two are
included as Elmdoners. If a London-based commuter and his wife
moved into Elmdon and then left three years later, the fact that

during that time they had a child born in Elmdon did not alter their position as short-stay incomers.

A more satisfactory way of looking at the position is through the 114 households in Elmdon in 1964. If the household heads are divided into those with Elmdon village kin connections and those without, we are likely to get a fairer view of how far incomers had 'taken over' Elmdon by 1964. Table 64 (a) shows that exactly half the heads had kin connections in the village outside their immediate household, while table 64 (b) shows the nature of these connections. If we go a stage further, and include all the members of each household as well as the head, to cover the whole population, we find that the proportion with Elmdon village kin connections rises to 57 per cent, as against 43 per cent for those with no connections, which is a reversal of table 60, showing that 41 per cent of the population were born in Elmdon compared to 59 per cent outside.[2]

Occupations

The professional class[3]

If Robert Wilkes in 1964 had wanted to find out how far the various occupational groups present in Elmdon in 1861 had changed (see chapter 1, table 3), he would probably have started his investigations at the Old Vicarage, where he himself had been born, and had lived for forty years before moving to Lofts Hall. Here he would have had his first shock, for he would have found the house occupied, not by the vicar, but by another professional man, a land estate agent and magistrate of a London juvenile court, whose work lay entirely outside Elmdon. When he had finally tracked down the present incumbent in the new, smaller vicarage up by the church and had discovered, perhaps to his secret disappointment, that the latter was not descended from the son-in-law to whom he had presented the living in 1872, he would have been further surprised to learn that the advowson was no longer even in the gift of the Wilkes family, and that the benefices of Elmdon and Wenden Lofts, which were separate in 1861, had been united. In Robert Wilkes's day, the professional class living in Elmdon was limited to his fellow clergymen. By 1964, however, membership had broadened to include not only the occupant of the Old Vicarage, but people working in university teaching and research, the arts, publishing, journalism, accountancy and the like,

Table 64
(a) *Household heads, Elmdon village, 1964, by kin connection with Elmdon*

	no.	%
Household heads with Elmdon village kin connections	57	50
Household heads without Elmdon village connections	57	50
Total household heads	114	100

(b) *Analysis of Elmdon village household heads with Elmdon kin connections, 1964*

	kinship		total heads	
	paternal no.	maternal no.	no.	%
A. Household heads descended from *at least* 1 parent and 1 grandparent born and raised in Elmdon village	21	9		
Non-Elmdon household heads whose spouses were descended from *at least* 1 parent and 1 grandparent born and raised in Elmdon village	9	4	43	75
Household heads descended from *at least* 1 parent born and raised in Elmdon village	—	2	2	4
	30	15		

	no. of heads		
B. First generation to be born/raised Elmdon, with			
1 generation of descendants in the village, 1964	2		
2 generations of descendants in the village, 1964	1	6	10.5
3 generations of descendants in the village, 1964	1		
No descendants in Elmdon village, 1964	2		
C. Other kin links, through			
Spouse's former husband, as Elmdon village resident	2		
Spouse born in Elmdon village	1		
Spouse's cousin married into old Elmdon village family	1	6	10.5
Inheritance/gift of property in Elmdon village from an aunt	2		
Total household heads with Elmdon village kin connections		57	100

Sources: Elmdon parish registers. Elmdon survey notebooks.

as table 65 shows. An even more remarkable event, in Robert Wilkes's eyes, would be the appearance of the three women who now came within this category, and represented nearly a third of its members.

Farmers and farm workers

If Robert Wilkes, on leaving the new vicarage, had gone on up the hill to Elmdon Bury, he would at first have felt much more at home, for the occupant of the farmhouse, Mrs Ida Wilkes, was his grandson's widow, and the farm itself was also owned by a family

Table 65
Full-time occupations of Elmdon village inhabitants, 1964

	men	women
Professional		
Clergy	1	—
Teaching and research	1	1
Publishing, journalism, lecturing, the arts	3	2
Insurance, advertising	3	—
Chartered accountant/solicitor	1	—
Land estate agent	1	—
	10	3
Agriculture		
Farmers	7	—
Farm foremen	1	—
Farm workers	32	—
	40	—
General services		
Policeman	1	—
Post Office employees	—	3
Water Board employee	1	—
Bus employees	6	—
Taxi operators	—	1
Roadmen	2	—
RAF	1	—
	11	4
Craftsmen, tradesmen, artisans, factory workers, trainees		
Blacksmith/mechanic	1	—
Mechanics, electricians, engineer	7	—
Builders, painters, carpenters, timber dealers	7	—
Factory workers	8	3
Newspaper employees	1	—
Drivers	1	—
Odd job men	1	—
Licensed victuallers and assistants	1	2
Butchers	1	1
Shopkeepers	1	1
Salesmen	2	—
Trainee representative	1	—
Clerical	1	2
Draughtsmen	1	—
	34	9

Source: Elmdon survey

connection, having been passed on to Mrs Wilkes's nephew, Major Rippingall. But he would soon have discovered that it had been halved in size since the survey carried out for him in 1860, and that all the Elmdon farms were now owner-occupied, instead of only one in 1861. He would then realise that the whole basis of landownership in Elmdon had changed, and that the role of a

Table 66
Part-time occupations of Elmdon village inhabitants[i], *1964*

	men	women
Professional		
Teaching and research	–	1
Agriculture		
Farmers	–	2
Farm workers	3	–
Fruit pickers and pruners	–	14
	3	16
Employment in private households		
Maintenance and handymen	3	–
Gardeners	10	–
Living-out domestic help	–	16
Au pair	–	1
	13	17
General services		
Taxi driver	1	–
Craftsmen, tradesmen, etc.		
Factory workers	–	2
Dressmakers	–	1
Licensed victuallers' assistants	1	–
Shop assistants	–	3
Clerical and secretarial	–	2
	1	8

(i) 3 men and 7 women had two part-time jobs each.

Source: Elmdon survey, 1964

landed proprietor leasing farms to tenants, which he himself had filled, had now disappeared.

Up at the Bury, a farm which in 1964 was devoted entirely to arable farming and carried no livestock, Robert Wilkes would also see the full effects of mechanisation. Where in his day the harvesting had been done by teams of men twenty or more strong, and had taken up to six weeks to complete, now with good weather the whole operation would be over in a few days. Tractors and combine-harvesters had replaced the horses in the stables, and with a work force of five men, four full-time and one part-time, all of whom were in their late 50s or 60s, the 350-acre farm was considered to be heavily overstaffed. It would not take him long to discover, however, that four of the five men were descended from parishioners he had known in 1861, while the fifth was a family connection, through marriage, of one of the other workers. To find a farm labourer who, in 1964, had come to Elmdon from a different part of the country he would have to go over to Jack Cross's property, based on Hill and Freewood Farms, where seven of the work force of fifteen men and boys had come from more than five miles away from Elmdon, some of them from quite different regions such as Northamptonshire or Scotland.

Robert Wilkes would also notice a change in the employment of women on the land. In 1861, most village women took part in gleaning and in other seasonal tasks on Elmdon's farms. Twelve of them were full-time field workers. In 1964, fourteen Elmdon women were still working part-time in agriculture, giving occasional help with specialised jobs (see table 66), but most of their work was done outside the parish on fruit farms in the district, either picking or pruning. The two part-time women farmers, one of whom was in partnership with her son and the other helping her husband, were nothing new, for Rebecca Perry and her farm bailiff had run Poplars for thirty years or so in the nineteenth century.

Employment in private households

The change in the employment of domestic servants would also become obvious to Robert Wilkes while he was at Elmdon Bury. Even though the farmhouse was large, with six bedrooms and a wealth of what estate agents now call domestic offices, his grandson's widow, at this time in her late 70s, not only had no living-in domestic help but had also surprised the village by learning how to cook. Indeed, there were no living-in servants in the whole village, apart from the Italian *au pair* who has already been mentioned, and only four village-based women worked full-time by day in Elmdon houses or at Lofts Hall. Where Robert Wilkes himself had employed a personal manservant, a butler, a coachman and a head gardener, the only men employed privately full-time in 1964 were a maintenance worker who went over to Lofts Hall each day, and a gardener *cum* general assistant who worked for a physically handicapped employer.

In 1964, Elmdon girls no longer left home for domestic service in neighbouring villages or towns before marriage, as they had done a century ago. But although full-time work in private households had decreased considerably, part-time work in this area was important both to men and women in Elmdon in 1964 as a supplement to the family income. Sixteen women did domestic work for a few hours each week, and ten men worked as gardeners in their spare time. All these men either were, or had at some time been, farm workers.

General services

Elmdon in 1861 had its general services, but the policeman who patrolled the parish was also responsible for Wenden Lofts and had his house there, while the two roadmen who dealt with the worst of the ruts and potholes lived in Duddenhoe End. A hundred years later, Elmdon housed the local policeman and two council roadmen; Post Office business in the village was undertaken by three women, instead of by Mr Crisp, the grocer and draper; and the two Elmdon carriers had been replaced partly by a taxi-service run by the wife of an Elmdon bus conductor, with the occasional help of her father, and partly by a major bus company. This company had an influence on the working lives of Elmdoners out of all proportion to the six jobs which it provided for men living in the village, since its daily services to nearby towns enlarged the area in which Elmdon men and women could find work, and allowed incomers, like the Water Board official working in Saffron Walden, to live in the village but work outside it.

Craftsmen, tradesmen and other industrial workers

The occupational group in which Robert Wilkes would find some of the greatest changes, comprised those who were self-employed in a small way of business, or who worked as employees in shops or industry outside agriculture. Even though the proportion of those working in this broad category had changed comparatively little over the hundred year period, the kind of work undertaken was very different. Robert Wilkes would have looked in vain for the specialist thatchers, bricklayers, tailors, full-time dressmakers, and girls making straw bonnets who were working in Elmdon in 1861. Instead of eight blacksmiths and wheelwrights, he would find only one, who spent his time repairing agricultural machinery for Jack Cross, and who in fact gave up his job a year or two later since he found there was not enough work to keep him fully occupied. True, Elmdon still boasted a grocer and two butchers, although one of the latter worked on a very small scale, and there was a choice of two public houses, but it was no longer possible

233

to buy drapery in the village, and both the bakeries had disappeared. Some of these vanished services had been replaced by vans visiting Elmdon from neighbouring towns, and some new facilities were enjoyed, like those offered by the mobile fish-and-chip shop, but these came from outside the village and did not help to create employment within it.

What then were people in this group doing to earn their livings in 1964? The men were working as mechanics, electricians, engineers and, above all, factory workers, mainly in the Spicer paperworks at Sawston and Whittlesford. There were still painters, builders and carpenters living in Elmdon, but they all went outside to their jobs. One man commuted nightly to London to work in a newspaper office on the delivery side, and two more did office jobs in Saffron Walden and Baldock. Women, too, had taken jobs in the new areas of factory and office work.

Working inside and outside Elmdon

By now, Robert Wilkes would have realised that one of the reasons why Elmdon had become so much quieter by day was because a large proportion of its work force was employed outside the village. In 1861, virtually everyone worked either in Elmdon itself or in the surrounding fields, and as four of the six farm homesteads lay within 300 yards of Cross Hill, there was inevitably much coming and going of men and boys, carts and horses throughout the day. By 1964, just over half the male work force (54 per cent)[4] and four out of ten working women were employed outside Elmdon.

It was not only the incomers who went outside the village to work. Men born or raised in Elmdon had also taken advantage of the opportunities opened up by improved transport facilities, and a little over half of them (52 per cent) left the village each morning, to return at night, compared with 55 per cent of the incomers. The rather surprising implication of these figures, however, is that even in 1964 nearly half (46 per cent) of all the working incomers had found employment in Elmdon itself, despite the fact that work opportunities in the village were contracting, rather than expanding. As table 67 shows, the greatest number of them were engaged in agriculture. The disappearance of the old tenant farmers had brought in owner-occupiers from outside, while Elmdon men were increasingly taking work in nearby towns or factories, or on the buses, leading to a labour shortage on the

234

Table 67
Employment within Elmdon, 1964

| | males | | females | |
	born or raised Elmdon	incomers	born or raised Elmdon	incomers
Professional	—	3	—	—
Agriculture				
Farmers	1	6	—	—
Farm workers(i)	16	11	—	—
Employment in private households	—	1	1	2
General services	2	1	1	3
Craftsmen, tradesmen, etc.	1	4	1	3
Total	20	26	3	8

(i) 9 farm workers who lived in Elmdon in 1964, and are therefore included in tables 65, 66 and 68 were working on farms outside the parish or in Duddenhoe End.

Source: Elmdon survey.

farms. The old 'closed shop', whereby farm-labouring jobs in 1861 were filled by those born in the village or with close kin connections, had broken down, and farmers were filling their vacancies with men whose origins lay far outside Elmdon.

In other respects, though, something of the old pattern remained. The professional category, whether its members worked in or out of Elmdon, was still filled entirely by incomers, and the majority of shopkeepers, publicans, Post Office workers and the like were from outside. The male Elmdoners, by birth or upbringing, who still worked in the village in 1964 were outdoor men, for they were all farmers, farm employees or roadmen, occupations which their forebears had filled for generations before them.

Occupational change, 1861–1964

The first main feature of occupational change or continuity between 1861 and 1964 was that agriculture had declined as a major employer. True, as table 68 shows, in 1964 it gave direct employment, either as farmer or farm worker, to 43 per cent of all male workers living in Elmdon, but just over a hundred years earlier, the proportion had been 71 per cent, and at that time a number of craftsmen, like the blacksmiths and thatchers, had also been dependent on the land for earning a living.

Table 68
Proportion of full-time working population in different occupational groups, Elmdon village, 1964

	male		(1861)	female		(1861)	total		(1861)
	no.	*%*	*(%)*	*no.*	*%*	*(%)*	*no.*	*%*	*(%)*
Professional	10	10	(1)	3	15	–	13	11	(1)
Agriculture									
Farmers	7	7	(5)	–	–	(2)	7	6	(4)
Farm workers(i)	36	36	(66)	–	–	(25)	36	30	(57)
Employment in private									
households	2	2	(3)	4	20	(44)	6	5	(12)
General services	11	11	(–)	4	20	(–)	15	12	(–)
Craftsmen, tradesmen, etc.	34	34	(25)	9	45	(29)	43	36	(26)
Totals	100	100	(100)	20	100	(100)	120	100	(100)

(i) Includes 3 elderly part-time workers for purposes of comparison with 1861.

Source: Elmdon survey, chapter 1, table 3.

Second, employment outside agriculture had changed very considerably in its nature. The professional category had risen from 1 per cent to 11 per cent of the working population. New types of work, in transport, in factories and in offices had replaced the old small crafts carried out in the village itself. As a result, more than half the male work force, including those born or raised in Elmdon, were now in jobs in other villages and towns.

A third change was in women's employment. Although a slightly smaller proportion of all females living in Elmdon in 1964 was at work full-time than had been the case in 1861 (12.5 per cent compared to 18 per cent), the nature of the jobs had altered. In 1861, nearly three-quarters of these working women had been doing hard manual work either in the fields or in domestic service. By 1964, eight out of ten were employed in professional work, or in factories, shops, small businesses and offices, and only a fifth were working full-time in private households.

Finally, there was one respect in which the pattern of employment in the nineteenth and early twentieth centuries could still be recognised in 1964. Those born and raised in Elmdon who continued to live in the village, with a few exceptions, still filled the lower-paid jobs, whether within their own community or outside it. In Elmdon itself, they were the farm and council workers; outside, the majority worked on the buses and in the factories.

236

Status and power

A visit to Lofts Hall would finally have convinced Robert Wilkes that the days of the Squire were over. Instead of the sixteenth century house in which he himself had lived, he would have found a building-site. Mr Graham Watson, a London stockbroker, and his American-born wife had bought the Hall in 1934, only to see it destroyed by fire soon after. They moved into one of the lodges while deciding what action to take, but before they were ready to start rebuilding, they were overtaken first by the Second World War and then by building restrictions, so that in 1964 the new Hall was only half-finished. Mr Graham Watson still retained the Lordships of the Manors which Robert Wilkes himself had held in 1861, but the Manor Courts no longer sat and the titles were purely nominal. Mrs Graham Watson farmed the Home Farm attached to the property, but she and her husband owned no other land in Elmdon parish, and unlike Robert Wilkes in 1861, they had no control over local farmers, or Elmdon houses and cottages. Nor were the couple accorded any special status locally beyond that which would normally be enjoyed by the well-to-do owners of a property which had long been closely associated with the village. As Audrey Richards remarks in her Introduction, the special status associated with the Squire had been reserved for Jack Wilkes, who early in the 1930s had returned to Elmdon Bury from his self-imposed exile in Wiltshire after the estate sale. He continued to behave as the Squire up to his death in 1958, and he was able to do so because the great majority of people in the village accepted that he should, but he no longer had any sanctions at his disposal with which to maintain his position. Although his status remained, his power, which had resided in the fields of employment and housing, disappeared from the moment he sold the estate in 1927. With his death came the end of the squirearchy in Elmdon. His nephew by marriage at Elmdon Bury, although always helpful when approached on behalf of a village organisation, considered himself to be primarily a farmer, and had no desire to assume a squire's role.

The first major inheritors of the Squire's power when the estate was sold were the farmers. They had always played an important part in the running of Elmdon's daily affairs, first through the Vestry and later the elected Parish Council, and their influence as employers of labour had been great, but up to 1927 those of them

237

who farmed on Lofts Hall estate land were dependent on the renewal of their leases every seven years. The presence of the Squire was always there, and he was in a position to exert pressure on his tenants, however little he might choose to do so. From 1927 onwards, the owner-occupiers of Elmdon's farms were free from any interference in their control over the majority of jobs available in the village and the allocation of about 15 per cent of the village housing through the tied cottage system.

By 1964, much of this power had disappeared. Although the farmers remained major employers of labour, it became increasingly difficult to find farm workers, and it was no longer a case of Elmdon boys hoping to be taken on by a farmer, but rather the other way round. Then, too, the building of twenty-five council houses over the years had given some farm employees an alternative to the tied cottage. Even in the area of village administration through the Parish Council, the farmers were losing ground. True, in 1962 both the chairman and vice-chairman of the council were farmers, but the other three members representing Elmdon village, rather than Duddenhoe End, consisted of an electrician from an old Elmdon family, a commuter, and the land estate agent from the Old Vicarage, while the clerk was the wife of a bus inspector. In 1964, no one individual or group was in control to the exclusion of others.

Conclusions

No village can expect over a period of a hundred years to be shielded from social and technological changes which have affected the whole country. The shift in age structure in Elmdon from a predominantly young to a mainly middle-aged and elderly population only mirrored in slightly exaggerated form what had happened in England as a whole over the same period,[5] as did the change from larger to smaller households. Mechanisation in agriculture and the resultant reduction in the labour force were common to all arable farms in south-east England. The changes in women's employment in Elmdon reflected nationwide trends.

Any village within fifty miles of London, and lying only four and three-quarter miles from a mainline railway station, could expect an influx of commuters prepared to make the daily journey to the capital to work, and many villages found that improved local transport facilities enlarged the job opportunities of their inhabi-

238

tants. In Elmdon's case, the interest lies not so much in the changes that took place as in the continuities. Even as late as 1964, more than half its population was linked with the village through birth, upbringing, marriage or other kin connection. What were the factors which had allowed this degree of continuity to take place?

Kinship and marriage. Looking back from 1964 to 1861, a constant pattern can be discerned whereby a limited number of individuals from a core of families with firm Elmdon connections through birth or kinship remained in the village; those native-born Elmdoners who could not find work or, later, housing, emigrated; while on the periphery other families previously unconnected with the place came and went. New names would appear in the parish registers and recur in succeeding generations, to show that the divide between insiders and outsiders could be bridged, as happened when Henry Clark arrived from Heydon in the 1890s, with his wife and family of young children, to be employed as a blacksmith by John Brand. In this case, the Clarks had no known kinship link with an Elmdon family when they arrived, but four of their children married into the numerous Hammond family of farm workers, thus cementing their position in the village.[6] More often, however, an incomer would himself become connected with Elmdon through marriage, as Fred Starr did in the 1930s when he came from a neighbouring parish to work as a farm labourer. He married Violet Hayes, whose ancestry in Elmdon can be traced back nine generations,[7] and headed the largest household in Elmdon in 1964, by which time one of his sons was already married and settled in the village with a son of his own. Again, the close kin links which existed between farmers on the Lofts Hall estate in 1861 were reinforced by the continuing tendency of the farmers and their children to marry locally up to the end of the nineteenth century. Although this pattern changed radically in the twentieth century, as far as the farmers were concerned, it was followed in general by the lesser craftsmen and artisans throughout the whole period we are considering. To this section of the community, it was more important to marry someone who was already part of Elmdon or from its immediate vicinity than to maintain social position by taking a husband or wife from a similar occupational group. In the same way, as Marilyn Strathern shows in *Kinship at the core*, kinship links among the farm labourers became increasinly complex, and young married couples found themselves more and more closely tied to Elmdon, provided the husband could retain a job and a house.

The influence of the Squire. Just as Elmdon's population between 1861 and 1964 formed two distinct parts, one stable and the other constantly changing, so land and house property in the village up to 1927 could be divided roughly into two, half belonging to the Lofts Hall estate headed by a resident Squire, and half to a multiplicity of owners, many of whom did not live in the village themselves. As chapter 6 showed, there was a marked association between the stable population and the Lofts Hall estate on the one hand, and the transient population and the property outside the estate on the other. Successive Squires, whether through self-interest or genuine concern for individuals known to them all their lives, or a mixture of both, tended on the whole to prefer established families as their tenants and workers, except where custom demanded that outsiders should be brought in, as in the case of the top workers in private service at Lofts Hall itself. The transient population, on the other hand, was associated with property outside the estate, and with businesses which demanded a bigger outlay of capital than most Elmdoners could afford. For instance, there were four different owner-occupiers of Baker's (Elmdon Lodge) Farm between 1860 and 1920, none of them known to be related, and only one coming from within the parish, while within the same period farm tenancies under the control of the Squire passed from father to son in no fewer than nine cases, taking the estate as a whole. Even when it came to the farm-labouring families, such evidence as there is would indicate that up to 1927, the chances of remaining in the village were higher if work could be found on estate property. Certainly in the nineteenth century the Hayes men working for Lofts Hall estate farmers survived in the village rather than those employed at the owner-occupied Baker's Farm.[8]

The paternalism of successive Squires and their preference for established Elmdon families was felt not only throughout the occupational hierarchy from the farmers, down through the craftsmen and tradesmen to the labourers, but also through all the age groups. An eye was kept on the school children's progress, and an interest taken in their future careers; advice was given on marriage partners, and some of the elderly were awarded small pensions or rent-free accommodation. Once a job and a cottage connected with the estate had been acquired, a man's place in the village for life was more or less assured.

The post Lofts Hall estate period. If the part played by the Squire in maintaining the position of established Elmdoners was so great, it might be expected that the stable core of families linked to the village through birth, upbringing or other kinship connections would break up once the estate was sold. Yet such a core was still in existence in 1959, and had decreased in proportion to the total adult population by only 20 per cent or so since 1861. If we look at where changes did occur, we find that the farmers were the group most affected by the sale. The Brands in Elmdon, the Primes and all but one of the large Smith family in Duddenhoe End and Wenden Lofts, and the Piggs in Chrishall disappeared from the scene, to be replaced ultimately by owner-occupiers from outside, some of whom, of course, were later to set up dynasties of their own. One or two of the estate's tenant shop-keepers and tradesmen held out in Elmdon a few years longer, but all had disappeared by 1964. The continuity after 1927 came from the property-less farm labourers in the main. How did they manage to survive the upheaval, given that in the past many of them had relied on the Squire and his tenant farmers both for jobs and for housing?

Employment. It is true that during the depression years of the 1930s Elmdon boys who found it difficult to get work may have missed Jack Wilkes's habit of looking out for suitable school-leavers and offering them employment on the land. However, during the same period, these boys' fathers were largely able to hold on to their jobs. Although the first tractors appeared in Elmdon in 1930, horses were used to some extent throughout the decade, and a good deal of hand labour was still required. With the outbreak of war in 1939, any need for the Squire's patronage in the employment field vanished. Throughout the war, the national effort directed towards food production ensured that there was work for all Elmdon's farm labourers. After the war, the greatly increased mechanisation of farm work, resulting in fewer jobs, was more than compensated for by the increased employment opportunities for Elmdon residents outside the village. These outside opportunities were taken up by Elmdon

241

farm labourers and their children to such an extent that the demand for new agricultural workers to replace those who retired could only be met by bringing in men from outside. Elmdon boys leaving school in the late 1940s and 50s found themselves in demand both for work on the farms, and as factory hands or bus workers. It must be noted, however, that in taking these jobs, the Elmdoners of the 1950s were not so different from their forebears. Although they now had a wider choice of employment and could work either in or out of the village, most of them, like the farm workers and smaller craftsmen of 1861, remained in the lower paid jobs.

Housing. As far as housing was concerned, the established Elmdon families survived because to a large extent the local authority through its council houses, and the national government through its housing legislation, took over the functions of the Squire in this field. The Lofts Hall estate workers did not buy the cottages they were occupying at the time of the sales in 1927 and 1930, either because they could not afford even the very low prices ranging from £30 upwards which were realised, or because the low rents they were accustomed to paying encouraged them to suppose that there were better ways of spending any money they had accumulated. Even before the dispersal of the estate, tenants of low value unfurnished rented accommodation, other than tied cottages, had been given a measure of protection both in relation to rent increases and security of tenure through the Increase of Rent and Mortgage Interest (War Restrictions) Act of 1915, and legislation of this nature continued to be in force in one form or another right through the period we are considering.[9] At the same time, council housing in the village increased from the six dwellings built in 1922 to the twenty-five units available in 1964, and provided an alternative for workers who did not wish to live in a tied cottage, as well as accommodation for other members of established Elmdon families. As a result of these policies, household heads who did not own their own homes were positively encouraged to stay in Elmdon, since the rights they enjoyed applied only to the dwelling they occupied, whether rented privately or from the council. While an owner-occupier was in a position to move out of Elmdon when he felt inclined, since he could sell his house there to pay for another, an Elmdon tenant without capital and on a low wage knew that if he were to leave his rented premises to settle elsewhere he would either find him-

242

self at the bottom of the council waiting list in the place to which he moved, or he would have to search for increasingly scarce and expensive rented accommodation.

The position in 1964. For the reasons just given, Elmdoners who were household heads at the time of the Lofts Hall estate sale were able to maintain their position, and by 1964 a number of them were still living in the village. The position, however, was not so easy for their children when they came to marry, for a variety of reasons. First was the increasing lifespan of the village population as a whole, resulting in continued occupancy of a house or cottage by an individual for a considerably longer time than had been usual in the past. In 1861, only 26 per cent of all household heads were 60 years of age or over; by 1964, the proportion had risen to 46 per cent. Moreover, there were more than twice as many heads who were over 70 years old than there had been a hundred years ago. Young Elmdoners were therefore having to wait longer before houses, whether council-owned or rented, became available. The council tried to meet this problem by building six bungalows especially for old people, so that the larger council houses could be released for young families, but this only partially solved the problem. Because Elmdon had not been designated a development village by the local planning authority, large-scale building which might provide cheap homes for young married couples was ruled out. Furthermore, as house prices rose, any tenanted house which became vacant was at once sold by its landlord to an owner-occupier, thus reducing the number of dwellings formerly available to Elmdoners. The very success of local and national government policies in maintaining one generation of villagers in Elmdon was acting against that generation's successors, and it is arguable that by 1964 the seeds of change, leading to a final break in the pattern we have observed in Elmdon itself for over a century, had already been sown.

Epilogue

This book has looked at continuity and change in one small village in south-eastern England from 1861 to 1964, and shown how, regardless of national events, a core of established working families maintained their position there throughout the period. But 1964 now lies some years in the past. How far has the old stability weakened already, and what lies in store for the children of Elmdon's families today? The first question will be answered in a chapter by Frances Oxford in the companion volume to this book, *Kinship at the core,* in which she covers the thirteen years from 1964 to 1977. As to the second, a new pattern evolving directly from the old is already faintly discernible.

The Elmdon-born child of today differs from his predecessor of 1964 in that his schooling takes place entirely out of the village. As a primary school child, he is taken by bus to Chrishall where he meets children from other nearby villages. At 11, he transfers to secondary school in Saffron Walden and again is in touch with other children from a fairly wide local area. When he leaves school, he will be more likely to go to work in light industry in Sawston, Whittlesford or Duxford, all within eight miles of Elmdon, than he is to work in Elmdon itself, but he will be able to go on living at home until he marries, since his work place will be easily accessible by public or private transport. He may well choose his marriage partner from the young women he knows either from his school-days or at work, and since in both places he has met girls from a number of local villages his choice is by no means confined to an Elmdoner. If on marriage he wants to buy his own house, or obtain a council house, his chances of doing either will be better in one of the nearby development villages or in the market town of Saffron Walden than they will be in Elmdon itself. It seems, there-fore, as if everything will push him to break with Elmdon, and that the old stability must disappear. In practice, however, what is happening is that he is following a pattern very similar to his predecessors in Elmdon, but that this pattern holds good over a wider geographical area. In fact, the single village as the main social unit is being replaced by the 'neighbourhood'. Within this larger unit, he is likely to go to school, work, marry and raise a family, just as his forebears did within Elmdon village itself in 1861. Moreover, the kinship ties and obligations which were so important to Elmdoners in the past will still be observed, since the telephone and the private car have made communication with parents living five miles away as quick and easy as they were when a daughter lived at the other end of Elmdon from her mother. What now appears to be change may later come to be seen as continuity.

Notes

Abbreviations: ERO: Essex Records Office; PRO: Public Records Office; MAFF: Ministry of Agriculture, Fisheries and Food.

Foreword

1   A.F.J. Bryant, *Essex at Work*, 1969, pp. 1-4.
2   *A New and Complete History of Essex*, by a Gentleman, 1770, p. 81.
3   Bryant, *Essex at Work*, p. 5.
4   Ronald Blythe, *Akenfield: Portrait of an English Village*, 1969, p. 22, G.E. Evans, *Ask the Fellows who cut the hay*, 1966, p. x; R. Parker, *The Common Stream*, 1975, p. 254.
5   *Royal Commission on Historical Monuments*, 1908, vol. I, p. 3 and vol. III, p. 24.
6   For instance, a cottage bought at £700 in 1964 was valued after conversion, at £22,000 in 1978.
7   Only the wealthy or reasonably well-off were able to afford stone tombstones before that date.
8   G. Benjamin, M. Strathern (née Evans), R. Riordon, and A. Strathern.
9   F. Harwood, Lithmore Ottowanga, P. Roberts and E. Schildkrout.
10 R Dean (née Winton) and A. Whitehead.
11 V. Maher and P. Cresswell.

1   Elmdon in 1861

1   Census, 1861. Returns for Elmdon and Wenden Lofts parishes, PRO RG9/1121. The schedules completed at the time of the 1861 census provided information on every person then present in Elmdon and Wenden Lofts parishes. Individuals were grouped into households; the household head was described as such; and the relationship of any other people in the household to the head was shown. In addition, information was given on each individual's marital condition, age, sex, occupation, and parish of birth, and details of certain physical infirmities were noted. Farm acreages were listed, together with the number of employees, both on the land and in other businesses. In some cases, the enumerator gave the name of the house in which a family lived; in others, he only named the road or area in which the household was to be found.

Although the 1861 census returns covered the whole of Elmdon parish, it is possible to distinguish between those living in the north, centred on Elmdon village, and those in the south, who looked to the hamlet of Duddenhoe End. In this book, unless otherwise stated, 'Elmdon' refers to Elmdon village, and not to the whole parish.

Information provided by the 1861 census taken in Elmdon parish has been used so extensively throughout the book that no further reference will be made to it in footnotes. The use of the date '1861' in the text indicates that the census has been taken as the basic source.

2   Private communication from Mr A.F. Graham Watson to Dr A.I. Richards, 27 June 1974.

3   Sale catalogue, Lofts Hall estate, 1927, Jackson Stops, in possession of Major G.J.F. Rippingall.

4   Survey of the Lofts Hall estate, 1860, by Carter Jonas, Cambridge. ERO D/DU 508/2.

5   Private communication from the National Society for Promoting Religious Education, 21 May 1975.

6   Manorial Court rolls, ERO Ws M9 14.

7   Sale catalogue, ERO B 2831.

8   Title deeds of 'The Old Stores', Elmdon, kindly made available for inspection by Mrs G. White.

9   Elmdon and Wenden Lofts Enclosure Award, 1829. ERO Q/RDc 26A.

10   *Crockford's Clerical Directory*, 1860.

11   Lofts Hall estate survey (1860).

12   Lofts Hall estate survey (1860).

13   Vestry minute book, 1852-91. ERO D/P 13/2.

14   Census, 1851. Returns for Elmdon and Wenden Lofts. PRO H 0107/1786.

15   Lofts Hall estate survey (1860).

16   *Post Office Directory of the Six Home Counties, viz. Essex, Herts, Kent, Middlesex, Surrey and Sussex*, 1862.

17   Title deeds, 'The Old Stores'.

18   Vestry minute book, 1852-91.

19   *Parliamentary Papers*, 1861. L583, p. 630.

20   *Parliamentary Papers*, 1861. L583, p. 586.

21   J. Kitteringham, 'Country work girls in nineteenth century England' in Raphael Samuel (ed.), *Village Life and Labour*, History Workshop, Oxford, 1975, p. 13.

22   *Census of England and Wales for the year 1861*, vol. II, HMSO 1863, p. x.

23   Lord Sandon's Education Act of 1876 (see *Encyclopaedia Britannica*, vol. 7, 1973, pp. 998-9).

24   W. Page and J.H. Round (eds.), *The Victoria History of the County of Essex*, vol. II, 1907, p. 556.

25   Private communication, The National Society for Promoting Religious Education, 21 May 1975.

26   Ray Barnes, *Elmdon Village School. A short history*, 1973. Duplicated document.

27   See chapter 11, p. 220, table 57.

28   *Census of England and Wales for the year 1861*, vol. III. HMSO 1863, p. 33.

29   Census, 1861. Returns for Saffron Walden Union Workhouse. PRO RG9/1122.

2   Links with the world outside

1   Much of the information in this section on the carriers, and in the

following section on the early Post Office, has been obtained from: *Post Office Directory of the Six Home Counties, viz. Essex, Herts, Kent, Middlesex, Surrey and Sussex,* 1845-78; *Kelly's Directory of Essex, Hertfordshire and Middlesex,* 1883-1926; *Kelly's Directory of Essex,* 1929-37; supplemented by reference to the Censuses for Elmdon parish for 1841, 1851, 1861 and 1871 (PRO H 0107/340, H 0107/1786, RG 9/1121, RG 10/1708), and to Elmdon parish registers.

2   R. Bucknell, *Our Railway History,* 1970, p. 87.

3   Censuses for Elmdon parish, 1841-71.

4   *Encyclopaedia Britannica,* vol. 3, 1973, pp. 594-5.

5   R.C.K. Ensor, *England 1870-1914,* 1949, p. 166.

6   Information provided by Messrs Spicers (Stationery) Ltd, Sawston, 1 June 1971.

3   Landownership in Elmdon, 1739-1930

1   Survey of the Lofts Hall estate, 1790, ERO D/DU 508/1.

2   The account of Elmdon at the time of the Domesday Survey is based on the work of Margaret McKie. See also J.H. Round in H.A. Doubleday and W. Page (eds.), *The Victoria History of the County of Essex,* vol. I, 1903, p. 471.

3   For an account of differing theories, see A.R.H. Baker and R.A. Butlin in A.R.H. Baker and R.A. Butlin (eds.) *Studies of Field Systems in the British Isles,* 1973, chapter 14. Other sources used have been Lord Ernle, *English farming, past and present,* 1961; C.S. Orwin and C.S. Orwin, *The Open Fields,* 1967; and J. Thirsk, 'The Common Fields' in *Past and Present,* xxix, 1964.

4   G.M. Trevelyan, *British History in the Nineteenth Century and After,* Pelican Books, 1971, p. 159.

5   Maps of the open fields in Elmdon and Wenden Lofts parishes. ERO D/DQy 33, 34.

6   Enclosure Act for Elmdon and Wenden Lofts, 1824. 5 Geo. IV cl-21, p. 53.

7   Elmdon and Wenden Lofts Enclosure Award, 1829. ERO Q/RDc 26A.

8   Sale catalogue, ERO B 964.

9   Survey of the Lofts Hall estate, 1860, by Carter Jonas, Cambridge. ERO D/DU 508/2.

10   Sale catalogue, ERO B 2340.

11   Between 1838 and 1860, the estate in Wenden Lofts and Elmdon grew by only 77 acres, compared with some 1,973 acres between 1790 and 1838.

12   Probably because of the opportunity afforded by the Enclosure Award for farm reorganisation, the sizes of farms in Elmdon and Wenden Lofts in 1861 were well above the average in the adjoining county of Cambridgeshire in the same year. While 69% of the farms in Cambridgeshire were below 200 acres, only 41% of the Elmdon and Wenden Lofts farms fell into this category; and while just over half the farms in the two parishes contained between 200 and 499 acres, less than a quarter of the Cambridgeshire farms did so. (Sources. *Census of England and Wales for the year 1861,* vol. III, HMSO 1863, p. 140; 1861 Census, Elmdon and Wenden Lofts parishes, PRO RG9/1121; Lofts Hall estate survey, 1860.)

13   Title deeds of Poplars Farm, kindly made available for inspection by Mr George Wood.

14   Sale catalogue, ERO B 2831.

15   1851 Census for Elmdon and Wenden Lofts parishes, PRO H 0107/1786.

16   Elmdon and Wenden Lofts Enclosure Award, 1829.

17   Note (ms) on 1860 survey, dated 1867, stating that the farms were now let at their full value.

18   Ernle, *English farming, past and present*, pp. 377-92.

19   Henry Ffiske, *The Fiske Family Papers*, 1902, chapter IV. Published privately.

20   Lofts Hall estate cash accounts, ERO D/DU 508/4-5-6-8.

21   P. Morant, *The History and Antiquities of the County of Essex*, vol. II, 1768, p. 477 (note).

22   *Shooting Times and Country Magazine*, 17 July 1971 p. 24.

23   W. Page and J.H. Round (eds.), *The Victoria History of the County of Essex*, vol. II, 1907, p. 585.

24   Elmdon Bury livestock and cropping books, ERO D/DU 508/11-13.

25   Sales catalogues, ERO B 2830, B 2831 and B 2858.

26   Lofts Hall estate cash account, ERO D/DU 508/10.

27   Sale catalogue, Lofts Hall estate, 1927, Jackson Stops, in possession of Major G.J.F. Rippingall.

28   Private communication from Mr A.F. Graham Watson to Dr A.I. Richards, 27 June 1974.

29   Pencilled note on Lofts Hall estate sale catalogue, 1927.

30   Sale catalogue, Lofts Hall estate, 1930, Knight, Frank and Rutley in possession of Major G.J.F. Rippingall.

4   The men on the land, 1860-1930

1   Survey of the Lofts Hall estate, 1860, by Carter Jonas, Cambridge. ERO D/DU 502/2.

2   ERO Wills, vol. III, 1721-1858, p. 760.

3   Lofts Hall estate cash account, ERO D/DU 508/4.

4   Lofts Hall estate survey (1860).

5   Sale catalogue of the Lofts Hall estate, 1922, Knight, Frank and Rutley, in possession of Major G.J.F. Rippingall.

6   Lofts Hall estate cash account, ERO D/DU 508/10.

7   Rev. P.A. Wright, 'A little-known Essex murder', *Essex Countryside*, vol. 7, no. 31, 1959, p. 195.

8   Lofts Hall estate cash account ERO D/DU 508/3.

9   *A century of agricultural statistics. Great Britain 1866-1966*, MAFF, 1968, p. 63.

10   Audrey Richards and Jean Robin, *Some Elmdon Families*, 1975. Published privately.

5   Farms, farmers and farm workers, 1930-64

1   Audrey Richards has described in the Introduction (pp. xxiii-xxvi) how the 1964 Elmdon Survey came into being. The sample used was based on the Register of Electors for Elmdon village in that year. The farmers included on the Register, and therefore within the scope of the Survey, were as follows:

     Elmdon Bury farm   Major G.J.F. Rippingall, born Norfolk.
     Elmdon Lodge farm   Messrs L. R. and W. Fison, born Ely.

Hill Farm	Mr J.E. Cross, born Edgware.
Church Farm	Mr G.R. Turner, born London.
Poplars Farm	Mr G. Wood, born Gt. Chishill.

The owner of Elmdon Lee, Mr Albert Duke, was on the Duddenhoe End Register for 1964, and so he was omitted from the Survey. On the other hand, as the proprietors of Lofts Hall had played so important a part in Elmdon over such a long period, the owners in 1964 were interviewed, even though the Hall lay in Wenden Lofts. Mrs Graham Watson, the wife of the Hall's owner, was farming the Home farm in 1964, and she has been included here with the Elmdon farmers.

Enough is known of the remaining farms formerly belonging to the Lofts Hall estate to be able to say that in 1964 none were tenanted, but information on the individual owners was not collected, being outside the scope of the Survey. They are therefore not considered in detail in this chapter.

2   Edith H Whetham, *British Farming, 1939-1949*, 1952, p. 1.

3   Ibid. p. 13

4   Ibid. p. 120.

5   *A century of agricultural statistics*, MAFF, table 27.

6   J.T. Coppock, *An agricultural geography of Great Britain*, 1971, p. 27.

7   Ibid. p. 28.

8   *A century of agricultural statistics*, MAFF, table 70.

9   The figure of thirty-six farm workers in 1964 includes thirty-three full-time workers, three of whom were under 21, and therefore not interviewed by members of the Elmdon Survey team; and three part-time workers who were all over 60 years old. These last have been included in the sample, since the 1861 work force, with whom comparisons are made, contained men over 60, some of whom may not have been doing a full day's work.

Of the thirty-six workers in 1964, nine were working on nearby farms in the neighbouring parishes of Ickleton and Wenden Lofts, or on Duddenhoe End properties. The farms on which the 1861 labour force worked are not known for the individuals concerned. For this reason, all farm workers living in or near Elmdon village in 1964 have been included in the sample, whether or not they worked on farms within Elmdon.

10   Howard Newby, *The Deferential Worker*, 1977, p. 172.

6   Non-farming occupations

1   Extensive use was made of the following material throughout the preparation of this chapter: *Post Office Directory of the Six Home Counties, viz, Essex, Herts, Kent, Middlesex, Surrey and Sussex*, 1845, 1874 and 1878; *Kelly's Directory of Essex, Hertfordshire and Middlesex*, 1886-1926; *Kelly's Directory of Essex*, 1929-1937; Registers of Electors, Elmdon parish; Elmdon parish registers.

2   Isabella Beeton, *The book of household management*, 1861, p. 8.

3   Sale catalogue, Lofts Hall estate, 1927, Jackson Stops, in possession of Major G.J.F. Rippingall.

4   Title deeds, 'The Old Stores', kindly made available for inspection by Mrs G. White.

5   Title deeds, 'Baker's Cottage', kindly made available for inspection

by Mr and Mrs C. Macdonald.

6 Ruth D'Arcy Thompson, *The Remarkable Gamgees*, 1974, p. 12.
7 Survey of the Lofts Hall estate, 1860, by Carter Jonas, Cambridge. ERO D/DU 508/2.

7 Marriage

1 Ffiske, *Fiske Family Papers*, p. 273.
2 W.J. Pinks (ed. E.J. Wood), *The History of Clerkenwell*, 1881, p. 314.
3 G.O. Rickword, 'John Wilkes in Essex in 1783', *Essex Review*, vol. 49, 1940, pp. 99-100.
4 The information on the Fiske family which follows has been obtained from Ffiske, *Fiske Family Papers*, chapters IV and V.

8 Status and social mobility in Elmdon

1 Letter from Messrs. Robbins, Olivey and Lake, Solicitors, to the Rev. F.T. Dufton, Vicar of Elmdon, 23.1.78.
2 Survey of the Lofts Hall estate, 1860, by Carter Jonas, Cambridge. ERU D/DU 508/2.
3 Lofts Hall estate cash account, ERO D/DU 508/3.
4 Lofts Hall estate cash account, ERU D/DU 508/6.
5 Lofts Hall estate cash account, ERU D/DU 508/3.
6 Sale catalogue, Lofts Hall estate, 1927, Jackson Stops, in possession of Major G.J.F. Rippingall.
7 Lofts Hall estate cash account, ERO D/DU 508/3.
8 Elmdon school log book, 1874-1915, and Elmdon school punishment book, 1900-34.
9 Lofts Hall estate cash account, ERO D/DU 508/3.
10 Returns by Church of England clergy concerning Non-conformist Meeting Houses. ERO O/CR 3/1/107.
11 Returns by Church of England clergy concerning Non-conformist Meeting Houses. ERO O/CR 3/2/27.
12 Wenden Lofts school log book, 1906-12. ERO E/ML 30.
13 Louis Golding, *A Dictionary of Local Government in England and Wales*, 1962, pp. 410-11.
14 Vestry Minute Book 1852-91. ERO D/P 13/2.
15 Elmdon Parish Council Minute Book, 1894-1925.
16 Ffiske, *Fiske Family Papers*, chapter V.
17 The information in this paragraph is taken from Ruth D'Arcy Thompson, *D'Arcy Thompson — The Scholar Naturalist, 1860-1948*, 1958; and *The Remarkable Gamgees*.
18 ERO Wills, vol. I, 1400-1619.
19 ERO Wills, vol. II, 1620-1720.
20 ERO Wills, vol. III, 1721-1858.
21 ERO Wills, vol. III, 1721-1858.
22 Enclosure Act for Elmdon and Wenden Lofts, 1824. 5 Geo. IV cl-21, p. 53.
23 In 1813, the Vicar of Elmdon spent the next seven years' income from the Trust Fund left by Thomas Crawley, the founder of Elmdon school in 1559, on repairing the school building, with the result that there was no money to pay a master until 1822. (Barnes, *Elmdon Village School. A short history*.)
24 In the possession of Mr Walter Brand of Chrishall.
25 In the possession of Mr Walter Brand of Chrishall.

26   William Brand's will, in the possession of Mr Walter Brand of Chrishall.

9   Migration in the mid-nineteenth century

1   Full schedules giving details of each individual in Elmdon parish are at present available only for the years 1841-71, as the rule preventing publication of individual names for 100 years from the date of the census is in force for the years 1881 onwards. Because of the limitations of the 1841 census, it is only possible to distinguish between the inhabitants of Elmdon village and Duddenhoe End, both in the parish of Elmdon, for the years 1851-71. For this reason, population figures outside this period have to be used for the parish as a whole.

2   A.K. Cairncross, 'Internal Migration in Victorian England',. *Manchester School of Economic Studies*, vol. XVII, 1949, pp. 67-81.

3   The period 1851-61 has been taken for this turnover study in preference to 1861-71 because of deficiencies in the 1871 census.

4   John Harrison and Peter Laslett, 'Clayworth and Cogenhoe', in *Historical Essays 1600-1750 presented to David Ogg*, ed. H.E. Bell and R.L. Ollard, 1963, pp. 157-184.

10   The changing population

1   It would be helpful to use the Registers of Electors not only to assess population changes at ten-year intervals, as is done in this chapter, but to show how many voters came into the village during a decade but left again before the ten years were up. This information is not available for the years between 1851 and 1861, however, so that no basis for comparison between the mid-nineteenth and mid-twentieth centuries exists in this respect. For this reason short-stay immigrants of this type are not considered here.

2   *Encyclopaedia Britannica, Macropaedia*, 1943-1973, vol. 6, p. 528 and vol. 19, p. 912. Women of 30 years and over were enfranchised in 1918.

3   Given the information available in the Registers of Electors, the question arises of how best to divide up the twentieth century to provide significant comparisons of migration trends. The division into decades from 1899 onwards which has been adopted covers the main events listed on p. 201 without much overlapping, i.e.

1899-1909:   recovery from the great depression of the last years of the nineteenth century.

1909-19:   breakdown of peaceful international relations; First World War.

1919-29:   the depression of the 1920s, and the first sale of the Lofts Hall estate in 1927.

1929-39:   The acute agricultural depression of 1929-1933, and the sale of the residue of the Lofts Hall estate in 1930.

1939-49:   The Second World War; the introduction of daily bus services to and from Elmdon.

4   Register of Electors, Elmdon parish, 1918.

5   *Kelly's Directory of Essex, Hertfordshire and Middlesex*, 1926.

6   Richards and Robin, *Some Elmdon Families*.

7   ERO Wills, vol. II, Hoy, 1684; vol III, Hoy, 1741, 1775, 1812; Hayes, 1744.

8   D'Arcy Thompson, *The Remarkable Gamgees*, p. 11.

9   The 1861 Census showed that there were four uninhabited houses in Elmdon parish, but as the agricultural depressions of the last quarter of the century took effect, the number rose until it reached twenty-five in 1901, when records of uninhabited houses ceased to be kept.

11   Elmdon in 1964. The continuity and the change

1   The Rev. F.T. Dufton, *The Church of St. Nicholas, Elmdon*. Pamphlet, 1st edition, 1977.

2   Although 'outsiders' headed 50 per cent of Elmdon's households in 1964, many of them either had grown-up children who had already left home, or were living alone. As a group they therefore had fewer dependents living with them than did established Elmdon householders.

3   The term 'professional class' is used here in a broader sense than its strict limitation to the three learned professions of divinity, law and medicine, and the military profession.

4   This figure includes three elderly male part-time farm workers.

5   **Age structures of Elmdon and England, 1861 and 1964**

Age group	0 - 14 %	15 - 29 %	30 - 44 %	45 - 59 %	60+ %	not known %
1861 Elmdon	41	24	13	12	10	—
1861 England	36	27	19	12	7	—
1964 Elmdon	19	18	16	20	25	3
1961 England	23	19	20	20	17	—

Sources: 1861 Census, Elmdon parish. *Census of England and Wales for the year 1861, vol. II*, HMSO, 1863, p. x. 1964 Elmdon Survey notebooks. *Census 1961, Great Britain, summary tables*, HMSO 1966, table 4.

6   Richards and Robin, *Some Elmdon Families*, pp. 64-5.

7   Ibid. pp. 90-3.

8   Ibid. pp. 97-8.

9   A.J. Lomnicki, *A Summary of Landlord and Tenant Law*, 1975, pp. 67-70.

Bibliography

Official publications

Enclosure Act for Elmdon and Wenden Lofts, 1824. 5 Geo. IV cl - 21.
Census of England and Wales for the year 1851, vol. I, HMSO, 1854.
Parliamentary Papers, L.583. HMSO, 1861.
Census of England and Wales for the year 1861, vols. II and III, HMSO, 1863.
Census 1961, Great Britain, summary tables, HMSO, 1966.
A century of agricultural statistics. Great Britain 1866-1966, Ministry of Agriculture, Fisheries and Food, 1968.
Long-term Population Distribution in Great Britain — a Study, Department of the Environment, 1971.
Public Records Office:
    Census returns for Elmdon and Wenden Lofts: 1841: H 0107/340;
                                                                  1851: H 0107/1786;
                                                                 1861: RG9/1121;
                                                                 1871: RG10/1708.

Essex Record Office

The Lofts Hall estate
Survey of the Lofts Hall estate, 1790. D/DU 508/1.
Survey of the Lofts Hall estate, 1860. D/DU 508/2.
Lofts Hall estate cash accounts, 1888-1920. D/DU 508/3 — 10.
Elmdon Bury livestock and cropping books. D/DU 508/11 — 13.

Sales catalogues
The King's Head, 1821. B 964.
Rockells Farm, 1838. B 2340.
Baker's Farm/Elmdon Lodge, 1858-76. B 2830, B 2831, B 2858.

Wills
Vol. I: 1400-1619.
Vol. II: 1620-1720.
Vol. III: 1721-1858.

Maps of the open fields in Elmdon and Wenden Lofts parishes. D/DQy 33-4.
Elmdon and Wenden Lofts Enclosure Award, 1829. Q/RDc 26A.
Returns by Church of England clergy concerning Non-conformist Meeting Houses, 1829. O/CR 3/1/107 and O/CR 3/2/27.

253

Manorial court rolls, Elmdon Bury, 1744-1899. Ws M9-14.
Vestry minute book, Elmdon parish, 1852-91. D/P 13/2.
Wenden Lofts school log book, 1906-12. E/ML 30.

Elmdon records

Parish registers, in possession of the Vicar of Elmdon.
Parish Council minute book, 1894-1925.
Registers of electors, 1899-1964.
School log book, 1874-1915.
School pubishment book, 1900-34.
R. Barnes, *Elmdon Village School — a short history*, 1973 (duplicated document).
Rev. F.T. Dufton, *The Church of St. Nicholas, Elmdon*, 1977 (duplicated pamphlet).

Reference books

Crockford's Clerical Directory, 1860
Encyclopaedia Britannica, 1943-73.
Post Office Directory of the Six Home Counties, viz. Essex, Herts, Kent, Middlesex, Surrey and Sussex, 1845-78.
Kelly's Directory of Essex, Hertfordshire and Middlesex, 1883-1926.
Kelly's Directory of Essex, 1929-37.

Books

Baker, A.R.H. and Butlin, R.A., (eds.), *Studies of Field Systems in the British Isles*, 1973.
Beeton, I., *The book of household management*, 1861.
Bucknell, R., *Our Railway History*, 1970.
Coppock, J.T., *An agricultural geography of Great Britain*, 1971.
Doubleday, H.A. and Page, W., (eds.), *The Victoria History of the County of Essex*, vol. I, 1903.
Ensor, R.C.K., *England 1870-1914*, 1949.
Lord Ernle, *English Farming Past and Present*, 1961.
Ffiske, H., *The Fiske Family Papers*, 1902 (published privately).
Golding, L., *A Dictionary of Local Government in England and Wales*, 1962.
Harrison, J. and Laslett, P., 'Clayworth and Cogenhoe', in H.E. Bell and R.L. Ollard (eds.), *Historical Essays 1600-1750 presented to David Ogg*, 1963.
Kitteringham, J., 'Country work girls in nineteenth century England' in R. Samuel (ed.), *Village Life and Labour*, History Workshop, Oxford, 1975.
Lomnicki, A.J., *A Summary of Landlord and Tenant Law*, 1975.
Morant, P., *The History and Antiquities of the County of Essex*, vol. II, 1768.
Newby, H., *The Deferential Worker*, 1977.
Orwin, C.S. and Orwin, C.S., *The Open Fields*, 1967.
Page, W. and Round J.R., (eds.), *The Victoria History of the County of Essex*, vol. II, 1907.
Pinks, W.J. (ed. E.J. Wood), *The History of Clerkenwell*, 1881.
Richards, A. and Robin, J., *Some Elmdon Families*, 1975 (published privately.
Thompson, R. D'Arcy, *D'Arcy Thompson — the Scholar Naturalist, 1860-1948*, 1958.

Thompson, R. D'Arcy, *The Remarkable Gamgees*, 1974.
Trevelyan, G.M., *British History in the Nineteenth Century and After*, Pelican Books, 1971.
Whetham, E.H., *British Farming, 1939 – 1949*, 1952.

.Journal articles

Carincross, A.K., 'Internal Migration in Victorian England', *Manchester School of Economic Studies*, vol. XVII, 1949.
Rickword, G.O., 'John Wilkes in Essex in 1783', *Essex Review*, vol. 49, 1940.
Thirsk, J., 'The Common Fields' *Past and Present*, vol. xxix, 1964.
Wright, Rev. P.A., 'A little-known Essex murder', *Essex Countryside*, vol. 7, no. 31, 1959.
Shooting Times and Country Magazine, 17 July 1971.

Index

256

257